The Songwriter's and Musician's Guide to Nashville

Revised Edition

SHERRY BOND

ALLWORTH PRESS
NEW YORK

PH BR

© 2000 Sherry Bond

04   03   02   01   00   5   4   3   2   1

Published by Allworth Press
An imprint of Allworth Communications
10 East 23rd Street, New York, NY 10010

Cover design by Douglas Design Associates, New York, NY

Page composition/typography by SR Desktop Services, Ridge, NY

ISBN: 1-58115-047-4

Library of Congress Cataloging-in-Publication Data
Bond, Sherry, 1941–
        The songwriter's and musician's guide to Nashville / Sherry Bond.
            p.   cm.
        Rev. ed. of: The songwriter's & musician's guide to Nashville / edited by
Sherry Bond. Cincinnati : Writer's Digest Books, 1991.
        Includes index.
        ISBN 1-58115-047-4 (pbk.)
        1. Country music—Tennessee—Nashville—Vocational guidance.   I. Title.
ML3790.B66   2000
781.642'09768'55—dc21   00-021666

Printed in Canada

Contents

Acknowledgments

My heartfelt thanks to Fred Koller, who got me this gig; dear friend and great writer/artist Betsy Meryl Hammer, who edited with a fine-tooth comb; and my wonderful sons Robert and Jeff. Without them, I wouldn't be who I am today—they are an unlimited source of support and encouragement!

Introduction

Y ou may have heard that Nashville is a tight-knit clique completely closed to outside writers. Nothing could be further from the
truth.

Nashville loves songs. Nashville loves songwriters. Nashville welcomes you with open arms.

On your first trip to Nashville you will learn what true southern hospitality is all about. When someone asks, "How are you?" (as they frequently
will), they really, truly want to know how you are, how your family is, how
your life is going. An important part of doing business in Nashville is sharing personal concerns with each other.

This book reads like many how-to books. It's filled with lots of do's
and don'ts. Please remember that these rules are simply general guidelines
for you to work from. Your success is basically going to depend on a single
factor—your own people skills. If you are positive, enthusiastic, and love the
process of pitching your songs as much as you love writing them, you are
bound to succeed. That is, *if* you are a *great* songwriter, artist, or musician.

The hardest thing for Nashville to deal with is someone who doesn't
have the faintest idea how to write a good song; someone, in fact, who
doesn't even know the difference between a good song and a bad song. An
astounding number of people fall into this category. They have written
what they believe is a good song, and they think that now all they need to

do is get someone in the music business to listen to it. They think that once someone listens to it, that'll be it; the song will be recorded, become an instant hit, and they'll get rich! Consequently, Nashville is bombarded with amateur songwriters trying to get someone to listen to their tapes. Unsolicited tapes are almost always returned unopened.

The purpose of this book is to prevent you from falling into the category described above. Nashville *does* listen to zillions of tapes—demo tapes of amateur, developing, and professional songwriters. By using the right approach, you can get your songs heard and you can start developing working relationships with music business professionals. Ultimately, you will be interacting with many different people who can help you get your song to the right artist. It's a long and difficult process, one that takes your continued effort and dedication.

This book will tell you more than you can possibly imagine about pitching songs, but my best advice is to try *not* to make pitching your very first priority. In Nashville, songs are usually discovered in the process of working with them, while cowriting, recording in the demo studio, or listening to them at a live performance. Relax and enjoy the creative atmosphere of Music City. Listen and learn how things are done, then slowly ease your way in.

You are truly welcome in Nashville, so I hope you'll come on down soon. Please stop by to see me when you do!

ABOUT THE AUTHOR

SHERRY BOND has a B.A. in music from the University of California at Santa Barbara. After receiving her degree, she took over the copyright and

Photo by Teddie West

royalty administration for the music publishing companies of her father, artist/writer Johnny Bond ("I Wonder Where You Are Tonight"), and the legendary Tex Ritter ("High Noon"), both of whom are members of the prestigious Country Music Hall of Fame. The catalogs of Johnny Bond Publications include the works of The Delmore Brothers ("Blues, Stay Away From Me"), Tommy Duncan ("Stay All Night, Stay a Little Longer"), and Harlan Howard ("The Blizzard"). In 1983, Sherry moved from Los Angeles to establish offices in Nashville. Since moving to Nashville, she has had songs recorded by Johnny Cash ("Going by the Book"), Marty Stuart ("Burn Me Down"), and Lyle Lovett ("There's More Pretty Girls Than One").

After writing the first edition of *The Songwriter's and Musician's Guide to Nashville* in 1991, Sherry became the fourth executive director of the NASHVILLE *entertainment* ASSOCIATION (NeA), and during her tenure, she nurtured the organization into a nationally recognized trade organization for aspiring artists and musicians. NeA Extravaganza showcased over four hundred acts from all genres of music before top industry professionals from Los Angeles, New York, and London. NeA Music City Music, a country music showcase, was created and produced by Sherry to assist the Nashville record industry in its search for new talent. As a result of this showcase, several acts were signed to record deals, including Chad Brock (Warner/Reprise), Dean Miller (Capitol), and SHeDAISY (Lyric Street).

Sherry left the NeA in 1998 to return to music publishing in the new climate of Americana and alternative country music. She is a graduate of Leadership Music, a nonprofit trade organization in Nashville, and an active member of the Country Music Association, Academy of Country Music, Nashville Songwriters' Association International, National Academy of Recording Arts and Sciences, and SOURCE, a networking organization for top female industry executives.

1

An Overview of Nashville

Nashville!

The name evokes all kinds of images . . . A place where everyone walks around wearing cowboy boots, hats, and jeans adorned with big silver belt buckles, carrying guitars over their shoulders. A place where you can come to see your favorite country artists performing at the local bars around town. A place where songs are written about drinkin' and cheatin' and the grittier side of life.

REALITY VERSUS MYTH

You will be really surprised when you arrive in Nashville. It is nothing like those fantasies mentioned above. The perception of Nashville, created by songs from a long-gone era, is quite different from the reality of Nashville today. In fact, this false perception has impeded the efforts of city government officials to attract new industries to Nashville. Fortunately, they have been able to overcome this obstacle and have led the city to remarkable growth and prosperity. New industries continue to relocate here, giving the city a next-to-zero unemployment rate for several years running. Nashville recently built one of the nation's top arenas and a state-of-the-art football stadium, home of the Tennessee Titans (formerly the Houston Oilers).

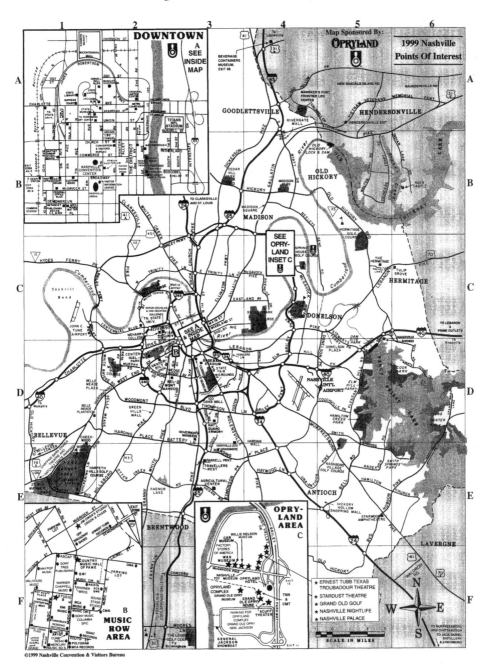

The only "cowboys" you'll find in Nashville are the tourists or aspiring artists trying to look the part. You'll find them wandering around downtown, on Broadway and Second Avenue North, away from the country music industry district, where industry executives and artists/musicians wear anything but boots, hats, and big belt buckles. Country artists are almost unrecognizable in their casual clothes.

The biggest surprise for tourists is the fact that there is very little country music performed here. The likelihood of hearing one of your favorite artists is very remote. True, Nashville's best-kept secret is that the city has a vibrant live music scene. Any night of the week you can go into any one of the many music venues and hear an awesome performance. But it's not country. Jazz, blues, rock, pop, swing, and alternative music thrive in Music City because the session musicians who record country music in the studios during the day go out and create their own original, non-country music in the clubs at night. Also, the city attracts outstanding musicians looking for studio gigs, and they are playing in the clubs as well. It is a wonderful opportunity to hear the greatest musicians ever, but most tourists don't take advantage of it because they came here expecting to find country music.

The music of Hank Williams, Patsy Cline, and Loretta Lynn is such an important part of our country-music heritage, it is difficult to break away from the stereotypes. While the "Nashville Sound" has progressed to contemporary themes, the legendary artists remain as popular as they ever were. This creates a huge problem for the country music industry: gaining recognition for a new, modern sound without diluting the past. Treading lightly through this tricky situation has caused the country music industry to remain stuck in time. Today's country music is much more modern and complex than it is perceived to be.

Although Nashville is located on the fringe of a loosely defined southern territory, it possesses all the charm and hospitality of a sophisticated southern city. Lush, rich greenery and spectacular blooming foliage frame stately brick mansions standing on their own acres of land. Many residential neighborhoods are divided by majestic stone walls built by slaves for erstwhile plantations. They are protected today as important works of art. Many a building contractor has altered architectural plans to incorporate history into the landscape. No visit to Nashville would be complete without a drive through its residential areas.

The Layout of the City

Nestled in the center of middle Tennessee (the state is divided into three sections: east, where Knoxville and the Smoky Mountains are located; middle; and west, where Memphis is found), Nashville is Tennessee's second-largest city (after Memphis), with a population of over one million people, and is the state capital. Located in the heart of the Bible Belt, the city's main industry is printing, primarily Bibles and hymnals. Hospitals, many of them corporately based in Nashville, are also a major industry of the city. Because of the Grand Ole Opry, Fan Fair, the Country Music Hall of Fame, and other attractions associated with country music, tourism is a major source of income for Nashville.

There are two separate tourist areas: downtown and the Opryland Hotel complex. Downtown Nashville thrives and bustles with activity almost every night. Weekends bring gridlock to the two main streets, Broadway and Second Avenues North and South. The blue lights on patrol cars blaze away while the police try to keep the traffic moving along. There is a congenial mix of locals and tourists roaming the streets and enjoying the great variety of restaurants. Locals head to their favorite bars to play a game of pool and sample one of the numerous beers offered by micro-breweries. Later in the evening they will club-hop among the various dance clubs. Or, if they are in the mood for music, there is a lot going on in the live music venues downtown. During the summer, there are a lot of outdoor music festivals at Riverfront Park, a huge hillside facing a stage on the Cumberland River.

There are numerous tourist attractions downtown, including a host of interesting shops and street vendors. Hard Rock Cafe, Planet Hollywood, and the NASCAR Cafe each offers their own distinctive charm. Unique to Nashville are the Wildhorse Saloon, Tootsie's, and the Ryman Auditorium.

The Wildhorse Saloon is a tourist's best chance to see a rare performance by a country star. Only occasionally will country artists perform at one of Nashville's two larger venues, the Arena or the First American Music Center (an outdoor amphitheater).

Tootsie's is a small bar located in the middle of a honky-tonk area the locals named "Lower Broad," because it is at the end of Broadway, away from the river. Here you will find a dense population of aspiring country artists performing in the hopes of being discovered. Tourists and locals alike provide enthusiastic support for these hopefuls. Some have attracted record label attention, most notably Arista recording act BR5-49. Tootsie's is the most famous of the honky-tonks because of its back entrance into the stage of the Ryman Auditorium. Opry performers used to sit in Tootsie's while waiting to go on stage. Their faded and tattered pictures adorn the walls today. In those days there was no live music performed in Tootsie's—it was added in recent years to keep pace with the surrounding clubs. Tootsie's also has the coldest beer in town.

The Ryman Auditorium was the original home of the Grand Ole Opry before it moved out to the Opryland Hotel complex. Originally a church, it has been beautifully restored and houses an interesting museum on Opry's history. Today the Ryman hosts a variety of outstanding musical offerings. Extreme care is taken to ensure the highest quality of performances on the Ryman stage. No trip to Nashville would be complete without attending a concert or a musical event at the Ryman just to enjoy the superb acoustics and historical significance. Other attractions of historical country music importance are the Country Music Hall of Fame, currently in the process of moving from Music Row to downtown, and Studio B, the original RCA recording studio where Owen Bradley created the Nashville Sound.

The Opryland Hotel complex is located northeast of the city, near the airport. It was at one time the largest convention hotel in the United States. An Opryland theme park was unique in its mix of fast rides, quality food courts, and many music stages throughout the beautifully landscaped park. Being one-of-a-kind is difficult, though, and competition with faster, scarier theme parks prompted Opryland decision makers to take a different course. They closed the park and began construction on Opry Mills, a huge shopping mall and entertainment center. At the printing of this book, Opry Mills was still under construction, but should be checked out as a possible source to see live performances of country artists.

For tourists and conventioneers, the Opryland Hotel has much to offer. The hotel itself is spectacular, especially during the Christmas holidays. Several huge arboretums grace the interior, along with waterfalls, clusters of little shopping and restaurant communities, and an indoor boat ride. Lots of live entertainment is offered. The General Jackson Showboat offers dinner cruises on the Cumberland River. The Springhouse Golf Club has one of the more popular eighteen-hole courses in the city. The award-winning country radio station WSM-AM/FM is a part of the Opryland complex and broadcasts live from the stage of the Grand Ole Opry.

The Grand Ole Opry is a unique show all its own, a very exclusive fraternity unlike any other. The Opry is presented every Friday and Saturday night, in half-hour segments, each segment hosted by a different celebrity. Performers wander on and off stage casually, as if it were a radio show only, and not the live performance that it really is. Family and friends of the performers sit onstage in a special section reserved for them. There are regulars on the show, and Opry members take turns performing throughout the year. Although membership in the Grand Ole Opry does not impel artists' careers, acceptance into the fraternity is still a very important milestone for them. While Nashville's tourism industry is perceived to be all about country music, the most interesting tourist attractions are far removed from the music industry. The Cheekwood Botanical Garden and Museum of Art, once the private estate of the Cheek family of the Maxwell House Coffee fortune, is now home to a valuable collection of eighteenth- and nineteenth-century paintings and decorative art, featuring prominent American artists. The many different gardens are breathtaking. Civil War enthusiasts will want to visit the Carnton House in nearby Franklin, where a family fought the battle in their own back-yard. President Andrew Jackson's home, The Hermitage, is located in Nashville, as well as the elegant Belle Meade Mansion and Carriage House. In the summer, you can enjoy a picnic while listening to jazz on the lawns of these two magnificent estates.

Residents of Nashville are very blessed indeed. Their graceful, attractive city provides an easygoing lifestyle, with lots to do evenings and weekends. Everyone is friendly and moves at a slow pace. It's easy to get around if you have a car, but one important warning: Street names change at random. For example, Wedgewood becomes Blakemore, which then becomes 31st Avenue South—all in just a two-mile stretch. Broadway splinters off into West End, which eventually becomes Harding Road, before it splits into two highways, 100 and 70 S. So do as the natives—slow down your pace and stop to enjoy life. That's easy to do in Music City, U.S.A.

A Brief History of Music in Nashville

The Nashville music scene has changed drastically from the days when the Ryman Auditorium was the home of the Grand Ole Opry. Back then, in the 1930s, the Opry was an important part of the country music scene, and the Opry's live show on WSM was the most significant of many live radio broadcasts across the country. Performers would vie for a chance to appear on the Opry, as this was where record labels looked for new talent. Numerous country legends such as Hank Williams, Roy Acuff, and Ernest Tubb launched their remarkable careers from the Ryman stage.

Downtown Nashville was where the action was. Every Friday night performers and others in the music industry stood and chatted in the hallways of the Charleston Hotel (no longer there). Other artists, such as Dolly Parton and Country Music Hall of Famer Uncle Dave Macon, stayed at the Merchant's Hotel on Broadway, downtown's main street. (Merchant's is no longer a hotel, but an elegant restaurant.) Everyone, including dynamic Brenda Lee, fondly remembers hanging out at Linebaughs' sandwich shop (no longer there, a courtyard next to Merchant's marks the spot). John Hartford immortalized Linebaughs' and the changing times by writing the lament, "Nobody Eats at Linebaughs' Anymore," recorded by himself and the New Grass Revival. Hartford's song is a fitting tribute to the era many fondly remember, when the nearby Printers Alley was a one-block alley filled with bars featuring live country bands.

By the mid-1950s Nashville was well-established as a leading music center and was dubbed "Music City, U.S.A." by a pop radio station disc jockey. Hank Williams's "Jambalaya" and "Your Cheatin' Heart," Red Foley's "Chattanooga Shoe Shine Boy," and many other country songs crossed over to the pop charts. Legendary producer Owen Bradley made the very first record in Nashville (Zeke Clements' "Night Train to Memphis") at a studio built in the WSM radio station on the top floor of the L&C Tower at Fourth and Union Streets. Then, in 1958, RCA Records asked Bradley to build a studio for the label in Nashville. They chose a site close to downtown, now known as Music Row. (Studio B, as it was called, is now part of the Country Music Hall of Fame Museum.) Bradley has a park on Music Row named after him in honor of the man who established Nashville as the center of country music.

Once RCA established offices in Nashville, others quickly followed suit. Visionary music publishers Jack Stamp (formerly of Tree Music Publishing, now Sony/ATV Tree) and Bill Hall (formerly of Welk Music Group, now Universal Music Group) situated their offices nearby. BMI, the first performing rights society to collect performance royalties for country music, opened a Nashville office. The Country Music Association was founded in 1958, and ground was broken for the Country Music Hall of Fame and Foundation in 1964.

But, while the tiny Music Row community continued to grow, the impact of rock 'n' roll took its toll on country radio. As Fats Domino, Chuck Berry, and Elvis Presley dominated the airwaves, the number of country music stations began to dwindle. The Grand Ole Opry and other live radio shows lost their importance in establishing country artists. As in many cities, Nashville's downtown district began to seriously deteriorate. The Ryman Auditorium was no longer the center of activity for country music throughout the nation or in Nashville. (In 1974, the Opry moved out to the newly built Opryland Complex of hotel, theme park, and auditorium, preserving the Ryman as a museum.)

Still, Nashville continued to make great records, and somehow, the music got out there. The industry discovered that demand for music revolved in cycles, making pop/rock popular for a while, then shifting to country music. Then, it cycles back to pop/rock or rap or Latino; then back to country. Now the market is changing drastically. With the deregulation of the airwaves, smaller radio stations are being bought at a frightening pace. Radio programmers who once determined the playlists for forty stations now program five hundred stations. The Internet is changing the way music is marketed and sold.

There will always be changes in the country music industry. But one thing is constant. A great song, a great singer, a great musician all stand the test of time. And Nashville will always be on the lookout for great new talent.

ABOUT MUSIC ROW

The Nashville music industry is tucked into a quiet residential district just southwest of downtown, on 16th, 17th, 18th, and 19th Avenues, between Blakemore/Wedgewood and Broadway and Division Streets, two miles deep and less than a mile wide. Ninety-nine percent of everything to do with the country music recording industry takes place within this small area. A few recording studios are located outside these boundaries but, for the most part, the business of music takes place here.

Once upon a time, not too long ago, the bulk of the music industry was located in beautiful old houses along Music Row. They were not recognizable as publishing companies, artist management companies, and other music-related businesses. Then along came Garth. The country music boom began. Major record companies built big new buildings and others followed suit. The landscape of Music Row changed drastically. Whereas ten years ago you could stand in the middle of Music Row and feel like you were in a residential area, today there is no mistaking the presence of successful music businesses.

It is impossible to calculate what portion of income the city derives from the country music recording industry, since much of the income it generates is collected and reported in other states, through main corporate offices. There are no statistics available on how many people travel to Nashville, work in the city's service occupations, and patronize its hotels, condos, restaurants, and stores because of the country music industry. But you don't need statistics to tell you that the impact of country music on Nashville is astounding. You will be amazed at the number of people you meet in service capacities who are aspiring songwriters or artists. You will especially be astounded at the remarkable talent everywhere you turn—not only performers featured in special showcases, but even those just "sitting in" at a corner bar. The competition is incredible and the city is saturated with talent. How you interact with this competition and present your own special gifts is very important.

That's what this book is all about. You will learn how to display your own particular talent in the best possible light and how to time your approach to give yourself the very best advantage. Most important of all, you will learn how the Nashville music industry thinks. The purpose of making a trip to Nashville is not to learn about the music industry. It is assumed that you already know the difference between a manager and a booking agent, between a producer and an engineer; the function of a performing rights society (and can name all three), of an A&R executive, and of a publisher; as well as what a publisher can do for you and a little bit about copyright protection.

If you are a country music singer and/or musician or if you are a songwriter of almost any kind of music, frequent visits to Nashville are a must. It may not be the best place for you to perform or showcase your talent, because sometimes it is best to be discovered outside of Nashville, in your own setting, but the business end of country music is centered on Music Row. All major record labels have divisions in Nashville, independent of their New York or Los Angeles offices. The signing of country acts, A&R representation, promotion, and marketing are run by these divisions. The same is true for publishing companies. Most country music publishers are located in Nashville because the people they are trying to reach on a daily basis work in Nashville.

Other music-related businesses, such as management, booking, legal representation, and other matters that do not require daily contact and socializing can be located just about anywhere; it really doesn't matter. What does matter is that you go to Nashville and meet the decision makers. Find out who they are, how they think, and what they want. They are the ones calling the shots. They are the ones who control country music. You need to know what their needs are and whether you can fill that need. If not now, perhaps in the future.

MAP OF MUSIC ROW

This bird's-eye view of the heart of Nashville's music industry (on the following two pages) highlights the major companies on the Row. Of course, there isn't room to list every single company, and the ones you are looking for might not be listed here, but this will help you to get your bearings. If you are able to do nothing else on your first trip to Nashville but familiarize yourself with a few of the businesses on this map, you will have accomplished a great deal.

It would be a good idea to take one morning or afternoon just walking around the Row with this map, making notes as you go of the companies you plan to visit. Note that Music Square West is actually 17th Avenue South, and Music Square East is 16th Avenue South. The street names and numbering system change once you pass Grand Avenue.

To Hillsboro Pike and the Bluebird Cafe

ACKLEN STREET

Acklen St. Post Office
SUNSET GRILL
PANCAKE PANTRY
Mail Boxes Etc.
The TRACE
IGUANA
CREATIVE TRUST
BELCOURT AVENUE
HARLAN HOWARD SONGS
CAPERS AVE.

21st AVENUE SOUTH

PEABODY COLLEGE
SCARRITT-BENNETT CENTER
VANDERBILT UNIVERSITY

17½ AVENUE SOUTH

BIG TRACTOR MUSIC
OASIS CENTER
BMG RCA LABEL GROUP
MANATT, PHELPS & PHILLIPS
MUSIC ROW MAGAZINE
WRENSONG PUBLISHING
ALMEBACH PUBLIC RELATIONS
GENL. FUERE MGMT.
MORRIS NANAS ENT.
APARTMENTS

18th AVENUE SOUTH

BOB DOYLE MGMT.
BLUE HAT RECORDS
MAINE BROS. MUSIC
BALMUR ENTERTAINMENT
BILLY SHERRILL
CO-HEART MUSIC
CRITERION MUSIC
STEVE CROPPER
APARTMENTS
CHET ATKINS
MALACO MUSIC
AMERICAN SONGWRITER
MUY BUENO MUSIC
BARRY BECKETT
CHIP PEAY ENT.
17 GRAND
RAY STEVENS
ERV WOOLSEY

WEDGEWOOD AVENUE

BEST BUILT SONGS
KEN LEVITAN MANAGEMENT
CROSSFIELD MUSIC
GURLEY & COMPANY
MUSIC SERVICES
PLA MEDIA
MALLOY BOYS STUDIOS
PLATINUM ENT.
DOUBLE J
OASIS CENTER
BORMAN ENT.
ANARICA
ISLAND BOUND PUBLISHING
HOUSE OF DAVID
OCEAN WAY
INGRAM-LEBRUN STUDIOS
APARTMENTS
LEE GREENWOOD
GLEN CAMPBELL BLDG.
ROGER MARRAH MUSIC
FAME
EMERALD MUSIC
AFTRA SAG
SUN TRUST BANK
DEATON-FLANIGEN PRODUCTIONS
API
GRAND AVENUE

16¾ AVENUE SOUTH

APARTMENTS

BELMONT UNIVERSITY

ARISTO MEDIA
RANDY TRAVIS MANAGEMENT
DREAM WORKS RECORDS
FORERUNNER MUSIC
JACKS TRACKS
HORTON AVENUE
SGA
SUSSMAN & ASSOC.

EDGEHILL AVENUE

PAUL WORLEY PROD.
HUNTSMAN ENTERTAINMENT
KIMS MARKET
SCHATZ PROD.
BUG MUSIC
FALCON-GOODMAN
HOT MUSIC
617 MUSIC SQUARE

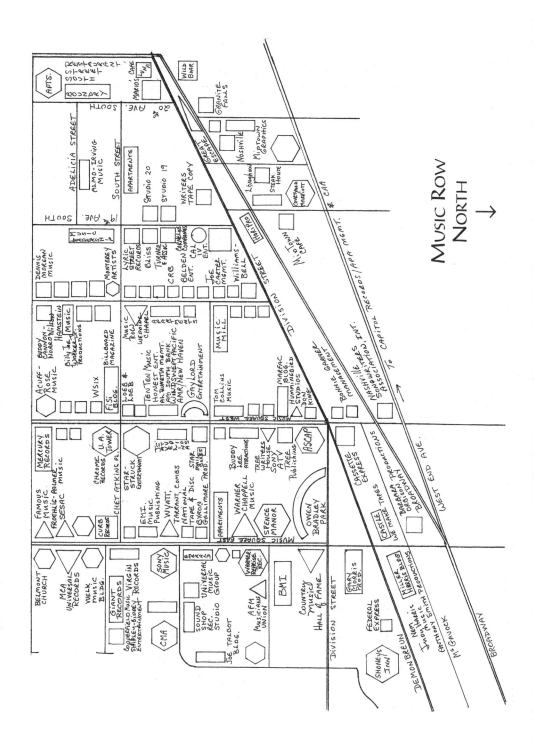

2

A Crash Course on the Music Industry (As It Pertains to Nashville)

opyright protection is one of the biggest concerns of a songwriter making his first trip to Nashville. What if someone hears his great idea, takes the hook, changes the lyrics, and thereby steals his song? It's a catch-22 for writer and publisher alike. Everyone has to be careful and wary. You have to find your comfort zone.

COPYRIGHT PROTECTION

A song is protected from the moment of creation. The problem is proof of creation. If you have unlimited funds, register every song with the Copyright Office of the Library of Congress, which almost always has the final say.

However, most Nashville publishers do not register a song with the Copyright Office until there has been some strong interest in it. Only if they are certain that a song will be recorded, will they go ahead and register it. If every demo in Nashville was registered, the Library of Congress would need a new building just to hold all the cassette tapes! Waiting until you are further along in the process is a good idea, because your songs are probably going to go through some changes before they are finally recorded with the Copyright Office.

What you can do, whenever you put any of your songs in print, is to protect them with a copyright notice: © 2000 John Doe; all rights reserved (on a small cassette with limited room © 2000 will do). Such notice might be effective as a deterrent to potential plagiarizers. What you should *not* rely upon is the "poor man's copyright." Poor man's copyright is the practice of putting your songs into a sealed envelope and mailing it to yourself using certified and return receipt requested forms. Songwriters may think that because the envelope carries a date stamped by a division of the U. S. Government, it will be accepted as proof of time of creation, should copyright ever come into legal question. Although this may seem a logical deduction, the practice is not considered reliable or provable. Therefore, it is a bad idea to put your trust in "poor man's copyright."

If you are really worried about your songs falling into unscrupulous hands, go ahead and spend the money to register them legally. Do whatever you deem necessary to protect them, and when you get to Nashville, stop worrying about it. It will be essential for you to share your songs with as many people as you possibly can. Sing them, give them to songwriters, give them to publishers, give out as many copies as possible. Give away all you brought with you.

THE ROLE OF A MUSIC PUBLISHER

Under the Copyright Law, every song has to be published, and the publisher keeps 50 percent of the total earnings of the song for a minimum of thirty-five years, depending on what he can negotiate. So even if you write a song and your best friend Garth Brooks records it, you still have to have a publisher for your song. Have you heard that you should probably try to keep your own publishing? Don't even think about it. Nashville publishers are your best contact in Nashville. You can meet with producers and A&R execs directly; you can pitch directly to artists. But you are still going to need a publisher. Every song must have a publisher, and even if you've legally set up your own publishing company, it doesn't carry much weight in Nashville.

It's the publisher's job to demo songs (with his own money, not yours!), pitch the song to the right artists, and register the song with the Copyright Office. (The publishing company holds the copyright to the song, not the writer. If the songwriter previously registered the song, the publisher re-registers it in the company's name and gets an assignment of copyright from the writer.) The publisher registers the song with the proper collection agencies (there are lots of them), collects royalties, negotiates synchronization licenses (TV and film), markets the song to film companies, TV and cable shows, etc., and gives 50 percent of all earnings to you, the writer.

Nashville publishers do a lot more: They encourage developing writers and artists to build relationships with other artists in order to better understand what types of songs they relate to, set up cowriting opportunities, and generally help their writers network in the community. Nashville publishers are worth their weight in gold!

THE ROLE OF THE PROS

Performing rights organizations (PROs) collect money every time a song is played on the air. Mostly, collections come from radio airplay, but they also come from large and small music venues, TV, movies, restaurants, jukeboxes, and the Internet. They come from any place that uses music to attract business. PRO income is *more than half* of a songwriter's royalty income on a hit song single, the other half collected by publishers for mechanical and print royalty income.

ASCAP, BMI, and SESAC use very different systems for discerning who gets paid what, but their age-old methods are rapidly changing with the advent of watermarking technology. They will wear you out trying to convince you that their method is the best! Currently in Nashville, the importance of the PROs lies more in networking opportunities, since it's hard to determine who pays the most royalties. But that may change as the use of technology makes monitoring more accurate. Study each PRO thoroughly, talk to other writers, and take your time before you sign on with one company. Publishers belong to all three PROs, but a writer can only join one of them.

Each PRO office in Nashville is actively involved in finding hit songwriters, artists, and musicians and directing them to the best publisher, artist manager, or booking agent. Therefore, all three of the PROs should be an important stop in Nashville.

THE ROLE OF AN A&R DEPARTMENT

A&R stands for "Artist and Repertoire." Each record company has an A&R department. Its job is to assist each artist with selecting songs for her next album project and to coordinate the various outside parties that are also involved in the song selection process. Besides the artists themselves, who will often make appointments with publishers to go into their offices and listen to songs, other people who are looking for songs include record producers (usually not part of the record company) and artist managers. Also, most artists write or cowrite songs for their album, so they have their own publishing company which is connected with one of Nashville's major publishing companies. That publisher may help the artist look for songs from other companies as well as their own catalogs, a very common practice in Nashville. The artist's A&R rep has to coordinate all the songs collected from these different sources.

Once the A&R rep has determined that a good number of songs are under consideration, he will call a meeting of all those concerned: artist, producer, and maybe the artist manager as well. They will decide which songs they are serious about, and then the A&R rep will call the publishers of the songs and put the songs "on hold." The hold policies of record companies and producers often come under fire from Nashville's music publishers. Once a song is put on hold for an artist, the publisher is prohibited from pitching it to another artist, tying up a great copyright. Publishers object to this practice when the A&R rep puts too many songs on hold (more than can be recorded) and the recording session date is a long way off. The danger is that when they finally get in the studio they change their minds and don't record the song after all. In the meantime, the publisher has lost an important opportunity to pitch the song to another artist. An opportunity to pitch a great song to the right artist doesn't come along very often, considering that an artist may only record one album a year.

Usually, an A&R rep helps the artist decide on a direction for an album project. A ten-song album should have a common theme, some balance in tempo that includes a mix of up-tempo, mid-tempo, and ballads, and it should be consistent with the image of the artist.

The A&R department also helps coordinate all the different internal departments of the record company that affect an album project—marketing, promotion, and publicity. Each of these separate departments work closely together to sell an artist—and the songs are a very important part of that sales pitch. It's the responsibility of the A&R reps to make sure the selected songs fit into the total picture of an artist's entire career, a big job when you consider how many different individuals are working separately to find songs for the artist.

THE DIFFERENCE BETWEEN AN ARTIST MANAGER AND A BOOKING AGENT

Although an artist manager and a booking agent have clearly defined roles, their jobs are intricately intertwined, making it essential for the two to cooperate. An artist manager has creative control over an artist's image: what songs to record, what clothes to wear, what clubs to play, what interviews to grant, what TV shows or films to do, what products to endorse, and all other issues which affect an artist's career.

The booking agent books all dates for the artist, which may sound simple on the surface, but is really a complicated process. An agent must handle moving an artist and his entourage across the country from city to city, booking the best clubs and state/county fairs, spacing performances so that the artist isn't overbooked or facing too much downtime, and must execute all of this in the best, most cost-effective manner. The booking agent books the dates, but the artist manager works with the artist's road manager, who makes sure all the stage equipment arrives and gets set up in time for the show, supervises concessions, and performs endless other tasks.

OTHER IMPORTANT PROFESSIONALS

It doesn't stop here. Artists need several more people on their payroll. They are:

An Entertainment Attorney

Entertainment attorneys are needed to negotiate those very complicated recording contracts. They cover not only the percentage points an artist will make on the sale of each album, but controlled compositions (a kickback to the record company on songs the artist writes), video costs, special markets like record clubs, and many more factors that cut into the potential earnings for the artist. In the music industry, and in Nashville particularly, an entertainment attorney is an integral part of an artist's career. In fact, if you are an artist or musician looking for a record deal, a great entertainment attorney may be a good place to start.

A Business Manager

There are so many people on an artist's payroll, and so many different sources of income, it's a full-time job just keeping track of it all. Most artists turn this big job over to a business manager. It's not unusual for an artist to be put on an "allowance," with the business manager deciding how much can be spent on a house, on clothes, and even on dinner Friday night!

An Accountant

A business manager doesn't file the complicated tax returns required for an artist. He'll need an accountant to do that and the long-term investment planning.

A Publicist

The record company handles most of the publicity needs for the artist, but an outside publicist can make a big difference in an artist's career. Again, for the artist or musician looking for a record deal, a great publicist can be just the place to start.

There are so many people on the artist's payroll—so many taking a piece of the pie—that it takes a rather long time for the artist to start realizing any substantial income. From the record company expense-side alone, an artist who sells 500,000 albums will just break even. Artists selling under that amount are usually dropped from the label after two or even one album release.

THE COUNTRY CHART SYSTEM (WITH COMMENTS BY MARC DRISKILL, DIRECTOR OF BUSINESS AFFAIRS, NASHVILLE ASCAP)

The Nashville major record labels use one predominant method of marketing their product: They heavily promote a single song chosen from an artist's current album to be played on targeted country radio stations across the country. They work closely with the station program directors who sometimes control the programming for as many as five hundred stations. In the early 1980s, when record labels were told that new technology could monitor exactly how many times a single had been played, the record companies rejected that system and went with one that was more easily manipulated. Technology won. Today, record companies are starting to use "fingerprinting" to trace the use of their product.

According to Marc Driskill:

"Record companies that use *Billboard's Country Airplay Monitor* to chart the progress of their country singles encode each single with a non-audio digital watermark or 'fingerprint,' which is then given to Broadcast Data Systems (BDS). BDS monitors 154 radio markets, with each market having ten to fourteen radio stations in it. BDS monitors 1,085 radio stations total and just acquired Media Base which monitors 671 stations. This increases their base by 50 percent.

"There are 2,500 stations that play country music in all, so BDS is now monitoring more than half of all country radio.

"BDS calculates how many spins each single receives and reports these figures in *Billboard's Country Airplay Monitor.* It's pretty amazing to see how many spins the Top Ten or Top Twenty singles get as compared to anything lower. For example, the Top Ten songs get 37 percent of the airplay; the Top Twenty get 26 percent. That's over 50 percent of total airplay for those twenty songs. Combined, the Top Twenty-five songs get 74 percent of airplay; songs which chart from fifty-one through one hundred get only 3 percent of airplay. If you just get a chart position of fifty or so, you're not really in the game. Those levels are not going to pay much.

"A Number One hit is pretty much determined by the artist. If you have a single by Garth Brooks or George Strait, the song will shoot straight up the chart. The less time it's on the chart, the less you get paid. So a Number One song can pay anywhere from $150,000 to $300,000 at ASCAP, depending on how long it stays on the chart. Payment is doubled with time spent going up the chart.

"The biggest portion of income from performances comes from radio. What radio is required to pay has gone down substantially. Collections are around 3 percent of the advertising budgets of the stations.

A rate court decides how much will be paid to each of the three PROs. Our goal is to give adequate compensation for the use of our copyrights, but we are seeing that rate reduced. Radio is saying that song spins are going down, that they are not playing as much music. Radio is saying that people do not listen to the radio for the music.

"The generation out there now is used to having something in their hands. But that is rapidly changing. We are moving away from paper and over to technology. There will come a day when we can buy the right to listen to a song one time; thirty days, etc. The industry will be completely different than the way it is today."

ABOUT DIGITAL WATERMARKING

A digital watermark or "fingerprint" is a non-audio code that is embedded into sound and video recordings. The term comes from the watermarking system that already exists for high-quality stationery and currency. In those industries, a watermark serves as a code of excellence and authenticity. Audio watermarks are more specific. They contain information about copyright ownership and can include as much information as desired: date, copyright registration numbers, publisher, writer, and so on. This code becomes an integral part of the music itself as it travels through any transmission media, including radio, television, cable, satellite, Internet, CD, DVD, and cassette tape. There are many different companies creating their own fingerprinting systems.

The music industry has been very resistant to new technology in the area of digital watermarking. The industry has claimed that digital watermarking will interfere with superior sound quality, which is the industry's first priority in the area of new technology. Two major factors convinced music industry executives to change their minds: 1) continued loss of revenue due to illegal duplication and 2) the rapid growth of downloadable music on the Internet. Once the music industry decided to accept the practice of digital watermarking, the question became, "which one?" Today, the industry struggles to find the right answer to that question.

DIFFERENT SOURCES OF INCOME AND HOW IT IS COLLECTED

For a songwriter, there are two primary sources of income: performance and mechanical. Performance money is collected by one of the PROs and paid directly to the writer. The publisher will share in 50 percent of the performance earnings, but the PRO will pay the writer and publisher separately.

Mechanical earnings come from the sale of CDs and cassettes. There is a statutory rate for all mechanicals, so everyone is paid the same for each three minutes of recorded music. The record companies issue a royalty statement four times a year, one each quarter; and they categorize their mechanical earnings according to publishers, including songs from several different CDs and cassettes on one royalty statement. Because this could get very confusing, the National Association of Music Publishers set up a clearinghouse for publishers called the Harry Fox Agency. Most publishers belong to this agency. The record company sends their royalty statement to the Harry Fox Agency, which reviews the statement, keeps 4.5 percent for the effort, and then sends the money and statement to the publisher.

The publisher then creates its own royalty statement, which lists all of the writer's songs and all of the different record companies who have paid mechanicals on these songs. The publisher keeps 50 percent of the earnings and sends the other 50 percent to the writer. It would be unethical for the publisher to deduct any fees or services—demo costs, for example—from the writer's 50 percent share. All costs incurred in the marketing of a song are the publisher's responsibility. It is a generally accepted practice to deduct the Harry Fox fees off of the top, with the publisher and the writer absorbing 2.25 percent each. Although the publisher collects from Harry Fox four times a year, the writer gets paid only twice a year: on February 15 for the collection period of July through December, and on August 15 for the period of January through June.

The terminology of publishing income is very confusing. If a song earns $100, the publisher and writer each receive $50. However, the 50 percent share of the publisher is referred to as 100 percent of the publishing. So if a publisher says he has one hundred percent of a song, he means he will get fifty percent of the earnings from the song. Usually, there is more than one publisher for a song, and two publishers will generally split the earnings 50/50. Splits for other than equal shares are very rare. The same applies for cowriters. If you decide to share your ideas with another writer and you end up writing most of the song, be prepared to give away 50 percent of the song anyway. It's just the way it's done, and if you aren't willing to share 50/50, your cowriter will feel like she's been treated unfairly.

Artists have lots of different sources of income: They are paid a certain number of percentage "points" for each CD sold (this can vary widely depending on what an artist is able to negotiate; that's why you need that great lawyer!). The sad thing is that almost everything a record company spends on an artist—the master recording, videos, costs associated with TV appearances, and advances to help the artist get by until he starts establishing an income—are taken out of the artist's royalties. So an artist really won't make anything unless he sells over 500,000 units; that's usually the break-even point. A record company is almost like a lending company, putting up the money to launch an artist's career. Other income for an artist comes from concerts, merchandise sales, songwriting, and some publishing revenue if he's lucky enough to establish his own publishing company.

Here is the most startling thing about this industry . . . an artist does not get paid for radio airplay! Only the writer and the publisher are paid for all that wonderful music we hear on the radio. That's why artists want to write and publish their own music if they can. What they usually wind up doing is cowriting with a hit songwriter. The hit writer may bring the most expertise to the table, but he is almost assured of getting his song on the album in return.

Musicians don't earn any royalties at all. They get a flat fee and that's it. There is a set union scale, and session musicians earn double, triple, or more. Once the record is cut, that's it. It doesn't make any difference whether it sells 50 or 500,000. But down the line, if the master session they played on is used in a film or some other source, musicians are paid the same fee again.

In Nashville, most of the live music clubs are considered "writers" clubs—so the club owners get away with not paying anything at all for the great music performed in their clubs night after night. Clubs vary greatly in the way they book and pay bands. For the clubs that allow a cover charge, the band usually gets to charge at the door and has some kind of agreement to share the earnings with the club owner. Other clubs don't allow bands to charge a cover, so those bands have to rely on a tip jar set up at the front of the stage. Another famous Bradley, Harold Bradley, brother of Owen, is president of the local musicians' union, the AFM (American Federation of Musicians). Since taking on presidential duties, he has worked hard to try to help musicians get paid in Nashville clubs. There is a reasonable club rate set by the union that can be used as a negotiating tool, but the chances of getting paid to play are still slim.

I hope that this chapter has given you a quick overview of the music industry, so that you have an idea of how things work when you come to Nashville to pitch your songs. However, a more comprehensive understanding of the music field—applicable law, possible careers, technological advances, etc.—is always desirable and useful. For information about these and other aspects of the music business, see Recommended Reading.

3

How to Know If Your Talent Measures Up to Nashville Standards

O K, we know. Your mom loves your songs (or spouse, or kids). There is an intrinsic special quality to your songs, because they are a part of you. It is wonderful that you have a gift to share your thoughts, feelings, and emotions through songs. However, they may not be commercial.

LITMUS TEST FOR SONGWRITERS

You need an objective opinion in order to evaluate your song's commercial potential, and here is how to get one:

1. Have your song evaluated by the Nashville Songwriters Association International (NSAI). Their Web address is *www.nashvillesong-writers.com.* You will probably have to join in order to take advantage of their song critique service, but it will be worth it. Joining NSAI is the most important step you can take in the advancement of your Nashville songwriting career.

2. Have your song evaluated by a songwriters' organization in or near your hometown. Join every songwriters' organization in your vicinity. Start going to as many meetings as you possibly can, performing or playing your songs for members, critique sessions,

anything that can get you some feedback from other writers or publishers. If you don't know of any organizations near you, then call NSAI at (800) 321-6008 and ask them for the one closest to you. They have NSAI chapters all across the country. Come to think of it, information about the chapters is also posted on their Web site.

3. Attend songwriting seminars, workshops, and conferences. There are many of these held all across the country every month. Start seeking them out and attending as many as you possibly can. You will learn a lot and meet some very important people who may influence your songwriting or artistic career. How can you find them? Try songwriter magazines, music magazines, the Web, and the PROs.

4. Get professional advice from the PROs. ASCAP and BMI have offices in New York, Los Angeles, Chicago, Atlanta, Miami, London, Puerto Rico, and Nashville; SESAC in New York, London, and Nashville. If you are close enough to any one of these cities to visit their offices, then do so and ask for an *honest* evaluation of your songs. You want to know if they would be willing to invest time in the advancement of your career. If they think you are talented, they will want to help you as much as they can, because they make money when you are successful. If they don't see any potential in your music, then you have to ask yourself why. They are an excellent barometer for your songs.

5. Call and ask permission to send a song for evaluation to the Nashville PRO offices. You have to ask for a writers' representative by name, so it will take a little research on your part to learn who writers' representatives are. BMI has a policy to give an evaluation if asked. ASCAP and SESAC might be a little tougher to get someone to agree to listen, but they are both worth a try.

6. Enter a song contest. Again, you will have to track them down through songwriter magazines, music magazines, the Web, and the PROs.

7. Contact recording studios in your immediate area and ask for their feedback. They are in the song business—what do they think of your songs?

8. Try to get a local band to perform or record your songs. Who are you writing for? People who love your music! They don't have to be just the top recording artists. Your songs could shine with an unknown artist. Which bands and artists are the most popular in your area? What do they think of your songs?

LITMUS TEST FOR ASPIRING ARTISTS AND MUSICIANS

In order to attract the attention of Nashville record labels, you are going to need a pretty awesome track record as a performing artist. They will be looking for experience—it helps if you've played in bands for years, and maybe won some awards (local contests). If you are packing them in at the local watering hole on weekends, it won't be difficult to get someone from Nashville to come and see your act. Aim for the top. What label do you think you'll fit in the best? Call that company and let it know what's going on in your hometown. What producer do you want to work with? What publisher? What artist manager? What booking agent? Call these people if you really have a strong following in your local club and can count on a good enthusiastic crowd.

They are looking for a unique quality. It is very, very important that you have a strong self-image. Contrary to what you might have heard, the record labels will not shape you into what they want you to be. You have to decide who you are and stick to it. That is harder than it sounds, because you probably can and have sung and played all styles of music. But they are listening to what you are trying to tell them—your own personal message.

You must perform original music for the music industry. You probably have a great repertoire of country favorites that you perform regularly in a local club; fans like to hear the hits. But the industry wants to hear new songs. If you don't write your own material, then you will have to find some great writers who will let you perform their songs. If you can find some writers who can't perform their songs themselves, then you have a perfect situation. You will be helping each other.

How much time have you spent in a recording studio? It is much harder than you might think to get your message across in a studio. There is a lot going on that has nothing to do with you, but it will distract you and interfere with your performance. Just picking the right microphone for your voice is a major challenge. The more experience you have had in this area, the better. You might want to hang around local studios and offer your free services if you need more studio time under your belt.

4

A Basic Understanding of Music Row

Probably the one thing that is going to surprise you most about Nashville is how helpful everyone is. The main topic of conversation for just about everybody is "Who's looking for songs right now?" Not only will your peers share this information with you, they will actually tell you how to get a song to whoever is looking. Although it is a highly competitive field, everyone on Music Row will go out of their way to help you succeed. It is a true fellowship; a camaraderie not found in any other highly competitive field.

The reason for this is that *the best song wins.* When it comes right down to it, it really doesn't matter who you are, who you know, or whether you've had songs recorded before. All that counts is that your song says what a particular artist wants to say, in the way she wants to say it.

THE WRITING ENVIRONMENT

The biggest mistake most songwriters make when they go to Nashville is to spend all their time trying to get appointments to play their songs for someone. As hard as this may be to understand, appointments with publishers or producers should not be your highest priority. Spending as much time as possible in the writing environment should be your primary goal.

You will find yourself in the writing environment as soon as you step off the plane, hop off the bus, or pull your car up beside the motel door.

Everyone in Nashville is a songwriter, or knows someone who is. Be open, be friendly to everyone you meet—they are going to be exceptionally friendly to you. And it's not just lip service—they mean it. Your Nashville experience starts the minute you arrive. The person you meet in the airport terminal might turn out to be the most valuable contact you make on your entire trip. Don't allow yourself to miss an opportunity by having certain expectations; be open to just about anything. Of course, there are places where songwriters hang out, and you will want to spend as much time in these spots as possible. They are:

- Writers' nights and open mic nights (chapter 4)
- Publishing companies (chapter 5)
- Music Row area restaurants (chapter 10)
- The Acklen Station Post Office (chapter 10)
- Golfing, fishing, playing tennis (chapter 10)

Surprisingly enough, you are not likely to find songwriters in Nashville's tourist areas. All the places you've just read about—the Wildhorse Saloon, Tootsie's, the Grand Ole Opry—don't attract aspiring songwriters, artists, and musicians, unless there is a specific industry showcase taking place. This book will tell you how to figure out where to go to hang out with the industry, and how to tell the difference between an industry gathering and a tourist gathering.

THE IMPORTANCE OF COLLABORATION

Ninety percent of the songs recorded in Nashville are cowritten and copublished. This is one more demonstration of the strong emphasis that Music Row places on networking and working together. The first question a publisher will ask a writer is "Who do you write with?" Cowritten songs are taken more seriously in Nashville. There are many reasons for this phenomenon:

- Cowriting provides expanded opportunities for pitching the song.
- Cowriters challenge each other to do their best writing
- Cowriters bring different skills to the songwriting project
- Cowriting is a learning experience that can't be duplicated in the classroom
- A well-known cowriter provides name recognition for an unknown writer
- Cowriting is motivational
- Cowriting provides opportunities to write with someone closely connected to an album project, such as the producer or artist

INDUSTRY INTERVIEW WITH ROGER MURRAH

Photo by Beth Gwinn

"Professional songwriters as well as writers just getting started can greatly benefit from cowriting. That's why I do it myself. For a two or three-year period I was writing with a different writer every day, five days a week. Cowriting helps writers maintain a consistent number of quality songs by having the challenge of another writer sharing ideas. I will not cut quality to build up volume. I like to feel that the song has gotten my best before I let it go. Some people emphasize the importance of volume, others emphasize quality. I feel that the quality of your songs is more important than the volume of songs in your catalog.

"Writers just getting started often want to write with professional writers. I like to write with new writers. I may have to sort through a ton of them before I find one I like and want to work with, but they usually come up with things I haven't heard before. It may be a melody, or a line or two, or both. New writers seem to come up with fresh ideas, or fresh ways to write old ideas. If you look at the song today, you'll find that new writers are having hits with old ideas, written from a modern point of view. They don't even know their idea has been a hit before, because they weren't around at that time and haven't heard it.

"I've had writers call me and convince me that we should write together. Many times a new writer may have been recommended by another professional writer, an industry acquaintance, a friend, or a publisher. I may not know the writer personally, but I may trust his publisher. I feel one of the main responsibilities of a publisher is to help set up collaborations for his staff writers. Generally speaking, new writers need someone to toot their horn for them until they build their own reputations.

"Songwriting can be lonely work. That's another reason for cowriting: It's appealing to have another person in the room with you when you are writing. It is very motivational when you get the right two people together.

"Once two or more songwriters get involved in creating a song together it's almost impossible to tell who contributed what portion of the song. Songwriters can sometimes get into a dispute over royalty disbursement. The most common situation is an even split, although it is done several different ways, depending on the writers themselves. I've always split evenly, even if my cowriter only contributed a title. That way there is no doubt about fairness.

"I used to feel that it was important to have my name first—I was putting so much energy into my songs, I guess, I felt like I was contributing the most. But now I've changed, and I always put my name last. I guess my ego changed. Actually, I think new writers will benefit by putting their name first. The well-known writer will get his credit anyway. His name will automatically stand out. The decision on whose name goes first is up to the individual writers, but I don't think there is much gain either way—it's pretty much just an ego trip.

"One of the major advantages of cowriting is the expanded opportunities for pitching the song. Each writer and publisher has his own circle of acquaintances. The more opportunities for pitching the song, the better the chances of getting it recorded. This major advantage can also be a major disadvantage. One of the biggest problems that comes out of collaborations is the situation of overpitching. It is not uncommon in Nashville for a song to be put 'on hold' by two producers at the same time. This unhappy situation can make a lot of people very frustrated—the artists, record companies, producers, managers, not to mention the publishers and writers. What can happen is that ultimately no one records the song—everyone loses. We all have to communicate with the people who are working with us on that song. We don't want to lose a cut because somebody's running all over town with a song! Pitches are carefully planned, and you have to be cautious.

"The ultimate cowriting opportunity can be with the artists themselves. I had pitched songs to Waylon Jennings and he had recorded several of them. One day he just called out of the blue and said, 'I'm thinking about putting together an album about my life, and I'd like you to be involved.' Writing the album *A Man Called Hoss* was a joy! He'd show up at my office in a big Cadillac he called 'The Golden Nose,' and the first thing he would do was order Brown's hamburgers for everybody. We'd sit around and eat and he'd tell jokes. I tried to keep it a fun, lighthearted atmosphere. Waylon has a wonderful sense of humor, and he'll laugh at himself. Waylon enjoyed it so much, he even made the comment that he felt it was the best he had done. It was a wonderful opportunity for me."

What can a new writer expect at his first cowriting appointment?
"The first thing you do is meet and talk about ideas for an hour or so. Assuming you come up with a good idea, you'll set aside one full day to write. Usually it takes two days—one day to start and one day to finish. Sometimes it will come together in one day."

What happens if two writers start working on an idea and it doesn't work out?
"If I get together with a writer and we are working on an idea of his, if we can't come up with a viable product, then I feel he should have his idea back. Every writer may not feel that way if he has put a lot of time into the song, but to me it eliminates hassle. More than likely, if the two of you don't feel like you have something, you probably don't.

"The most important thing in cowriting is keeping your ego in check. It is imperative that egos be left outside the room. The sooner you shed that ego, the quicker you can get down to what's best for the song. You have to learn to chip away at your ego in the right spots, so your ego will allow you to make a living."

INDUSTRY INTERVIEW WITH KATHERINE DINES

Photo by Kay Williams

"I grew up in a warm and loving musical family. My dad taught himself to play the harmonica, ukulele, mandolin, and banjo, and my mom had a beautiful voice. They sang wonderful old-timey duets and, at family gatherings, our uncle and aunt joined them in four-part barbershop style. For special occasions, my parents wrote humorous lyrics to standard melodies for their friends. As a third grader, I beamed with pride when my mom brought her guitar to school and performed at our assembly.

"My mom passed her guitar along to me on my sixteenth birthday. The guitar had a very narrow neck, and the action was so high it hurt to play. So my Dad traded it for a beautiful 0-21 Martin plus some cash—if I promised to work hard to pay him back. It took two years and plenty of extra chores, but that guitar was worth every cent.

"In high school, I sang in a madrigal group called The 4's. My boyfriend's band played at local high schools and events, and during breaks, The 4's played acoustic sets—mostly folk songs—along with a few of our originals. After I graduated from high school, I performed solo at various coffeehouses for about two years. But from the first time I walked out on stage alone and every time after that, I was struck with *severe* stage fright. I'm talking about the 'toss-your-cookies-before-and-after-several-times' kind. So rather than trying to fight that, I left the stage and fled to my basement, where I wrote songs and began to learn all I could about the craft. And my boyfriend and I got married.

"Somewhere I read about the Los Angeles Songwriters' Showcase (LASS), a songwriter's organization. I immediately joined, and attended one of their conferences. It was a tremendous opportunity to meet with publishers, songwriters, producers, and peers in the music industry. For once I was with others who did what I did.

"I then entered songwriting contests. After winning the Kerrville New Folk Festival in Texas, I managed to place in the *Music City News* Song Contest, American Song Festival, and a couple of others. Many people criticize contests. For me, they were an important part of the process. With my husband's encouragement, I quit my job and drove to Nashville for the entire month of November—my guitar and notepads in hand. There, I managed to sublet a tiny duplex for $50 a month off of Edmondson Pike. It was freezing! The water bed had a leak and no heater. Since there were no appliances either, I cooked soup every day on a Coleman stove, and drank warm 7-Up. I wrote and wrote—sometimes all day and far into the night.

"I attended writers' nights three times a week, soaked up information from NSAI, the Songwriters' Guild, and other writers, and got as much feedback from publishers as I could. I met and mingled with as many industry people as I could, and became totally immersed in the Nashville music scene—learning about and trying to write songs for the country music market.

"A month later I returned to Denver. After all, I did have a husband, a home, and a life there! Periodically, I sent postcards to the people I had met—just to keep in touch. I carried around a book full of those contacts, and tried to keep tabs with all the Nashville goings-on. That was difficult from a distance—not simply because of the energy and time it took, but because people changed jobs so frequently. For the next three years in a row, I worked as a freelance graphic artist, and squeezed in as much songwriting as I could. I made annual treks to Nashville every November, and continued to Meet, Mingle, and Maintain, my personal '3Ms for success.' Positive feedback from publishers and all the new friends I met there kept me going.

"Slowly, publishers began taking an interest in my work. Maypop Music hooked me up with a writer and gave us each a $50 advance for a song we wrote in twenty minutes (I framed the check!). It was pitched to Alabama and some other artists. Two other publishers said they had holds on two of my songs, one with Barbra Streisand and the other with Madonna. But they were never cut. A producer and some other songwriter in Canada then rewrote two lines of my song ('True Love Is'). It was cut by an artist named Von and charted in Canada.

"Back in Denver, in my spare time, I wrote and rewrote songs. As soon as I'd arrive for my month in Nashville, I'd go straight to Jackie Cook's Song Cellar and demo as many songs as I could afford. Of the thirty songs I demo'd in three years' time, nineteen were eventually published . . . which isn't a bad percentage! If I had been in Nashville more often, and mingled there longer, I have no doubt that I would have gotten more cuts.

"On one of my yearly trips to Nashville, I met a woman at a writers' night. She had been in Nashville for a long time, and had just written a Number One song for Reba McEntire. She thought a few of my songs might be a good fit for a publisher named Aaron Brown. Aaron did like them, but instead of offering me a publishing deal, asked if I would be interested in writing lullabies instead. I told him, 'I don't know, but I'll try.' But secretly I thought, 'Wait! I don't have any children! How can I write a lullaby?'

"That same day I went to the library and checked out the only seven books I could find on the subject and browsed through stores in search of more. Very few were available. I visited mothers and fathers of new babies, and chatted with nurses at the Vanderbilt Hospital nursery. I got intensely excited about the project—probably because I wasn't able to have children myself.

"Then, about three days later, I was strumming away and mulling around the whole concept. Suddenly, this lyric and melody just 'flew into my head.' In less than ten minutes, I had the whole song 'Wings.' I put my guitar down and started to cry. Whatever had happened, it was my first 'A-Ha!' at what the process of songwriting is all about. That was a very riveting moment. The song came as a gift. I was simply the instrument that was open to receive it, and was now able to share it. That experience touched my being so deeply, it was a blessing.

"Soon after that, I wrote another lullaby. Then I went into the studio and demo'd both of them. I took the completed songs to Aaron, and he loved 'Wings' but said he wanted a rewrite on 'Someday Baby.' I said, 'I can't write any better than this! I have given you my best work!' He said, 'I'll give you three more days, and on your way back to Denver in the middle of Kansas, I'll bet you come up with exactly what I'm looking for. By the way, I would like to have the publishing, and will send you contracts for both songs—that is, if you get the last one right!'

"I really didn't know what that meant at the time. I was too new to the business. So I struggled with getting two tiny lines 'right' on the song 'Someday Baby' for three long days before I had to pack the car up and head to Denver. Sure enough, somewhere in the middle of Kansas, those lines came to me. I called Aaron from a pay phone (no cell phones in '86), and sang the revised lyric into his answering machine. He woke me at 2:00 A.M. the following morning and played the finished tracks to 'Wings' and

'Someday Baby.' He said that my two songs were so beautiful, they had made everyone in the studio cry!

"Both songs are now part of the album, *A Child's Gift of Lullabies*. It was nominated for a Grammy, went Platinum, and has been translated into five other languages. Aaron even changed the name of his publishing company to Someday Baby—after my song!

"While all this was happening, I tried to talk my husband into moving to Nashville. When he wouldn't budge, I decided to be content with the minor success I had had and to write songs more or less as a hobby. My guitar went back under the bed, and I said goodbye to what should have become an even more successful songwriting career. After about three months, I was so desperate for a music scene like the one I had experienced in Nashville, I decided to create one. So I founded the Rocky Mountain Music Association (RMMA). Then, I approached professionals in the music field and put together an amazing board of directors. We had just about every aspect of the music industry represented: newspaper, television and radio, club owner, booking agent, and promoter, recording studio, producer, engineer, songwriter, publisher, musician, attorney, music educator, and Yours Truly.

"The first event I conceived for RMMA was called MusicFest. We offered twelve seminars on various subjects pertaining to the business of music for a full day, showcases for two consecutive nights in twelve different clubs around the city, and a trade show with twenty-one booths. Over 750 people attended the seminars, and on both nights every club was jam-packed. Music industry professionals from Nashville, Los Angeles, and New York flocked to Denver to listen to the talent at MusicFest II. Two bands were signed to major labels: Big Head Todd and the Monsters and the subdudes.

"The RMMA board sent me to Austin, Texas, so I could meet and learn from the people involved in South By Southwest (SXSW—an extremely successful and profitable music conference). For an extra $25, I was able to fly back to Denver through Nashville, where I decided to make a three-day stop. One of those nights in Nashville, I was lying on a friend's futon, staring out the guestroom window, when I heard a loud 'voice' (woooeeeeoooo!) cry out: 'What are you doing with your life?' I just lay there in the dark and wept, because I had no idea how to answer that question. Then I heard 'the voice' again, and it said: 'Your destiny is to move to Nashville and be a songwriter!' To me, that voice was undeniably God talking. It was the truth I had been seeking my entire life. And from that moment on, my work with RMMA was finished. Also, my marriage ended in divorce, and I was finally free to follow my heart.

"During that three-day stop in Nashville, I made a point of visiting my old haunts. One of them was at ASCAP. Tom Long, who was a writers' rep there, was a brand new daddy. So I gave him a copy of *A Child's Gift of Lullabies*. After he listened to it, he asked me if I could write some children's songs for a theater group. I said, 'I don't know, Tom. I don't have any children. But I'll try!'

"For two weeks, I wondered and researched. I hung out with friends who had children, visited preschools, played in sandboxes and swung on jungle gyms with children. I asked them questions. I sat in backseats of carpools, listened to them, played with them, and observed them. When I finally picked up my guitar, a saying my grandmother used all the time when I was a child came into my head. 'KICK-ta-bill-icky-ALL-uh-guh-LOCKS-tuh-HUNK-ta-bunk-ta-boo-YOO-HOO!' It was a wonderfully playful word—fun and full of rhythm and rhyme, and at that moment, once again, my path took another sudden turn. I had never been so inspired. To this day, I truly believe that at that moment God allowed me to realize my gift: to write music for children.

"I wrote solidly for two or three days, came up with five songs, demo'd them at a Denver studio and sent them to Tom Long. He planned to use all of them until his project suddenly fell through. But that didn't bother me in the least because I loved writing them so much, and had finally found my niche.

"My Denver friends who had kids knew what I had been doing and invited me to perform at their children's birthday parties. I wrote a special song in honor of each one, and performed other originals. Strangely enough, in front of those brilliant, young, smiling faces, I had absolutely no stage fright. Parents began to ask where they could buy my music. During that time, I was having so much fun writing and performing songs in Denver, I had decided to ignore the voice I had heard in Nashville. Besides, why would I want to leave my home of thirty-eight years, my friends and family, and move to Nashville?

"In Denver, I made a lease/option deal on a loft in an old building. Just as I was ready to move in, the owner of the loft called to say that our deal was off. I had nowhere to go until a friend's friend hired me as a house sitter. I sat in the middle of her big empty house and wrote. Songs for children poured out of me.

"The second week I was there, I got three phone calls from Nashville in one afternoon. The first one was a job offer as director of the Songwriters' Guild. The next one came from a friend in real estate who said now was the time to buy in Nashville. The last call was about a position that was open at NSAI. I took all of these calls as an absolute sign that it was time to move to Music City, and that the voice could not be denied again.

"I flew to Nashville to interview with NSAI, and was hired on the spot. I moved there on June 1, and rented a house in Sylvan Park with another writer. I worked full time at NSAI for about eighteen months and then for another six as a consultant. Being at NSAI was a great way to meet publishers, producers, and all the really great (and not so great) writers in town. In my spare time, I wrote.

"My first paid gig came in 1992 from my younger sister who lived in Casper, Wyoming, with her three children—just the right ages for my music. At that point, I gave up my NSAI job. She arranged for me to perform at her children's elementary schools and three others in the community. I recorded my first album, *Hunk-Ta-Bunk-Ta BOO*. As a recording artist, I had attracted keen interest from Pam Lewis for management and had a contract to sign with her, but Garth Brooks managed to grab her attention. I spent hours on the phone chasing after every possible lead and sending out what seemed like hundreds of pieces of mail per month: promotional folders, cover letters, and *Hunk-Ta-Bunk-Ta BOO* albums. My postage and phone bills were astronomical.

"I was trying to decide what to call the next album, when I went to get my hair cut. While I was in the chair, I overheard a woman next to me chatting with her hairdresser about this 'wonderful music her kids had fallen in love with called Hunk-Ta-Bunk-Ta or something like that.' BOOM! It hit me! My grandmother's phrase now had a life of its own, and thereafter I would call all of my records 'Hunk-Ta-Bunk-Ta *something*.'

"Today I continue to travel the Hunk-Ta-Bunk-Ta™ path. With six award-winning albums for children ages four to twelve, activity guides, piano arrangements, television and radio shows, read-along booklets, and seven licensable characters, I am expanding the line, as well as writing for and licensing my songs to different companies. I also teach and perform for family audiences everywhere, with a target market of children ages four to twelve. More recently, I have been invited to present keynote addresses at educational conferences. I've learned a lot about selling records and more about the business side than I ever wanted to. It is a full-time job keeping up with inventory, invoicing and shipping. Every album is targeted to specific audiences, so I am able to market them more effectively, which translates into an increase in sales. In turn, the sales increases have expanded my market, given Hunk-Ta-Bunk-Ta more visibility and added more credibility to my reputation as an artist.

"Any successes I may have had are a result of my faith in God, family, and close friends, hard work, focus, and the personal contacts I have Met, Mingled with, and Maintained along the way (my 3Ms). In closing, I offer this encouragement to all songwriters: Music is indeed the language of the soul. There is one clear voice there that will guide you. Once it speaks and rings true, follow that voice—wherever it takes you."

KATHERINE DINES is a singer/songwriter from Denver, Colorado, who moved to Nashville to pursue a career in country songwriting and wound up taking several unexpected paths. Growing up in a talented musical family, Katherine felt destined to try to hone her skills in music. She learned to play the guitar and started singing in high school and college. Severe stage fright and an abundance of creativity in many other artistic areas led Katherine to put down her guitar and concentrate on the business side of the music industry. She founded the first songwriter's association in Colorado, the Rocky Mountain Music Association, and put together a two-day music conference, which led to the discovery of hit songwriter John Ims ("She's in Love with the Boy") and the major label signing of the band Big Head Todd and the Monsters.

Katherine's children's songs "Someday Baby" and "Wings" became big hits, creating more demand for children's material. *A Gift of Lullabies* was nominated for a Grammy, translated into five other languages, and went Platinum.

Today, Katherine has written and produced a series of albums targeted to children. She tours extensively in the United States and Europe, running her business as songwriter/artist, publisher, record producer, and record company executive. You can check out her Web site at *http:// songs.com/hunkta.*

INDUSTRY INTERVIEW WITH MIKE SETTLE

"My focus is to be as commercial as possible. 'But You Know I Love You' has had 2 million units of airplay. It's hard to top that!

"My first cut was 'Settle Down' by Peter, Paul and Mary. With the First Edition, I did the Johnny Cash show, performed at Nashville's Vanderbilt campus, and met lots of people in Nashville. I left the First Edition, and Bob Montgomery produced a solo album on me for the MCA/Uni label. I signed a publishing deal with Montgomery's publishing company, House of Gold, and met songwriters Kenny O'Dell ('Mama He's Crazy') and Larry Henley ('Wind Beneath My Wings').

"I loved writing for Bob Montgomery. As a publisher, Bob gave writers positive and encouraging feedback without making the writer feel that he didn't have any talent. I really believe that a publisher is a partner whose number one job is marketing the song, and his number two job is to help the writer keep the creative juices flowing. Montgomery was great at that. I would show him a line or two, or a chorus, and Bob would help me with the direction of the song.

"My album was released around the time of Elton John's first release—there were tons of pop singers and songwriters during that period. I stopped being an artist and stopped performing, and began concentrating on songwriting. As a writer/artist, it's no big deal to place songs on your album—but a true songwriter has the challenge of attracting an artist to record his songs.

"In the early eighties I realized that what I wanted to do was to write songs that had a universal appeal. I was writing with other writers in Los Angeles. They just weren't country; they were what I thought country was or what I wanted country to include. Basically, I wasn't speaking the right language. I had not absorbed the country field or the Nashville sound. I would come down, write a little bit, pitch a little bit. I wasn't writing with other writers. I got some cuts by Johnny Rodriguez, Charlie Rich, and others.

"I would come for two or three weeks at a time, three or four times a year. I would come for CMA Week and the Country Radio Seminar. These are good when you know a lot of people; but it is hard to get appointments around this time. Before I even bothered coming to town I'd make sure that people who didn't know me and had never met me before had listened to my songs and identified with them. A listener has to identify with the story of the song.

"The first place to explore is where you live. Try and find people who know someone in Nashville. Then use that name to get an appointment—'so-and-so said to give you a call.' In the songwriting organizations I met mostly big-hit writers—and they have a set group of people that they write with. It's hard to get to write a song with them.

"It's important that you write with a uniqueness, so publishers and other writers can see that you have a different point of view. I would go to all of the writers' nights that I could; go up and talk to as many of the performers as you can, especially the ones that you think are good songwriters. Don't be pushy; tell them that you just got to town. Be modest.

"Get up and sing your own songs. That is the best way to learn which of your songs are the most commercial. One way I test how I feel about a song, or to determine if it is finished or not is to perform it live in front of a crowd. Then I can feel in my gut whether or not I like this song. It helps seek out the special songs. Of course you like all your songs; you wrote them. But which ones will stand the test of time? Sometimes a song can make sense on paper, but it doesn't make sense when you are performing it and hearing it as the audience is hearing it. Write every day; don't let more than two days go by without writing. It keeps you contemporary and gets the thoughts out of your head, so that your heart can make a judgment on it.

"I finally decided to move to Nashville because I didn't feel I could make it without being a part of the everyday life it offers. Everybody can quote an exception to this rule; but they are exceptions. It's very hard for people to evaluate their own songs, but I knew I wasn't writing for the country market, so I basically listened to others when they said 'this is the way to go.'

I had to learn to make that evaluation for myself. If you go out enough and see what other people are doing, and you start absorbing, you'll see that what worked ten years ago in country music doesn't necessarily work anymore.

"What is the difference between pitching songs from Los Angeles and actually living in Nashville? I am much more cautious about what I play for people. I used to send songs without realizing that they were pieces of crap or that they were totally wrong for that artist.

"The best results I've gotten have come from people I've known before I even got in the business. For example, I went to high school with Chick Rains ['Somebody Should Leave,' Reba McEntire; 'Old Enough to Know Better,' Wade Hayes].

"Other than Montgomery, I've never met a publisher that I connected with; I still feel like a student. I don't have fifteen or twenty songs that people believe they can make a whole lot of money with. I'm holding back and keeping my publishing until I have a really big cut; then I will use that as leverage to get a great publishing deal.

"Staff deals are for people who need to meet more writers, and publishers get their money's worth just doing that for writers who need the money.

"But a publisher needs to be more than just a bank; he needs to be a partner. In publishing companies today, songs are done by committee. There are a lot of people involved in working with your songs.

"In signing a single-song agreement or exclusive contract, sign a deal where you get your song back in the shortest amount of time possible. Don't sign without a reversion clause. The most important thing is to do what's necessary to keep writing songs. Don't turn bitter toward the business side and let it affect the way you grow. It took me five years to get twelve songs I truly believe in. A good song will jump out at you.

"My cowriters and I write four or five songs to get to the one great one that we'll keep. There is a big difference between a well-crafted good song that is not marketable, and a great song that pushes universal buttons and is unique—musically and lyrically; a great song stands head and shoulders above the good stuff."

MIKE SETTLE is a former singer with First Edition, whose most famous member was Kenny Rogers; Mike is also the writer of the BMI Two Millionaire Award–winning song "But You Know I Love You," made famous by Dolly Parton.

ABOUT WRITERS' NIGHTS AND OPEN MIC NIGHTS
In June of 1982, an entrepreneur by the name of Amy Kurland opened a little restaurant in Green Hills (south of downtown), featuring musical

entertainment on weekends. She decided that, in a songwriting town of great stature, only original music would be played in her establishment. It became apparent rather quickly that the Bluebird Cafe was a room that was meant for acoustic music. She found as well that songwriters needed a place to share their songs with each other, so she set aside Sunday nights as "writers' night." The small restaurant, which has a capacity of only 100 people, soon became standing room only on Sundays. It became necessary to hold auditions, and soon, Sunday nights were booked months in advance.

Within a short time, the Bluebird became a full-time music club with live music seven nights a week, from 6:00 P.M. until the wee hours of the morning. Today, the Bluebird Cafe is world-renowned. Much of the footage for a recent major motion picture about a songwriter in Nashville, *The Thing Called Love,* was shot inside the Bluebird. Those scenes captured the true essence of the magic that takes place in this unique setting. Also, many songwriters have gone on from their performances at the Bluebird to sign record deals, the most famous being Garth Brooks. Garth had been seriously shopping for a record deal, had a great master recording that he had played for all the A&R reps and producers in Nashville, and was turned down by every label. He took the stage at the Bluebird to sing three of his songs at a writers' showcase. A representative from Capitol Records was in the audience, and the rest is history.

Amy has a strict policy concerning bookings at the club. All songs must be original material (no cover bands allowed), and songwriters must audition in advance either live or by tape submission. And when you are in the club either listening to the performers or waiting for your turn to go on, don't be surprised if you get shushed. There is no talking allowed during performances.

Another very important writers' club is Douglas Corner, on Eighth Avenue South. This club is always filled with writers, most of whom have had several songs cut by major artists. Writers have a very strong bond with their songwriting friends, and the majority of their time is spent playing their hits and their favorite songs (that may never get cut) with their buddies. All of the shows on the Douglas Corner stage are put on by full-time songwriters who actively cowrite, pitch, and play their songs. Just the people you want to meet.

You can't go wrong if you spend your evenings in Nashville in one of these two clubs, but there are many, many others to consider. Since one of your goals should be to perform your songs on a writers' night showcase, one of the lesser known forums might be easier to get a slot on the show. There are lots of different formats, as well. Here's what to look for:

Writers' Nights

Writers' nights are generally a one or two-hour rehearsed show. They vary greatly in format, but the common thread is that the shows consist of songwriters performing their own original material, usually by acoustic guitar. Songwriters audition live or by tape submission. It is especially interesting to be able to hear a well-known hit performed on an acoustic guitar by the person who wrote it. This has to be, without a doubt, the best classroom available for a developing songwriter.

Performing Rights Organizations' Writers' Nights

ASCAP, BMI, and SESAC all produce their own writers' nights, featuring their own writers (or writers they are hoping to sign soon). There is no predicting when they will hold a writers' night, so you might want to give them a call to see if they have one scheduled. If they do, make sure you don't miss it! The writers are guaranteed to be top-rate.

Publishers' Writers' Nights

Similar to performing rights organizations' writers' nights, publishers showcase their writers to the industry from time to time. Not only will the writers be some of the best in Nashville, but the audience will most likely be filled with industry executives, A&R, producers, other writers, and other publishers—another don't-miss-under-any-circumstances event. This kind of showcase will not be easy to find—this is where your networking skills will be put to the test. You will find hints about how to hone those skills later in the book.

Hit Songwriter Nights

Big-hit songwriters will put on a show from time to time, usually to raise money for charity, but sometimes just because they want to. They might sing a lot of their hits, or songs they just wrote. Either way, it's really interesting to see them perform. You'll find a lot of industry folks in the audience as well.

Writers in the Round

Whoever first started this format at the Bluebird Cafe really started something. Now it's the most popular format used. Four songwriters sit in a circle in the middle of the room and take turns singing their own songs and backing each other up. There's lots of ad-lib chatter and joking around, and more than a tad of competition between the four of them.

Musicians' Showcase

Many studio musicians who enjoy playing together perform with various bands they have assembled. It's almost always *not* country music! And again, it's hard to find out about these showcases unless you are really familiar with the individuals who are playing. One rule of thumb: If musicians are playing a non-country, non-songwriter showcase at the Bluebird, they are probably popular studio musicians. Almost everyone who performs at the Bluebird has some industry connection.

Writer/Artist Showcase

Hit songwriters who are looking for an artist deal put on live shows—these are well-rehearsed, polished, full-band showcases. Some serious money is put into the show to make it as perfect as possible. Studio musicians are normally used; a publicist is hired to make sure the industry attends; and there is most likely a publisher or an artist manager involved as well. An aspiring artist needs to make sure all the bases have been covered before attempting a writer/artist showcase for the industry (see chapter 18).

These various types of showcases are featured every night in Nashville. The best nights to find industry types in the audience are Tuesday, Wednesday, and Thursday. The industry usually doesn't come out on a weekend night unless it's for something very special, or for an event planned by one of the several professional organizations. A serious songwriter, aspiring artist, and musician should plan to spend as much time as possible in these clubs, for a variety of reasons:

- It is a firsthand look at the competition
- It is a great opportunity to meet other writers and set up possible cowriting appointments
- It is not unusual for publishers, producers and/or record executives to be in the audience
- It is your opportunity, and the best opportunity, Nashville has available to pitch your songs

Think of writers' nights as your first priority. Plan to be out in the clubs every night. The cover charge at most clubs is under $10. At most writers' nights the audience mainly drinks water or coffee. In fact, it's hard for a club owner to make money on writers' nights, because the audience is in a work mode instead of a party mode. So you can have a few beers or not drink at all and be perfectly comfortable in the writers' night environment. Nothing is expected, except that you be courteous to the performers and listen quietly, applaud generously, and try to laugh at their jokes.

Open Mic Nights

This is the best opportunity for songwriters and aspiring artists to perform on stage. open mic nights operate on a first-come, first-serve basis. Writers show up about an hour before the show time, sign up, and then wait for their turn to go onstage. The format is a two- or three-song acoustic guitar set, depending on the number of people that sign up. A piano is generally not available but there may be one or two extra mics set up if you want to have another guitar player, bass player, or vocalist for harmony. These songwriter forums are for original material only; no cover material is performed at open mic nights.

THE BLUEBIRD CAFE: WHAT TO EXPECT, BY AMY KURLAND

Country music may be in a little bit of a slump these days, but the phone at the Bluebird just keeps ringing. Songwriters and artists want their chance on stage. And we continue to try to find a way for them to play. Open mic on Monday provides a place for any writer, no matter their skills or credentials, to play. Each week forty or more writers arrive at the Bluebird before 5:00 P.M. to put their names in a hat, for the chance to play two songs. As long as the songs are original, and you can accompany yourself (no backing tracks) you are eligible. Will the open mic show be your ticket to wealth and fame? Probably not. But it is the place where an important door to the music business opens.

Open mic is good for three things:

1. A chance to try out your material on a friendly audience
2. A chance to work on your performing skills (and, please, learn to tune your guitar and remember your lyrics)
3. A chance to make friends, meet potential cowriters, and find your place in the music community.

My rule is, if you don't get out to play when you are in Nashville, you are wasting one of the greatest opportunities the city has to offer.

Sunday night writers' nights are different. For these shows you must pass an audition, and those are only held once every four months. What is the key to passing the audition? A good song. I have heard thousands of songs over the years, and my standards are pretty high. We are already booked months ahead on Sunday nights, so I want to pass only the best. So take the time to write a lot, try out your material at open mics, and take classes and workshops from the Nashville Songwriters Association International.

One other thing about the audition: Follow the rules. We ask you not to play introductions to the songs, or explain them, so don't do it.

We've had songwriters from as far off as Australia play at the Bluebird, and many, many people come from all over the country to play their three songs. I guess people want to play here because of our reputation. The songwriters' nights are really the first rung on the Nashville ladder to success. Another rung is our early set, which can function as a mini-showcase. The writers invite the publishers, and often a few show up. Our feature late-evening shows are very difficult to get on, even as an opener, but it's truly just a matter of working hard, writing extraordinary songs, and having the patience of a saint. Some of the success stories we claim are Garth Brooks, Vince Gill, Radney Foster, Hal Ketchum, T. Graham Brown, Sweethearts of the Rodeo, Kathy Mattea, Jill Sobule, Steve Earle, Michael Johnson, Kelly Willis, Kevin Welch, Pam Tillis, Ashley Cleveland, and many, many others.

Our songwriting successes are exciting also. My personal favorite, Mark Irwin, moved here from New Jersey and started washing dishes in the Bluebird's kitchen the third night he was in town. He had a Number One hit with Alan Jackson's "Here in the Real World." More and more writers that I know from the Sunday writers' nights are turning up with their names on the *Billboard* charts. Our former waitress Liz Hengber is now a very successful songwriter with multiple hit songs for Reba McEntire, including "And Still" and "For My Broken Heart." And Kim Richey, a former Bluebird cook, is now a marvelous artist with Mercury Records.

Somewhere in Nashville there is at least one songwriters' night every night of the week. And so the wise newcomer makes the tour: Bluebird on Monday, Douglas Corner on Tuesday, and so on. Writers have the opportunity to play for each other, improve their performance, test out their songs with an audience, meet other writers for cowriting and performing, enjoy a social life, and pray that there is a publisher or an A&R person in the audience. During their time off they make demos and go to appointments with publishers.

Is there an average "new songwriter" in Nashville? The age range is very broad, the majority are between twenty-five and thirty-five, but many are younger or older. Male and female are equally mixed, and there are some couples. Most are pretty well-educated, with some college, but they are ready to wait on tables, do carpentry, and work in sales to get by. I would estimate that there are at least a *billion* songwriters in Nashville, which has an overall population of about 500,000! Every housepainter, window washer, cook, dishwasher, temp, cab driver, and street person is a songwriter. Many of the lawyers, doctors, and stockbrokers are writing also. In fact, many of the staff at the Bluebird are aspiring music professionals—one bartender, three out of five waitresses, and one cook. How does this thing work? How do you move to Nashville and strike it rich as a songwriter? Forget about striking it rich. Like any other creative job, if you don't do it for the joy of the work, if you wouldn't go on with it even if it didn't pay, then you are in the wrong business. Love and commitment show, to every-one—to audiences, to publishers, to other writers.

Leave your ego at the city limits. Yes, back where you came from you probably did write songs that were miles better than anyone else's. But not here. Here you have a chance to share music, to learn from the others. It has been my observation that the newcomer is welcomed warmly by the writer who got here last month. This is probably because that guy is so glad to have someone around who knows less than he does. And the established writers will be friendly too, because they remember what it was like. But don't ask to write with them, don't give them tapes; you will only get a rep-utation as a pest. Your time will come, and the more patient you are the more quickly it will happen.

Write and play, write and play, write and play. It's like homework. The more songs you write, the better you'll get. Don't think that you need to keep playing your one masterpiece over and over; it's not the only good song you'll ever write. If you aren't going to go out and play your new songs for someone, you might as well have stayed at home. People tell me that the Bluebird is the difference between Nashville being a good or a bad experience for new writers in town, so come on down and play.

I love Nashville and recommend it as a swell place to live. The peo-ple are friendly, rents are not too bad, and it has a small-town atmosphere. But don't come here thinking that songwriting is like winning the Publisher's Clearinghouse Sweepstakes. It takes a long, long time before you will feel like you've had any success. But there is success in following your dream. I believe it is better to fail in doing something than to succeed in doing nothing.

AMY KURLAND, a Nashville native, received a B.A. in American literature from the George Washington Uni-versity in Washington, D.C., and returned to Nashville to open a small restaurant and nightclub in 1982. She recognized a need for a place where songwriters could meet and share their songs and ideas with each other. Writers' night at the Bluebird grew to such proportions that she decided to take the focus away from the restaurant and devote the club to music. Since she started the writers' night in 1983, others have cropped

Photo by Beth Gwinn

up in clubs all over town and have become an invaluable way for publishers, producers, and record executives to find new talent. The Bluebird has traveled with shows from New York to Los Angeles, and has a regular series at the Disney Institute in Orlando, Florida. The Bluebird Cafe can be seen in a weekly TV show, *Live From the Bluebird,* on the Turner South network.

How to Play the Bluebird Cafe

(These instructions are handed out at your first visit to the Bluebird.)

Open Mic

For writers who haven't played at the Bluebird and writers from out of town, open mic is the place to start. It gives songwriters a chance to play two of their own original songs, solo or accompanied by no more than two others on stage. Drums and backing tracks are not allowed. Open mic is a great place to try out new material, meet other writers, become a part of the songwriting community, and practice your performing skills. We recommend that all new writers play open mic here at the Bluebird as well as at the many other writers' clubs in Nashville, on a regular basis. Often, we have more writers come to open mic than we have time and space for. In this case, we offer writers a "play next time" ticket, so that if the writer doesn't get to play the first time he tries, he will definitely get to play the next time. Sign-up starts on Monday nights at 5:30. You must be signed up by 5:45. The lineup is announced at 6:00, and the show runs from 6:00 to 9:00.

Sunday Writers' Nights

These shows are scheduled by audition, and through this screening process, writers know that they have been selected to play along with other writers who show growing talent and maturity in their songwriting and performance skills. These shows feature between nine and twelve songwriters playing three songs each. Each show is hosted and ends with a special guest performance by a hit-writing songwriter from the Nashville music industry. Sunday nights are always well-attended, which gives the writer a chance to perform for a full room. This is a good chance to develop a following and collect names for a mailing list. The writers' performances are rated and filed for use by the Bluebird to determine when a writer might be eligible to perform during the week on our Early Shows and spotlight shows. All performances must be acoustic; no drums, backing tracks, and no more than three people on stage. Auditions are held quarterly, and are only open to Nashville residents, people residing within a hundred-mile radius of Nashville, and active members of an NSAI regional chapter. They are judged by Bluebird staff and professionals from the music industry. Call (615) 383-1461 to get the date of the next audition.

Early Shows: Tuesday through Saturday, the Bluebird Cafe features the best up-and-coming songwriters from our Sunday writers' nights in no cover-charge shows at 6:30 P.M. These shows are always acoustic: bands, drums, and large groups are not part of our Early Show. Writers who have played Sundays at least four times and at least one "Picks" night (the first Sunday of the month), and have high scores from our judges, are eligible to play on Early Shows. If you don't already have a following (a number of people who will come out especially to hear you perform), you should continue to play Sunday nights and open mics. Other writers who are eligible to play are staff writers from established Nashville publishing companies and touring artists with product and good press from out-of-town newspapers. We only book touring songwriters who we believe are as good or better than the best local Early Show writers. If your package does not include professional product and press, it will not be considered. To submit material for Early Shows, send to: the Bluebird Cafe, Early Shows, 4104 Hillsboro Road, Nashville, TN 37215. If you have played four Sundays and at least one "Picks" night, call (615) 383-1461 to see if your scores make you eligible for an Early Show.

Sunday Spotlights

The Bluebird Cafe does not offer many opportunities for bands to play. The exception is our Sunday Spotlight, a no-cover show each Sunday from 6:30 to 7:15 P.M. The same criterion applies as for our Early Shows—writers who have played Sundays at least four times, and have high scores from our judges, are eligible to play on Sunday Spotlights. Other eligible writers are staff writers from established Nashville publishing companies and touring artists with product and good press from out-of-town newspapers—but this slot is for bands up to six pieces including drums. The solo writer must have played an Early Show to be eligible to bring her band to play a Sunday Spotlight. To submit material for Sunday Spotlights, send to: the Bluebird Cafe, Sunday Spotlight, 4104 Hillsboro Road, Nashville, TN 37215.

FREQUENTLY ASKED QUESTIONS

• *I am a singer and I don't write my own songs. How can I play the Bluebird?*
Unfortunately, Nashville and the Bluebird Cafe offer very few showcases for singers. You may perform at an open mic with songs by local writers, as long as the songs have not been released by a major label or aired on the radio. You should see this as an opportunity to help a writer present his or her songs; this is not a show for the singers as much as it is for the songwriters.

• *What if I don't play an instrument?*
We do not allow backing tracks at any shows. Some choose to sing a cappella, but it is probably to your advantage to find a guitar player to back you on stage. That is one of the benefits of open mics and songwriters' nights: you will meet many people there who would be happy to help out on a show. The songwriting community is very supportive in this way.

• *Does the Bluebird provide instruments for the shows?*
No, sorry. You will need to bring your own guitar or keyboard. We do provide a good sound system and someone to operate it for you.

• *How are the late shows booked?*
Late show time slots are reserved for local or national acts with a large following. Openers for these shows are sometimes selected from the best Early Show performers, although these opportunities are extremely limited.

• *What is a showcase, and how do I get one?*
A showcase is an early evening show to which the performer invites members of the industry in the hopes of getting a recording deal. Many venues charge a substantial fee/rent for this. It is the Bluebird's policy not to rent our room for showcases unless the request comes directly from a major label representative, established manager, or publishing company.

• *What other resources do you recommend for songwriters?*
The NSAI and SGA are great organizations which offer many services to writers including seminars and classes, office and writing rooms, song screenings, and solid information and advice. Also, the bookstores are full of good material on songwriting; keep working and educating yourself all the time.

5

A Basic Understanding of Nashville's Music Publishers

I f you look at the listing of publishers on the *Billboard* country chart, you will find hundreds of companies listed there. In reality, there are only a very few publishing companies that are getting cuts in Nashville. Every large publisher has three companies: an ASCAP, BMI, and SESAC company. The songwriter is the one who determines into which company the publisher will put a song. If the writer is signed with ASCAP, the song goes into the publisher's ASCAP company, and so forth.

For example, the letterhead on my publishing companies' stationery reads: "Red River BMI/Crimson Creek ASCAP." When I publish the work of a writer who belongs to ASCAP, his song is published by Crimson Creek, but if he belonged to BMI, the publisher would be Red River. I don't have a SESAC company, but if I discovered a great new writer whose affiliation was with SESAC and I wanted to work with him, I would start a SESAC company as well. When people refer to publishing companies, it is not uncommon for them to identify them as, for example, "AMR/New Haven." People automatically know that refers to an ASCAP and a BMI company even if they rarely mention it.

About Nashville Publishers

Over the years, the large publishers have purchased valuable publishing companies, and although a song may be now owned by a new publishing company, the old company's name might still be used. For example, Cross Keys is the same company as Sony/ATV Tree, as well as many, many others owned by Sony. So many of the publishing companies listed on the charts may be owned by larger companies.

Once songwriters have consistent chart success (most of the writers on the *Billboard* charts), they are then in the enviable position of being able to keep a portion of their own publishing. So their publisher will enter into a copublishing deal with them. The writer will now earn 75 percent of his song royalties, instead of the usual 50 percent, with 25 percent of the earnings going to the writers' publishing company. It's just a way of giving the writer a larger portion of his own creation; in most instances, the writer isn't really running a publishing company. In fact, his publisher most likely administers his publishing company for him. The majority of publishing companies listed on the charts, especially those with really imaginative names, are songwriters' companies.

There are three different levels of publishing companies in Nashville that you should be aware of. On your first trip to Nashville, make it your goal to try to get an appointment with one company from each of these three categories.

NASHVILLE'S MAJOR MUSIC PUBLISHERS

**BMG Music Publishing (BMG/RCA Records,
BNA Records, aka RCA Label Group)**
1400 18th Avenue South
Nashville, TN 37212
Tel. (615) 858-1300
Fax (615) 858-1330

Curb Music Publishing (Curb Records)
47 Music Square East
Nashville, TN 37203
Tel. (615) 321-5080
Fax (615) 321-9532

DreamWorks Music Publishing Nashville (DreamWorks Records)
1516 16th Avenue South
Nashville, TN 37212
Tel. (615) 463-4600
Fax (615) 463-4601

EMI Music Publishing (Capitol Records)
35 Music Square East
Nashville, TN 37203
Tel. (615) 742-8081
Fax (615) 726-2394
Web site: *www.emimusicpub.com*

Sony/ATV Tree (Sony Music, CBS, Columbia, Epic, Lucky Dog, Monument Records)
Eight Music Square West
Nashville, TN 37203
Tel. (615) 726-8300
Fax (615) 726-8387
Web site: *www.treepublishing.com*

Universal Music Group (MCA Records, Mercury Records)
12 Music Circle South
Nashville, TN 37203
Tel. (615) 248-4800
Fax (615) 248-9300

Warner/Chappell Music, Inc. (Warner/Reprise Records, Atlantic Records, Giant Records)
21 Music Square East
Nashville, TN 37203
Tel. (615) 254-8777
Fax (615) 726-1353
Web site: *www.warnerchappell.com*

These publishing companies are owned by huge corporations and are linked to record companies owned by the same corporations. They account for more than half of all songs recorded in Nashville, but not necessarily on their own record label. Artists will go to all the big publishers in Nashville looking for songs, not just their own company. These publishers have big budgets, a highly respected general manager (usually someone who has been around Nashville for a long, long time), a creative manager, lots of song pluggers, a big staff of writers, a recording studio, and a production company.

There isn't any need to try to get to the top executive in this company; try to get a meeting with one of the song pluggers. Song pluggers can be found in the *Music Row Publications,* in both the "In Charge" edition and the "Publisher Special" edition. They are more accessible, and work with songs on a daily basis. And they are constantly focused on getting a great song to the right artist. Yours might be the one they are looking for.

NASHVILLE'S HOT INDEPENDENT MUSIC PUBLISHERS

Acuff-Rose Music Publishing
65 Music Square West
Nashville, TN 37203
Tel. (615) 321-5000
Fax (615) 321-5655
Web site: *www.country.com*

Almo/Irving Music
1904 Adelicia Avenue
Nashville, TN 37212
Tel. (615) 321-0820
Fax (615) 329-1018

Big Tractor Music
1503 17th Avenue South
Nashville, TN 37212
Tel. (615) 292-5100
Fax (615) 292-2934
E-mail: *tractorbig@aol.com*

Famous Music Corporation
65 Music Square East
Nashville, TN 37203
Tel. (615) 329-0500
Fax (615) 321-4121

Hamstein Publishing
914 18th Avenue South
Nashville, TN 37212
Tel. (615) 320-9971
Fax (615) 320-7835
Web site: *www.hamstein.com*

Starstruck Writers Group
40 Music Square West
Nashville, TN 37203
Tel. (615) 259-5300
Fax (615) 259-5301

Windswept Pacific Entertainment
33 Music Square West, #104B
Nashville, TN 37203
Tel. (615) 313-7676
Fax (615) 313-7670

Wrensong Publishing
1229 17th Avenue South
Nashville, TN 37212
Tel. (615) 321-4487
Fax (615) 327-7917
Web site: *www.wrensong.com*

These independent music publishers carry a lot of weight in Nashville. You would almost think they were one of the majors, considering how many cuts they get. They probably account for more than 30 percent of the songs cut in Nashville. They too have a large staff of writers, one or two song pluggers, demo studio and production company. If you can get an appointment with *anyone* in any one of these companies while in Nashville, you will have accomplished a great deal.

Industry Interview with Ree Guyer Buchanan, President/Owner, Wrensong Publishing

Photo by Alan L. Mayor

"My father was very involved in writing and recording songs in Minneapolis. He knew all the musicians, all the players in town. In the eighties, it was a hot music center with Sound 80 Studios—the Artist Formerly Known as Prince recorded there. Corporate headquarters for a lot of big companies like 3M, Pillsbury, and General Motors were located in Minneapolis; so musicians made an incredible living doing commercials. They also wrote songs, which wound up on the shelves. After a while there was a big catalog of songs just sitting there.

"The woman who ran the studio thought pitching songs would be a good idea, but after three months, she gave up. About that time I graduated from college and started working in pottery, but realized that what I really wanted was a sales position. I interviewed with Pillsbury and other companies. I had always been involved with my dad's businesses, so I started to work for him as a part-time consultant. A friend introduced me to Michael Johnson—he was at the top of his game at the time. He took me to lunch and said, 'You need to go to Nashville!' That's where he had recorded with Brent Maher, and knew everyone. He gave me a list of publishers to see—Pat Rolfe, Judy Harris, Celia Froehlig, Bob Doyle, Joe Moscheo, Karen Conrad, Tom Collins, Sue Patton, and Pat Higdon. (They are all my mentors today. This was in 1982, and today, in the new millennium, these nine people still hold very influential positions on Music Row.)

"I would come into town and stay at Shoney's Inn for two weeks at a time; I would have six meetings a day and then make demo tapes at night. I had twenty songs I was pitching, and they would help critique the songs. I looked at myself as an agent for these songs, and I wanted to broker them out to someone who knew what they were doing. But these people had their own staff writers and didn't need outside songs.

"I realized I had to become a publisher and would have to go directly to the producers. There were five producers in town at that time—Billy Sherrill, Ron Chancey, Jerry Kennedy, Ray Baker, and Bud Logan. You had to know those guys. If you didn't, you weren't going to get your songs recorded.

"I discovered that Billy Barber was the writer everybody was interested in, so I dropped off a tape of his to Billy Sherrill. He called me fifteen minutes later and said, 'Who are you; who is this guy?' It was not country, it was pop, and Sherrill wanted something that would be a pop success out of Nashville. Sherrill became my mentor and started working with Billy as an artist. Sherrill and (Los Angeles publisher) Al Gallico realized that Barber was going to be a big artist, and they started wining and dining me to get the publishing on him. Dinner at Mario's, the works. But I had worked so hard to get to that point, I decided to hold onto it myself.

"New York wouldn't take the project seriously since it was coming out of Nashville. The minute I realized New York was going to pass, I started pitching the songs. Bob Doyle, who was with ASCAP at the time, was really helping me a lot; and he helped me get one of Barber's songs on the bus with the Oak Ridge Boys—the song was 'Little Things.' The Oak Ridge Boys loved the song and planned to record it. They sent Noel Fox after me. He offered me the A-side single in exchange for the publishing. But I said no. It was the A-side single anyway and was a Number One record—my first cut.

"Meanwhile, I was still living two lives—one in Minneapolis and one in Nashville. In Minneapolis, I produced two music seminars. We had a boat trip and seminars during the day for developing songwriters. The lineup for the first seminar was hit songwriters Dennis Morgan and Kye Fleming; the industry speakers were Jim Black, Aaron Brown, Buzz Cason, Joe Moscheo, and John Sturdivant. Jon Vezner attended the seminar.

"I was still spending two weeks here in Nashville and two weeks at home. So we bought this building on Music Row for $100,000. I kept one office and rented the rest; we still rent the upstairs. In November of 1985, I had an open house and a Number One party for 'Little Things' at the same time, and moved here permanently. Jon Vezner also decided to make the move to Nashville, and in January of 1986, I signed him as my first staff writer. It was so incredible to see Jon Vezner grow; we got cuts by Mel McDaniel, Lorrie Morgan, Ronnie Milsap. I also took some song-by-song contracts with other writers. One was John Kurhajetz, who wrote 'Gonna Take a Lot of River' with Mark Henley.

"Jon Vezner wrote with Don Henry quite a lot; one day they invited me into their writers' room to listen to a new song they had written called 'Where've You Been.' Jon says he'll never forget when he played it for me. I was standing up, and by the time the song was over I was on the floor crying. I said, 'Can I come back in a while and listen again?' When I heard it the second time I said, 'If we can't get this cut, I quit!' Kathy Mattea had heard the song but thought, 'I can't do a song like that!' So I pitched it for a year. Everybody was afraid of it; I wasn't.

"There was an important publisher/producer showcase every month at the Bluebird Cafe; it was really a big deal to be on the show at that time. Jon got chosen to be one of the writers, and he sang it live on the show. Kathy was in the audience, and said, 'What have I been thinking? I want to do that song!' The next day Buzz Stone called me and said he wanted to put the song on hold for Conway Twitty. So I called Kathy and said, 'Are you sure you are really going to record this song?' She said absolutely, so we told Conway it was already taken.

"When they went in and recorded the song, they cut an art piece. They were hesitant to release it as a single; they really were undecided. But they did, and it won every award that year. A Grammy, NSAI, CMA, ACM, everything. My mentor Bob Doyle was the publisher for the great song, 'If Tomorrow Never Comes,' which lost out on the awards because of this song. He said, 'You are kicking my butt!'

"From there, we just kept building it. We now have over three thousand songs, two BMI Million Air Award–winning songs, and countless singles in the catalog. It all comes down to songs. Great songs open doors. 'Little Things' is a great song. I know it's hard for writers to be objective about their songs, but you have to be. Pitch that one song.

"A lot of times if I hear someone who has a lot of potential, I'll sign them. I got where I am by developing people. I will always have a couple of developing writers. 'How Can I Help You Say Goodbye?' was referred to me by one of my writers. Neither Burton Collins nor Karen Taylor-Good had publishers at the time they wrote that song.

"I also got involved in the pop/rock field. Sherry Cathran started out as an intern here. I knew that her husband, Brian Reed, was in a band, and that Sherry wanted to be a star. Over the years, they developed their own songs and style, and started their own group called The Evinrudes. So we sat down and talked about how to launch a pop/rock act. Hootie and the Blowfish got a following in their region, then people came to them. So I said, 'Get out there and play, play, play. Just show that people like your music.' A local radio station played them, and they got so much audience response that people called in wanting to know about them, where to get their record. We sold five thousand EPs. It was neat. I went to labels in New York and shopped their record.

"I thought, 'If I can meet all the producers in Nashville, I can meet all the people in Los Angeles.' Heart, Bonnie Raitt, and others were cutting outside songs. Loretta Muñoz at ASCAP in Los Angeles helped me get started. I did the same thing in Los Angeles that I did in Nashville, made inroads at Capitol Records, and got 'Stranded' recorded by Heart. It went Top Ten in all formats.

"I started attending SXSW in Austin, Texas, met lots of people. Ten years later all those guys were running labels. I was able to get to them. Everything here is about relationships. When I was just getting started, I would read all the trades, see their faces, go up to them, introduce myself. I didn't have a hit writer; l didn't have a name. Yes, you have to have great music; but you also have to know who the people are. You have to make a name for yourself. People can help you, but at the end of the day you have to do it yourself.

"I found all my first writers at writer nights. I lived at the Bluebird. They joked that I should have a cot in the back. I met Sandy Ramos; met demo singers. Today, it's not happening as much. My job is just to get to everybody.

"I started a production company; it's a natural evolution of working with songwriters. Every songwriter wants to be an artist. I developed Sherrié Austin. The hard part is finding the package. 50 percent of it is having the drive. You need a unique voice and hit songs; but the drive has to be relentless. It's hard to find people who are that driven.

"My first love is for writers. People who can write by themselves. I stand in awe of it. People don't realize that Sherrié is a great writer. She started writing with one of my staff writers, Will Rambeaux. Will is an amazing writer ('Wild One' by Faith Hill). The song they wrote together, they think, got her the record deal. The demo they did is exactly like the cut. 'Lucky in Love' sold 100,000 singles (in an industry that doesn't even market singles!). I went to lunch with her before I even heard her sing and knew I wanted to sign her. She's amazing; she's a star! When she met with the record label, Tim DuBois said, 'Congratulations, honey.' And she said, 'Congratulations to you, too!' I talked Larry Fitzgerald into managing her.

"I don't believe in showcases; they are too manufactured. It's the kiss of death. There is nothing worse than playing for a music business crowd; they just stand there with their arms crossed. At Fan Fair, I study the performers, who they are. We don't need people who are manufactured.

"One of the things that my father taught me as a partner, from his success, is that you have to find a niche—you have to be different. If people are doing board games, do a plastic people game. If people are playing with balls, do an inside ball. It was really different—but it worked."

REE GUYER BUCHANAN was born and raised in St. Paul, Minnesota. She graduated in 1981 from St. Mary's University with a B.S. in Psychology and Studio Arts. Shortly after graduating from college, she held two jobs—a production potter for Sansei Pottery in St. Paul and a sales position for Wrensong Publishing, a newly formed division of her father, Reyn Guyer's, development company, Winsor Concepts (this company owns the patents on Nerf and Twister). The initial concept of Wrensong was to help professional jingle writers, like Billy Barber, in the Minneapolis/St. Paul area get their commercial songs recorded by major recording artists. Ree and her father initially signed single song contracts with these writers and began with twenty songs. Today, Wrensong is one of the top independent publishing companies on Music Row, with over three thousand copyrights and twelve staff writers and artists. Ree is known for developing writers and for being an excellent song plugger. She has focused on developing a catalog of unique, special songs ("Where've You Been," "How Can I Help You Say Goodbye?").

In the last three years, Ree has focused on developing artists as well as writers. Sherrié Austin is Wrensong's first artist to be signed to a major label. Ree introduced Sherrié to her producer, record label, and manager. Ree is currently shopping writer/artist deals for the Evinrudes, Blair Daly, and Sally Barris.

OTHER IMPORTANT INDEPENDENT MUSIC PUBLISHERS

There are zillions of music publishers in Nashville—almost as many publishers as there are songwriters, but not quite. The majority of independent music publishers are struggling hard to get their songs heard, and they know that a great song will make its way through to the top. There are many more great publishers than the ones listed here, and just because they are not included here does not mean that you should omit them from your own list of publishers. Hopefully, you have created your own target list of publishers by reading the label copy on CDs, reading the *Billboard Country Airplay Monitor,* and by information you have obtained from *Music Row* magazine, especially the "Publisher Special" edition. These are all very different companies, with varying styles of music and a completely different approach to the industry. You should learn as much as possible about each company, the songs in their catalog, and their team of writers, then match the companies to your own catalog.

Here is a list of recommended independent music publishers, with a few notes about each one.

Affiliated Publishers, Inc.
1009 16th Avenue South
Nashville, TN 37212
Tel. (615) 327-9050
Fax (615) 327-9027
E-mail: *apinc@earthlink.net*

Instrumental in the development of Joe Diffie's career. Run by publishers/producers Johnny Slate and Danny Morrison, the company also offers artist management.

Balmur Entertainment
1105 17th Avenue South
Nashville, TN 37212
Tel. (615) 329-1431
Fax (615) 321-0240
E-mail: *balmurent@aol.com*

Balmur is a Canadian-based company started by Anne Murray's original manager. Since opening its office on 17th Street, Balmur has done everything first-class. Many first cuts for unknown artists happen in the viable Canadian song market.

Beckett Music Group
1006 18th Avenue South
Nashville, TN 37212
Tel. (615) 322-9555
Fax (615) 322-9506

Publishing company of the famed Muscle Shoals keyboardist and producer Barry Beckett. His son Matthew runs the company.

Best Built Songs
1317 16th Avenue South
Nashville, TN 37212
Tel. (615) 329-1837
Fax (615) 327-3359

Proof positive that if you work hard and just keep at it, you will succeed. Larry Sheridan started out with nothing but drive, and has done very well.

Big Ears Music
33 Music Square West, #102B
Nashville, TN 37203
Tel. (615) 742-1250
Fax (615) 742-1360
Web site: *www.ohboy.com*
>Publishing company of John Prine.

Bluewater Music Corporation
1218 17th Avenue South
Nashville, TN 37212
Tel. (615) 327-0808
Fax (615) 327-0809
>Bluewater specializes in the international market. They provide full copyright collection, bypassing the massive Harry Fox Agency.

Brentwood-Benson Music Publishing, Inc.
365 Great Circle Road
Nashville, TN 37228
Tel. (615) 742-6824
Fax (615) 742-6994
>Brentwood Music represents all genres of music, which includes a wide expanse of Christian music since they acquired Benson Music.

Bug Music
1026 16th Avenue South
Nashville, TN 37212
Tel. (615) 726-0782
Fax (615) 726-0784
Web site: *www.bugmusic.com*
>Another innovative company, Bug Music administers writers' catalogs. Highly respected for managing the publishing rights of major self-contained acts, they have adapted to the Nashville climate by pitching artists' and writers' catalogs to other artists. Offices in Nashville, Hollywood, New York, and London.

Bugle Publishing Group
2410 Belmont Boulevard
Nashville, TN 37212
Tel. (615) 460-1112
Fax (615) 460-7300
>Publishing company of Sting's producer Miles Copeland.

Bursen Music Group, Inc.
2611 Westwood Drive
Nashville, TN 37204
Tel. (615) 297-3134

Publishing company of the Music Row veteran Dave Burgess.

Cal IV Entertainment
808 19th Avenue South
Nashville, TN 37203
Tel. (615) 242-4200
Fax (615) 242-6989

Cal Turner is a highly successful businessman and entrepreneur of Dollar General stores. He's trying his hand at music publishing and artist development.

CDP Music Group
3610 Mayflower Place
Nashville, TN 37204
Tel. (615) 292-9904
Fax (615) 292-9904

If you are looking for a woman who knows the ropes and has a great song sense, C. Dianne Petty is the one. She was in charge of writer/publisher relations at SESAC for many years.

Chrysalis Music
1204 16th Avenue South
Nashville, TN 37212
Tel. (615) 327-4797
Fax (615) 327-1903
Web site: *www.chrysalismusic.com*

Chrysalis Records music publishing, Nashville branch.

Co-Heart Music
1103B 17th Avenue South
Nashville, TN 37212
Tel. (615) 327-0031
Fax (615) 327-4175

Publishing venture of veteran hit songwriters Hank Cochran and Glenn Martin.

Collins Music
21 Music Square West
Nashville, TN 37203
Tel. (615) 255-5550
Fax (615) 256-6467
    Publishing company of Barbara Mandrell's producer Tom Collins.

Copperfield Music Group
1400 South Street
Nashville, TN 37203
Tel. (615) 726-3100
Fax (615) 726-3172
E-mail: *copperfild@aol.com*
    Publishing company of Kin Biddy, husband of the first female record company label head Sheila Shipley-Biddy (she was head of Decca, a now-defunct subsidiary of MCA).

Cornelius Companies
812 19th Avenue South
Nashville, TN 37203
Tel. (615) 321-5333
Fax (615) 321-5653
E-mail: *CoComps@Juno.com*
    Publishing company owned by Music Row veteran Ron Cornelius.

Creative Artists Agency Publishing
3310 West End Avenue, #500
Nashville, TN 37203
Tel. (615) 383-8787
Fax (615) 385-6933
    CAA is one of the biggest and most powerful artists' agencies in the world. And it has its own publishing company.

Criterion Music Corporation
1025 17th Avenue South, #C
Nashville, TN 37212
Tel. (615) 327-2146
Fax (615) 327-2626
    Father-and-son business (Mickey and Bo Goldsen) with offices in Hollywood and Nashville. The Goldsens represent major recording artists.

Crossfield Music
1311 16th Avenue South
Nashville, TN 37212
Tel. (615) 269-8661
Fax (615) 269-5999
E-mail: *crossfield@midtn.campus.mci.net*
 A true song-based company, representing all genres of music.

Crutchfield Music
1106 17th Avenue South
Nashville, TN 37212
Tel. (615) 321-5558
Fax (615) 321-5598
 Publishing company of Tanya Tucker's longtime producer Jerry Crutchfield.

Don King Music Group, Inc.
19 Music Square West, #V
Nashville, TN 37203
Tel. (615) 256-0580
Fax (615) 781-9176
 Publishing company of the father and son hit songwriters Don King, Sr., and Don King, Jr.

Double J Music Group
1227 16th Avenue South
Nashville, TN 37212
Tel. (615) 327-0770
Fax (615) 327-3281
E-mail: *doublej.music@nashville.com*
 Nashville veteran and songman Juan Contreras heads this multilevel company.

Drake Music Group
P.O. Box 40945
Nashville, TN 37204
Tel. (615) 297-4345
Fax (615) 297-1584
 Publishing company run by the widow of the legendary producer Pete Drake.

Electric Mule Music Publishing, Inc.
1420 Clifton Lane
Nashville, TN 37215
Tel. (615) 385-2729
Fax (615) 385-9481
E-mail: *emule1420@aol.com*
    Publishing company of the hit songwriter Jeff Moseley.

EMI Christian Music Publishing
35 Music Square East
Nashville, TN 37203
Tel. (615) 742-8081
Fax (615) 726-2394
Web site: *www.emimusicpub.com*
    Leading publisher in Christian Music; formerly Sparrow Music and Records. Same company as EMI Music Publishing, but run separately.

ESP Music
P.O. Box 121676
Nashville, TN 37212
Tel. (615) 753-0060
    Publishing company of the hit songwriter Even Stevens.

Fame Publishing
1103 16th Avenue South, #104
Nashville, TN 37212
Tel. (615) 320-5417
Fax (615) 322-9168
Web site: *www.fame2.com*
    Muscle Shoals comes to Nashville.

Forerunner Music Group
1308 16th Avenue South
Nashville, TN 37212
Tel. (615) 298-5499
Fax (615) 385-2611
E-mail: *Fore.runner@nashville.com*
    Publishing company of Garth Brooks's producer Allen Reynolds.

Fretboard Publishing Company
2814 Azalea Place
Nashville, TN 37204
Tel. (615) 269-5638
E-mail: *AUTOHARP@aol.com*
    Publishing company of the producers Mark and Andy Moseley.

Frizzell House
705 18th Avenue South
Nashville, TN 37203
Tel. (615) 320-5777
E-mail: *Frizzell@bellsouth.net*
    Publishing company of the recording artist Allen Frizzell, son of Lefty.

Froehlig Palmer Music
65 Music Square East
Nashville, TN 37203
Tel. (615) 329-0235
Fax (615) 321-4121
    Celia Froehlig ran Famous Music for many years. She has an awesome Rolodex.

Glen Campbell Music Group
1114 17th Avenue South, #102
Nashville, TN 37212
Tel. (615) 329-9886
Fax (615) 329-0423
    Marty Gamblin has done a great job representing this Los Angeles–based company in Nashville.

GMMI Music Group
1218 17th Avenue South
Nashville, TN 37212
Tel. (615) 329-8031
Fax (615) 327-0809
    Specializes in all genres of music, with offices in Nashville and Canada.

Great American Talent, Inc.
1010 17th Avenue South
Nashville, TN 37212
Tel. (615) 320-3009
Fax (615) 321-3090
Web site: *www.gatalent.com*
    Publishing company run by the Music Row veteran Merlin Littlefield.

Harlan Howard Songs
1902 Wedgewood
Nashville, TN 37212
Tel. (615) 321-9098
Fax (615) 327-1748
E-mail: *harlansongs@juno.com*

Harlan's wife, Melanie Smith-Howard, has done a great job representing the contemporary catalog of this legendary songwriter ("I Fall to Pieces," "Heartaches by the Number," etc., etc., etc.).

Harris-Gordon Music
118 16th Avenue South, #203
Nashville, TN 37203
Tel. (615) 254-2080
Fax (615) 254-2081

Publishing company of the superb song plugger Judy Harris.

Hayes Street Music
1514 South Street
Nashville, TN 37212
Tel. (615) 327-1991
Fax (615) 320-1991

Catalog of Don Schlitz ("The Gambler") and friends.

High Seas Music
1908 Wedgewood Avenue
Nashville, TN 37212
Tel. (615) 322-9881
Fax (615) 322-9946

Run by the highly respected Los Angeles transplant Tracy Gershon.

Horipro Entertainment Group
1819 Broadway
Nashville, TN 37203
Tel. (615) 329-0890
Fax (615) 329-1874

Once upon a time, every record produced in Nashville contained a song published by Bob Beckham. Beckham is honored by his peers as a man who helped create the Nashville Sound.

Ingram-Lebrun Music
1201 16th Avenue South
Nashville, TN 37212

Tel. (615) 320-7707
Fax (615) 329-2569
   A highly successful book publisher ventures out into music publishing.

Island Bound Music, Inc.
1204 16th Avenue South
Nashville, TN 37212
Tel. (615) 320-5440
Fax (615) 320-0849
   The dynamic duo of Brad and Julie Daniel have shown that they really know how to pitch songs.

J. Aaron Brown & Associates
1508 16th Avenue South
Nashville, TN 37212
Tel. (615) 385-0022
Fax (615) 386-9988
E-mail: *mail@lullabies.com*
   The king of lullabies.

Johnny Bond Publications
P.O. Box 158029
Nashville, TN 37215
Tel. (615) 297-7320
E-mail: *slbond@bellsouth.net*
Web site: *www.johnnybond.com*
   Publishing companies of the author.

Kicking Bird Music
1102 18th Avenue South
Nashville, TN 37212
Tel. (615) 321-5767
Fax (615) 321-5519
   Publishing company of businessman Tom O'Grady and David Corlew, Charlie Daniels's business manager.

Kim Williams Music
1207 17th Avenue South, #306
Nashville, TN 37212
Tel. (615) 321-0132
Fax (615) 321-3632

Kim is a wonderful hit songwriter and runs his publishing company with cutting-edge technology.

Life Music Group
Two Music Circle South
Nashville, TN 37203
Tel. (615) 259-4373
Fax (615) 259-0773
 Specializing in Christian music.

Little Shop of Morgansongs
1800 Grand Avenue
Nashville, TN 37212
Tel. (615) 321-9029
Fax (615) 321-3640
 Hit songwriter Dennis Morgan's publishing company.

Magnatone Music
1604 17th Avenue South
Nashville, TN 37212
Tel. (615) 383-3600
Fax (615) 383-0020
 Specializes in placing songs within the film industry.

Major Bob/Rio Bravo Music
1109 17th Avenue South
Nashville, TN 37212
Tel. (615) 329-4150
Fax (615) 320-4303
E-mail: *majorbob@earthlink.net*
 Bob Doyle's publishing companies. Bob discovered Garth Brooks.

Malaco Music Group
1012 18th Avenue South
Nashville, TN 37212
Tel. (615) 329-4150
Fax (615) 329-3964
 Publishing company of the blues/gospel Malaco Records in Jackson, Mississippi. "When in Rome . . ." Nashville office sticks to country songs only.

Milsap Galbraith Music Group
1223 17th Avenue South
Nashville, TN 37212
Tel. (615) 320-3030
Fax (615) 320-0290
Artist Ronnie Milsap's company, run by producer Rob Galbraith.

Monk Family Music Group
P. O. Box 150768
Nashville, TN 37215
Tel. (615) 292-6811
Fax (615) 292-7266
E-mail: *monkfamily@aol.com*
Publishing company of the Honorary Mayor of Music Row, Charlie Monk.

Moraine Music Group
2803 Bransford Avenue
Nashville, TN 37204
Tel. (615) 393-0400
Fax (615) 383-2375
Publishing company of the Judds' producer Brent Maher.

MRBI
1605 17th Avenue South, #200
Nashville, TN 37212
Tel. (615) 386-0025
Fax (615) 386-0026
MRBI and Murrah Music (address follows) are the publishing ventures of hit songman Roger Murrah. MRBI is a full-service company, including copyright management and royalty collection.

Murrah Music Corporation
1109 16th Avenue South
Nashville, TN 37212
Tel. (615) 329-4236
Fax (615) 329-4417
See above.

Muy Bueno Music Group
1000 18th Avenue South
Nashville, TN 37212

Tel. (615) 327-9229
Fax (615) 327-9234

Publishing company of George Strait's manager Erv Woolsey.

NEM Entertainment

15 Music Square West
Nashville, TN 37203
Tel. (615) 726-0046
Fax (615) 726-1004
E-mail: *Nemmusic@aol.com*

Offices in Los Angeles and Nashville.

New Company Song Group

21 Music Square East
Nashville, TN 37203
Tel. (615) 248-9629

Publishing company of Music Row veteran Chuck Neese.

Of Music

204 Burgandy Hill Road
Nashville, TN 37211
Tel. (615) 333-2872
Fax (615) 834-3660

Company with the most imaginative songs on the Row! President
Tom Oteri is the father of *Saturday Night Live*'s Cheri Oteri.

On the Mantel Music

1016 17th Avenue South
Nashville, TN 37212
Tel. (615) 320-1896
Fax (615) 320-1963

Publishing company of hit songwriter James Dean Hicks.

Paden Place Music

3803 Bedford Avenue
Nashville, TN 37215
Tel. (615) 292-5848
Fax (615) 292-9598
E-mail: *t.paden@worldnet.att.net*

Another company that proves staying power pays off!

Patrick Music Group/pa•TIL•son tunes
209 19th Avenue South, Suite 449
Nashville, TN 37203
Tel. (615) 256-7505
Fax (615) 256-7904
E-mail: *patpmusic@aol.com*
    Popular Music Row publisher.

Peermusic
1207 16th Avenue South
Nashville, TN 37212
Tel. (615) 329-0603
Fax (615) 320-0490
E-mail: *Peermusic_Nashville@compuserve.com*
    One of the most successful independent music publishers, with copyrights dating back to the 1940s. Offices in New York and Los Angeles, too.

Plug In, Inc.
563 Burgess Drive
Nashville, TN 37209
Tel. (615) 356-3048
E-mail: *songplugin@aol.com*
    Pitches writers' catalogs.

Randy Scruggs Music
2821 Bransford Avenue
Nashville, TN 37204
Tel. (615) 385-1744
Fax (615) 385-4013
    Publishing company of producer, writer, and artist Randy Scruggs, son of the legendary Earl Scruggs.

RBI Entertainment
2814 12th Avenue South, #202
Nashville, TN 37204
Tel. (615) 844-5678
Fax (615) 844-5680
    Run by three great song pluggers.

SDB Music Group
P.O. Box 158407
Nashville, TN 37215-8507
Tel. (615) 333-1174
Fax (615) 333-1174
Publishing company of Sherrill Blackman, who was the office manager for NSAI under the direction of the much-loved Maggie Cavender.

Singing Roadie Music Group
P.O. Box 120672
Nashville, TN 37212
Tel. (615) 780-2997
Fax (615) 599-9887
Web site: *www.songnet.com/srmg*
Los Angeles transplant Garth Shaw doing great in Nashville.

Southern Cow Music
23 Music Square East, #102
Nashville, TN 37203
Tel. (615) 251-9815
Fax (615) 255-7499
Another Los Angeles transplant, Steve Bloch, doing great, too!

Southern Writers Group USA
2804 Azalea Place
Nashville, TN 37204
Tel. (615) 383-8682
Fax (615) 383-8696
Publishing company of the Music Row veteran Buzz Cason.

Still Working Music Group
1625 Broadway, #600
Nashville, TN 37203
Tel. (615) 242-4201
Fax (615) 242-4202
Publishing company of the late, great, legendary Roy Orbison.

Street Singer Music
1303 16th Avenue South
Nashville, TN 37212
Tel. (615) 327-4425
Fax (615) 327-1077
Hays, Kansas, transplant Mark Meckel doing great also!

Talbot Music Group
2 Music Circle South
Nashville, TN 37203
Tel. (615) 244-6200
Fax (615) 254-8860
E-mail: *TalbotMusi@aol.com*
Publishing company of the Music Row veteran Joe Talbot, honored by his peers as a man who helped create the Nashville Sound.

Taste Auction/Linden House Music
1612 Linden Avenue
Nashville, TN 37212
Tel. (615) 356-5992
E-mail: *mmorgan@edge.net*
Publishing company of the producer and engineer Marshall Morgan.

Ten Ten Music Group
33 Music Square West, #110
Nashville, TN 37203
Tel. (615) 255-9955
Fax (615) 255-1209
Publishing company of the respected artist manager Barry Coburn.

To the Moon Music Company
P.O. Box 41643
Nashville, TN 37204
Tel. (615) 251-3205
Fax (615) 254-1976
E-mail: *ToTheMoon@Juno.com*
Publishing company of the dynamite song plugger Leslie Salzillo-Schmidt.

Tollesongs
P.O. Box 121242
Nashville, TN 37212
Tel. (615) 385-4554
Fax (615) 383-1197
E-mail: *Tollsongs@aol.com*
Publishing home for all those great Jim Glaser hits.

Western Beat Music
P.O. Box 128104
Nashville, TN 37212
Tel. (615) 383-5466
Fax (615) 383-6331

If your songs are Americana or very traditional country music, this is the company for you. Billy Block also produces a weekly artist showcase and radio show for Americana and alternative country music.

Zamalama Music Group
1100 18th Avenue South
Nashville, TN 37212
Tel. (615) 321-0033
Fax (615) 321-2244

Another company that would sign songs with character, outside-the-norm type material. Company of the writer and artist Kacey Jones.

Zomba Music Publishing
916 19th Avenue South
Nashville, TN 37212
Tel. (615) 321-4850
Fax (615) 321-0765
E-mail: *zomba@zombaontherow.com*

Highly respected on the Row; active in artist development.

ABOUT SONG PLUGGERS

There are people on Music Row who do nothing but pitch songs all day long to artists, producers, and A&R reps. They are called "song pluggers." The major publishing companies have several song pluggers and the smaller independents have one or two; every Nashville publisher has a song plugger or is a song plugger herself. This creates a highly competitive environment for publishers trying to get their songs heard by the right people.

All of the song pluggers know each other and, sometimes, even hang out together. Sometimes they even share inside information with each other. It's not uncommon for producers or A&R reps to call a special meeting with all of the song pluggers at one time, to play them some sides they recorded on a new artist in order to give the pluggers an idea of what they are looking for. Believe it or not, it is extremely difficult for artists to find great songs for an album project. Every time they go into the studio, artists will listen to thousands of songs. The songs may have been written by big hit writers and they may be great songs—but they are not necessarily exactly what the artist is looking for. Artists and record companies work closely with Nashville's top song pluggers to help speed up the process of looking for songs.

From time to time, song pluggers will organize themselves and form a song-plugging group. They hold monthly meetings and invite artists, producers, and A&R reps to come and listen to their songs. Or the industry folks will tell them about the current project they are working on and what they are looking for. Two very successful song-plugging groups (which may or may not be in existence anymore) are The Young Turks and Chicks with Hits. By working together, they give themselves an extra opportunity to pitch a song.

The fast track to getting your songs recorded is by signing a publishing contract with a publisher who has a great song plugger, or who is a great song plugger himself. This information needs to be researched before you talk to publishers about your songs. Without a great song plugger, the chance of getting the right exposure for your songs is very slim.

ABOUT STAFF WRITERS

All major Nashville publishers have a staff of songwriters under contract to write exclusively for their company. During the term of a contract, every song that a writer creates belongs to that publisher and remains with that publisher even when the writer leaves the company, even if the song was never recorded.

Staff writers are paid a nominal fee. The fee is based on anticipated earnings for one year, and with hit songwriters it is very easy to calculate a fee based on past earnings. Generally, the major publishers pay $12,000 to $24,000 per year for a development deal, and $25,000 to $50,000 per year in mid-range.

If the writer has a proven track record with several songs recorded (cuts), great contacts with artists, A&R, and producers, he or she may receive top level—over $50,000 plus copublishing.

These are the top-name writers, often an artist or a very close friend of one or more artists. These writers consistently produce chart-topping songs, and can open any door.

It is expected that the staff writer will be available full-time to write for the company and will be able to live on his advance. Contracts require ten to twelve whole copyrights turned in, which could mean twelve songs written only by the writer, or twenty-four cowritten songs, or thirty-six songs with three writers.

Term of contract is usually one year with a publisher's option for the next four years. Exclusive contracts are usually for one year, with a publisher's option to renew after a year for four or more years. Of course, if the staff writer is unhappy with his situation and wants out of his contract when the year is up, the publisher will most likely not use his option.

Staff salaries are an advance on future royalties, and all monies paid will be deducted from future income. So a staff writer can have a big hit on the charts, but never see the resulting windfall of money because he will have spent it already. On the plus side, if he leaves the company without ever getting a song recorded, he doesn't have to pay the money back. Song publishing makes for some very creative financial statements and is one reason the banks in Nashville have offices that specialize in the music industry.

Advantages of a Staff Writing Position

- Immediate access to a top publisher: As a freelance writer, much of a writer's time is spent looking for a publisher for each song. With a staff position, a writer can eliminate that worry and concentrate on writing songs. Immediate access to cowriters. There are no guarantees that staff writers will be compatible, but generally there is someone in the company who will make a good collaborator. If not, the publisher will help a staff writer find cowriters outside the company. A few companies do not allow their writers to cowrite with writers from other companies. If a cowriter is unpublished, he may be expected to sign his song over to the staff writer's publisher.
- Demo, showcase, and secretarial support
- A position "inside" the hub of activity

A staff writing position is very attractive to the developing songwriter. It pays him a little money, which in all likelihood won't be recouped; it's like going to school on a scholarship. However, as wonderful as a staff writing position sounds, there are some major drawbacks.

Disadvantages of a Staff Writing Position

- When a writer leaves the company, his songs stay behind. If his best songs are signed to a company that no longer is interested in him, the chances of getting his songs recorded are very slim indeed.
- Highly competitive writing environment. The pressure is on in a staff writing situation. The publisher can't possibly demo every song written, and has to make choices between songwriters on his staff.

• The same goes for pitching songs. The publisher will decide what songs to pitch and will expect his writers to check with him before pitching one of their own songs.

Although it may seem on the surface that a staff writing deal is a great way to go, there are many important factors that should be considered before signing on the dotted line. Make sure you have a lot of professional advice before entering into a staff writing commitment.

Getting a Staff Writing Position in Nashville

Staff writer is not a position you can apply for, so don't hurry to type up your resume. The best way to achieve a staff position is to keep a very close personal relationship with publishers. Plan to see them at least once a week, keep them informed as to new songs you've written and new cowriters you are writing with, and invite them to any writers' nights in which you plan to participate. In other words, act like one of their staff writers anyway. When a position does open up you'll know about it—and the publisher will have a good feel for you and whether or not you'll fit on his staff.

Industry Interview with John Van Meter, Director, Creative Services, Sony/ATV Tree Music Publishing LLC

"One of the most important stages in a songwriter's career is getting a staff writing position. I'd say it's pretty important for a writer on any level. Publishers have better access to artists, producers, and A&R, and are working with the writer on a daily basis.

"A song is a 50/50 partner-ship—for every dollar earned, the songwriter gets 50¢ and the publisher gets 50¢. For her 50 percent, the writer creates the song. For his 50 percent, the publisher:

• Helps come up with ideas for songs, by talking to producers and artists that have specific ideas about what they want to record
• Gives feedback on completed songs

- Helps set up cowriting possibilities
- Introduces writer to other industry professionals
- Demos the song
- Registers the song with the Library of Congress Copyright Office
- Gets the song recorded
- Places the song in a movie, TV show, songbook
- Collects royalties worldwide, including tough-to-find markets
- Gives the writer lots of support and encouragement

"How do I find writers to sign to a staff position? BMI and ASCAP will send over a writer they feel deserves a staff deal. NSAI will do the same. These organizations work with a lot of writers on a daily basis and have a pretty good idea of the ones who are writing great songs, or who have a lot of potential.

"I'll hear about writers through word of mouth—when a new writer hits town and has some great songs, the word travels fast on Music Row. I'll seek that writer out and get to know her and her songs.

"Cowriters are another great source for staff writers. Our writers are free to write with other writers outside of the company, so I'll always check out a cowriter to see if he is signed to another publisher, or available to sign with us.

"Nashville publishers are cutting back on signing developing writers because they take a lot of extra work. There's more time spent editing songs, more time spent in the studio helping them demo songs, and a lot more hand-holding going on because they are not familiar with the lay of the land. The song plugger is involved in the whole song process, from the first idea for a song to the completed demo. It can take a lot of work to go through the entire development of a song.

"All songs that are demo'd are approved by someone on the staff. Each writer is assigned a "point person," someone on staff that writers can check in with when needed. Based on a writer's past history, somebody on the professional staff will oversee the demo process. Once a writer has had two or three songs demo'd, they should be able to do it themselves.

"A good demo costs around $600 per song; usually the minimum recorded at one time would be around four songs—I normally go in with six. Six tracks would be a very good session. The more songs demo'd, the less cost per song. We use the top players in town, maybe not the A team, which are the major label session guys, but definitely the A– or B+ guys. It really makes a big difference; you get more work done and get a better quality sound. And you don't have to go back later and fix things. The type of demo you record depends on the song. You don't always have to have a full-blown demo; sometimes a guitar and a vocal will suffice.

"I really recommend that writers spend some time at writers' nights. The benefit of doing writers' nights is, that's the place where the word of mouth starts. Even though publishers might not be hanging out at writers' nights, the word gets back to them about really good writers. Another reason they are so important is that they expand cowriting possibilities. That's the place to network with writers and set cowriting appointments.

"Not many people are aware of the fact that Nashville publishers are also very active in helping to develop new artists. Every big publisher has a production arm. They will produce a master quality recording on an unsigned artist, and then shop that artist to the various record labels. Although the finished product is often as good as a record produced by the major labels, it is not expected that it will ever be offered for sale to the public. Instead, the publishing company will recoup their investment by publishing the artist's songs. Production companies are an important part of the development side of publishing.

"Of course, my biggest responsibility in working with staff writers is getting their songs cut. I really take pleasure in this side of my job. Success in song-plugging is summed up best by Ken Kragen, who defines the Fundamental Rule: Don't take 'no' from a person who can't say 'yes'.

"My biggest victories are getting unknown writers their very first cut. I was able to get a Pam Tillis cut for a writer I had been working with. It was her first song to be recorded, and I thought I was king of the world when I did it. It's really tough to get a cut on an unknown writer. When you are pitching a song, you provide the lyrics, and the artist or producer will glance at the lyrics as they are listening to the songs. You can see their eyes go right down to the bottom of the page where the writers are listed to see who wrote the song. A hit songwriter, especially the one whose songs they like, will carry a lot of weight.

"My best advice for any songwriter? Please remember this: *The publisher works for the writer, not the other way around!*"

A Kentucky native, JOHN VAN METER moved to Nashville in 1987 after graduating from the University of Kentucky. "When I found out that a man could make a living putting singers and songs together, that's all I've wanted to do," John says. A postgraduate internship led to a job in the tape-copy room of Tree International. Following three years of tape-copying and the occasional cut, John was hired by Malaco Music to head the creative department of their Nashville office.

From Malaco, John was hired by Zomba Music to pitch songs. He stayed with Zomba until he was lured away to return to Sony/ATV Tree as director of creative services. "To have such a great company come after you is very flattering," John admits, "especially after having worked there before."

Over the course of more than twelve years in Nashville, John has had cuts by artists ranging from Conway Twitty, the Oak Ridge Boys, and Alabama, to Pam Tillis, Faith Hill, and Tim McGraw. He has also been involved in the development of such writer/artists as Sara Evans and Andy Griggs. While representing such powerhouse writers as "Mutt" Lange, Tom Shapiro, Gretchen Peters, and Bobby Braddock, John has still developed a reputation for recognizing and nurturing talented and undiscovered writers, writer/artists, and writer/producers.

WORKING WITH PUBLISHERS ON A SONG-BY-SONG BASIS

There are so few staff positions available in Nashville that a full-time job is not something you can step into right away. There are many advantages to working with a publisher on a song-by-song basis. Publishing contracts are as varied as music publishers. Throw away the books you've read and go with your instincts. If a publisher is interested in pitching your songs, then work with him. Variables are:

Duration of Contract

Copyright reversion is a four-letter word to publishers, but it is something they've had to learn to live with. It takes a long time to get a song cut, even if the artist is interested from the day he hears it. A two-year reversion is the norm, but five years is not unreasonable. If he insists on no reversion (which will be the case with the majors), then look him in the eye and ask whom he intends to pitch it to tomorrow. It doesn't really take too long to get the song to the right artist if you have a firm idea about who should record the song.

Demo Costs

Publishers pay all demo costs. If you have already demo'd the song and it's a great song demo that the publisher wants to pitch, then you should be able to keep half of the publishing or be reimbursed for your costs. If the publisher has to re-demo the song in order to pitch it, then he absorbs the cost and keeps one hundred percent of the publishing. When you are looking for a Nashville publisher, it's not a good idea to get hung up on demo costs at the outset. Sign the song over 100 percent even if you've paid for the demo—but if it needs to be redone, the publisher pays. The Golden Rule is that the songwriter never pays costs that a publisher should absorb. But the reality is that a songwriter spends a lot of money just trying to get his song into the right hands. Walking a fine line, publishers sometimes take advantage of writers in regard to costs, but you can work together to get the job done.

Handshake agreements are not uncommon—the publisher likes your song, will pitch it for six months or so; if he gets a cut with a major artist, then he gets the publishing. This kind of agreement calls for a great deal of trust on both sides, but it focuses on what matters most—getting the song recorded. It's worth the risk, and the biggest risk lies with the publisher!

6

A Basic Understanding of Nashville's Record Companies

There are only five major record labels in Nashville and each of these are very small divisions of huge corporations, several owned by foreign companies. Although the Nashville labels have their own autonomy when it comes to marketing and promoting their artists, their budgets are subject to the financial health of their parent company. The threat of consolidation looms over the record industry, and the broadcast industry as well. The size of a label's artist roster will suffer the first impact of consolidation in either of these industries.

NASHVILLE'S MAJOR RECORD LABELS

In order to control a larger share of radio airtime and maintain a larger artist roster, major record labels divide into smaller labels, each with their own A&R, marketing, and promotion staff. Most of these smaller companies share the same offices, but some have separate offices. It will be very important for aspiring artists to familiarize themselves with the artist roster of each label, and have some idea of where they would fit in the best. Here is a listing of Nashville's major record labels and their biggest stars. Information for smaller divisions of major labels follows directly below the label data.

Capitol Nashville (EMI)
3222 West End Avenue, 11th Floor
Nashville, TN 37203
Tel. (615) 269-2000
Web site: *www.hollywoodandvine.com*
Home of the great Garth Brooks.

Virgin Records Nashville
48 Music Square East
Nashville, TN 37203
Tel. (615) 251-1100
Web site: *www.virginnashville.com*
    A Nashville Virgin label was started for producer extraordinaire Scott
Hendricks (Faith Hill, Alan Jackson, Brooks & Dunn).

RCA Label Group (BMG)
1400 158th Avenue South
Nashville, TN 37212
Tel. (615) 301-4300
Web site: *www.twangthis.com*
RCA: Alabama, Clint Black, Tracy Byrd. BNA: Lorrie Morgan, K.T. Oslin.

Arista Nashville
1400 18th Avenue South
Nashville, TN 37212
Tel. (615) 846-9100
Brooks & Dunn, Diamond Rio, Alan Jackson.

Sony Music Nashville (CBS)
34 Music Square East
Nashville, TN 37203
Tel. (615) 742-4321
Web site: *www.sonynashville.com*
Columbia: Chet Atkins, Mary Chapin Carpenter. Epic: Joe Diffie, Patty
Loveless, Collin Raye. Monument: Dixie Chicks. Lucky Dog: David Allen
Coe, Johnny Paycheck.

Warner/Reprise Nashville (Time/Warner)
20 Music Square East
Nashville, TN 37203
Tel. (615) 748-8000
Web sites: *www.warnerbros.com* and *www.reprise.com*
Warner Bros.: Faith Hill, Ronnie Milsap, Travis Tritt.
Reprise: Dwight Yoakam.

Atlantic
20 Music Square East
Nashville, TN 37203
Tel. (615) 733-1880
Web site: *www.atlantic-records.com*
John Mitchell Montgomery.

Asylum Records
20 Music Square East
Nashville, TN 37203
Tel. (615) 292-7990
Bryan White, George Jones.

Giant Records
1514 South Street
Nashville, TN 37212
Tel. (615) 256-3110
Clay Walker, Don Williams.

Universal Music Group
MCA/Nashville
Sixty Music Square East
Nashville, TN 37203
Tel. (615) 244-8944
Web site: *www.mca-nashville.com*
Reba McEntire, George Strait, Trisha Yearwood.

Mercury Nashville
66 Music Square West
Nashville, TN 37203
Tel. (615) 320-0110
Web site: *www.mercurynashville.com*
Billy Ray Cyrus, Kathy Mattea, Shania Twain.

DreamWorks Nashville
1516 16th Avenue South
Nashville, TN 37212
Tel. (615) 463-4600
Randy Travis.

NASHVILLE'S MAJOR INDEPENDENT LABELS
There are three very big independent labels with major label status:

The Curb Group
47 Music Square East
Nashville, TN 37203
Tel. (615) 321-5080
Web site: *www.curb.com*
Curb: Tim McGraw, Jo Dee Messina, LeAnn Rimes, Hank Williams, Jr.
Curb/MCA: Lyle Lovett. Curb/Mercury: Wynonna.

Maverick Mike Curb has built a strong roster and relationships with other labels. The Curb Web site is great too, with links to many of the other labels.

Lyric Street Records (Disney)
824 19th Avenue South
Nashville, TN 37203
Tel. (615) 963-4848

New in Nashville; no established artists at this printing.

Platinum Entertainment
1222 16th Avenue South
Nashville, TN 37212
Tel. (615) 327-0770

Intersound Country: Lynn Anderson, Bellamy Brothers, T. Graham Brown, Earl Thomas Conley, the Oak Ridge Boys, Billy Joe Royal, Rick Springfield. River North: Atlanta Rhythm Section, Peter Cetera, Kansas.

OTHER IMPORTANT INDEPENDENT RECORD LABELS

Many aspiring artists become extremely frustrated with Nashville and decide to start their own record label and market themselves directly to radio. This can be a very expensive proposition, and has a 99 percent chance of failure for many reasons, including:

- The airplay a country single gets is monitored by BDS (Broadcast Data Systems). In order to be picked up by BDS, your single must have a digital watermark recognized by BDS.
- The Nashville record labels have a very close relationship with the radio programmers and lobby heavily to move their current single up the chart. Radio programmers juggle chart positions between all of the labels listed above and rarely include singles from other companies, even those listed below.
- Even if you had a great hit single that was getting lots of airplay across the country, it wouldn't be monitored by BDS or the PROs. So you wouldn't earn back the money you spent producing and marketing your single. It's a vicious circle.

In spite of those grim odds, there are some independent record companies that are determined to find alternate ways to promote and market product. In the new world of technology and the Internet, the chances of success are brighter. Here is a listing of Nashville's current independent labels:

Compass Records
117 30th Avenue South
Nashville, TN 37212
Tel. (615) 320-7672

Specializes in folk/pop, jazz, acoustic, and world music. Interested in touring artists with national or strong regional fan base. No country.

Door Knob Records
3950 N. Mount Juliet Road
Mount Juliet, TN 37122
Tel. (615) 754-0417

Record company of producer Gene Kennedy—represents many aspiring country artists.

Step One Records
1300 Division Street, Suite 304
Nashville, TN 37203
Tel. (615) 255-3009

Artists: Jack Greene, the Whites, Gene Watson.

HOW TO APPROACH NASHVILLE'S RECORD COMPANIES

Most Nashville record labels, especially the majors, will not work with unknown writers or artists. They prefer to work with publishers, artist managers, or entertainment attorneys—business representatives of writers and artists. Whether you are a songwriter or an artist, you need someone to speak on your behalf.

If you've decided to start your own publishing company and pitch your own songs, then you will be approaching the record company as a publisher, not a songwriter. Each record company has its own policy regarding unsolicited material, but generally they will not accept songs unless they come from a publisher. Also, it must be stated very clearly on the cassette tape itself to whose attention it is directed. There are a couple of tip sheets that will give you some specific information on who is currently looking for songs, and to whom you should get your tape. They are:

Chuck Chellman's Parade of Stars

1201 16th Avenue South
Nashville, TN 37212
Tel. (615) 320-7270

Chuck has been publishing his tip sheet for a quarter of a century.

Music Row Publication's Row Fax

1231 17th Avenue South
Nashville, TN 32132
Tel. (615) 321-3617
Fax (615) 329-0852
E-mail: *news@musicrow.com*
Web site: *www.musicrow.com*

Comes to you via fax or e-mail, and includes the latest gossip on Music Row.

Both of these tip sheets are excellent, and will tell you about the artist, record label, producer, and recording date. You may have the greatest song in the world for Garth Brooks, but if he's not recording right now, it won't do any good to get it to him. Wait until he's looking for new songs. Your songs will have to be packaged just like all the other cassette tapes on Music Row (see chapter 9). Again, you really shouldn't be pitching your songs directly to record companies and producers—country songs need a Nashville publisher.

If you are an aspiring artist and you've got it all together—lots of live performance experience, a great local following, terrific original songs, a great 8″ × 10″ glossy, and an awesome CD—then you are probably itching to get your artist package to one of the major record labels. Stop! Before you go any further, the best thing you can do for yourself is spend as much time in Nashville as possible before you tip your hand and reveal that you are looking for an artist's deal. Can you spend a week? A month? Move here for a year or so? Get a feel for the environment and observe your competition. They are the people you will be working with if you do get an artist's deal. You want to start building relationships as soon as you can.

Music Row is a very tight-knit community, and the artists have to feel comfortable here. Artists have to be familiar with publishers and other writers, because they will be relying on publishers and writers to supply them with great songs. Even if you plan to write your own material, you will still want to cowrite with Nashville hit songwriters. So before you go marching into a record company office, get to know Nashville first.

Nashville record labels are interested in four specific things:

1) What is your unique quality?
2) How do you sound on tape?
3) Who is your support team?
4) How do you look and sound on stage?

#1—Your Unique Quality

What do you have that no one else has? A wispy sound? An extraordinary range? A booming bass? The labels will be looking for that something different from everyone else. What is the message you want to put across? You have to have a very strong sense of self—this is who I am and what I'm about. Are you a rebel? A strong woman? A kinder, gentler man? Contrary to what you may have heard, the labels will not shape you to fit their own mold. You have to let them know who you are and what you stand for. Stick to it!

#2—Your Artist's Demo

This is such an important part of your presentation to a record label that there is an entire chapter devoted to this topic (please see chapter 11, "Packaging Your Product"). No matter how great a performer you might be, it is how you sound on tape that will make or break your artist's career.

#3—Your Support Team: Nashville's Top Managers and Entertainment Attorneys

Record labels will not only be interested in you, but will want to meet with everyone connected with your career. Who has helped you along the way? Who do you work closely with to make important decisions about your career? Usually an aspiring artist has a family member or a close friend working as an artist manager—someone who "discovered" you and helped bring you along to where you are today. Even though you have an intense loyalty to your current team and they may be doing an excellent job, you should all be prepared to discuss other options with the label. The label will want to have a great deal of confidence in everyone connected with your career. Needless to say, the more people on your support team are from Music Row, the stronger your presentation to the label will be.

There are three areas of representation you should consider before you go straight to a record label. They are publishers, artist managers, and entertainment attorneys. We have already discussed publishers in depth; here is a little info about Nashville's artist managers and entertainment attorneys.

Artist Managers

It is next to impossible to attract the attention of an artist manager before you are signed to a record label. It's another catch-22 situation. Artist managers are paid a percentage of your live performance income, so you have to be able to demonstrate your ability to bring in enough income to make time they spend on your career somewhat lucrative. The truth is, artist managers work for practically nothing in the formative stages of an artist's career, often putting up their own money to help get you started. It takes a lot of work over a long period of time before the money starts coming in. An artist manager has to really believe in you as much as you believe in yourself to get involved in your career. Many top artist managers don't even live in Nashville, so don't make that your criteria for picking a good one. Here are some of Nashville's top artist managers:

Creative Artists Agency
3310 West End Avenue, #500
Nashville, TN 37203
Tel. (615) 383-8787
Fax (615) 383-4937
Probably the most powerful artist management agency in the United States. They have a very large staff of managers in Nashville, plus a publishing division.

Idea Productions & Publishing
25 Music Square West
Nashville, TN 37203
Tel. (615) 457-2000
Fax (615) 457-2828
Management, publishing, and production company of E. Michael Blanton and Dan Harrell, who have guided the careers of Amy Grant and Michael W. Smith.

Borman Entertainment
1208 17th Avenue South
Nashville, TN 37212
Tel. (615) 320-3000
Fax (615) 320-3001
Prestigious Los Angeles–based firm with star clients Faith Hill and Dwight Yoakam.

Frank Callari Management
209 19th Avenue South, #322
Nashville, TN 37203
Tel. (615) 742-6300
Fax (615) 742-6333
Clients include the Mavericks and Kim Richey.

Carter & Co.
P.O. Box 128195
Nashville, TN 37212
Tel. (615) 329-2145
Fax (615) 329-0416
    Joe Carter moved to Nashville from Beaumont, Texas, where he discovered Tracy Byrd.

William N. Carter Career Management
1028-B 18th Avenue South
Nashville, TN 37212
Tel. (615) 327-1270
Fax (615) 321-0802
    Former Secret Service agent and trial lawyer. Manages Ralph Emery and several country artists.

Keith Case & Associates
99 Music Square West
Nashville, TN 37203
Tel. (615) 327-4646
Fax (615) 327-4949
    Manager and booking agent for America's top bluegrass and folk acts.

Refugee Management Int'l
209 19th Avenue South, #347
Nashville, TN 37203
Tel. (615) 256-6615
Fax (615) 256-6717
    Stuart Dill manages Jo Dee Messina and the Bellamy Brothers.

Bob Doyle & Associates
1111 17th Avenue South
Nashville, TN 37212
Tel. (615) 329-1040
Fax (615) 329-1021
    Instrumental in launching Garth Brooks; manager for Brooks and other artists.

Falcon-Goodman Management
1012 16th Avenue South
Nashville, TN 37212
Tel. (615) 244-6994
Fax (615) 255-4585
    Gary Falcon and Jon Goodman manage Travis Tritt and others.

Fitzgerald Hartley
1908 Wedgewood Avenue
Nashville, TN 37212
Tel. (615) 322-9493
Fax (615) 322-9582
Mark Hartley heads the Los Angeles office; Larry Fitzgerald is in Nashville. They manage numerous top country artists.

Glen Campbell Management/Music
1114 17th Avenue South, #102
Nashville, TN 37212
Tel. (615) 329-9886
Fax (615) 329-0423
Marty Gamblin helped develop Alan Jackson; manages Bryan White and SouthSixtyFive.

Bonnie Garner Management
119 17th Avenue South
Nashville, TN 37203
Tel. (615) 259-9050
Fax (615) 259-1109
Former VP A&R for CBS Records/Nashville; manages Marty Stuart.

Dan Goodman Management
P.O. Box 120775
Nashville, TN 37212
Tel. (615) 661-9090
Fax (615) 370-1100
In management over sixteen years.

Merle Kilgore Management
2 Music Circle South
Nashville, TN 37203
Tel. (615) 742-3622
Fax (615) 742-1235
Manages Hank Williams, Jr., and wrote "Wolverton Mountain"; if you are looking for a manager with gusto, Merle's your man.

TKO Artist Management
4219 Hillsboro Road, #318
Nashville, TN 37215
Tel. (615) 383-5017
Fax (615) 292-3328
Clients: Sawyer Brown, Chris LeDoux, and others.

The Left Bank Organization
1100 17th Avenue South
Nashville, TN 37212
Tel. (615) 327-7920
Fax (615) 327-4667

Another Los Angeles megamanagement firm that recently opened offices in Nashville; Philip Kovac heads the office and represents Deana Carter.

Vector Management
1500 17th Avenue South
Nashville, TN 37212
Tel. (615) 269-6600
Fax (615) 269-6002

Ken Levitan manages Lyle Lovett, Patty Griffin, and others. Founded and ran Rising Tide Records which was doing just great until consolidation closed the label.

Moress Nanas Entertainment
1102 18th Avenue South
Nashville, TN 37212
Tel. (615) 329-9945
Fax (615) 321-3457

Offices in Los Angeles and Nashville; represents Donna Summer and K.T. Oslin.

Firstars Management
2410 Belmont Blvd.
Nashville, TN 37212
Tel. (615) 460-1124
Fax (615) 460-1136

Miles Copeland's company, run by Anastasia Pruitt (Mrs. Tony Brown). Clients are Sting, Human League, and others.

Creative Trust, Inc.
1910 Acklen Avenue
Nashville, TN 37212
Tel. (615) 297-5010
Fax (615) 297-5020

Dan Raines manages Steven Curtis Chapman and other Christian artists.

Senior Management
56 Lindsley
Nashville, TN 37210
Tel. (615) 244-3080
Fax (615) 244-3029
    Simon Renshaw manages Dixie Chicks and Janis Ian.

Mike Robertson Management
P.O. Box 120073
Nashville, TN 37212
Tel. (615) 329-4199
Fax (615) 329-3923
    Nashville manager for over seventeen years; current clients include BlackHawk and the Nitty Gritty Dirt Band.

AS is Management
209 19th Avenue South, #120
Nashville, TN 37203
Tel. (615) 255-8090
Fax (615) 255-1090
    Al Schiltz manages Billy Ray Cyrus.

Shipley Biddy Entertainment
1400 South Street
Nashville, TN 37212
Tel. (615) 846-0493
Fax (615) 846-0496
    Sheila Shipley Biddy was the first woman to head a record label—Decca—in Nashville. Decca was closed under consolidation of MCA and Mercury.

rpm management
209 19th Avenue South, #229
Nashville, TN 37203
Tel. (615) 256-1980
Fax (615) 256-1134
    Scott Siman manages Tim McGraw; former Senior VP of Sony Music.

Titley Spalding & Associates
900 Division Street
Nashville, TN 37203
Tel. (615) 255-1326
Fax (615) 254-4267

Bob Titley and Clarence Spalding guide the careers of Brooks & Dunn and Kathy Mattea.

Gold Mountain Entertainment
2 Music Circle South, #212
Nashville, TN 37203
Tel. (615) 255-9000
Fax (615) 255-9001
Burt Stein manages Nanci Griffith and Rodney Crowell.

DS Management
1017 16th Avenue South
Nashville, TN 37212
Tel. (615) 329-8020
Fax (615) 259-1109
Denise Stiff manages Alison Krauss and others.

The Erv Woolsey Company
1000 18th Avenue South
Nashville, TN 37212
Tel. (615) 329-2402
Fax (615) 327-4917
Erv manages George Strait and Lee Ann Womack.

Entertainment Attorneys

It will be a lot easier to find an entertainment attorney—they start at around $200 per hour. If you've got the money, honey, they've got the time. Actually that's not really true, because their reputation is on the line every time they take an aspiring artist to a record label. The more discerning about whom they represent, the better lawyers they are. So if you just walk in and they sign you up just like that, beware. It should be almost as difficult to convince an entertainment attorney to represent you as it will be to convince a record company to sign you.

Like an artist manager, the attorney you use doesn't have to be in Nashville. However, it is very, very important that your attorney is well-versed in entertainment law and, even more important, has worked with Nashville record labels. Record contracts, songwriting and publishing contracts, and copyright law are all highly specialized fields that require expertise. The State of Tennessee doesn't really certify "specialists," but there are definitely specialists in the entertainment industry. Here are a few of the top firms:

Craig Benson Law Offices
1207 17th Avenue South, #300
Nashville, TN 37212
Tel. (615) 320–0660
Fax (615) 320–0909
    In business twenty-three years, handles all aspects of entertainment law.

Frank & Frank, PLLC
1102 17th Avenue South, #300
Nashville, TN 37212
Tel. (615) 321–4707
Fax (615) 321–3722
    Richard Frank specializes in copyright law and is counsel for the CMA.

Gladstone, Doherty & Associates, PLLC
1222 16th Avenue South, #21
Nashville, TN 37212
Tel. (615) 329–1547
Fax (615) 329–2148
    Steven Gladstone represents artists, songwriters, publishers, and managers.

Gordon, Martin, Jones & Harris, P.A.
49 Music Square West, #600
Nashville, TN 37203
Tel. (615) 321–5400
Fax (615) 321–5469
    Rusty Jones represents Nashville's most famous writer, Garth Brooks.

Loeb & Loeb
45 Music Square West
Nashville, TN 37203
Tel. (615) 749–8300
Fax (615) 749–8308
    International law firm which recently set up offices in Nashville; Malcolm Mimms heads the office and is counsel to NSAI.

Manatt, Phelps & Phillips
1233 17th Avenue South
Nashville, TN 37212
Tel. (615) 327–2744
Fax (615) 327–2044

Ken Kraus represents some of Nashville's top artists and the Elvis Presley estate.

John Mason Partners, Ltd.
1107 17th Avenue South
Nashville, TN 37212
Tel. (615) 320-5150
Fax (615) 320-5410
Represents a long list of top music industry artists and label heads; has offices in Lake Tahoe and Los Angeles as well.

Sally Nordlund, Attorney-at-Law
P.O. Box 121859
Nashville, TN 37212
Tel. (615) 313-4166
Fax (615) 313-4174
E-mail: *nordlundlaw@mindspring.com*
Former attorney for Nashville's oldest music publisher, Acuff-Rose.

Wyatt, Tarrant, & Combs
29 Music Square East
Nashville, TN 37203
Tel. (615) 255-6161
Fax (615) 254-4490
One of the oldest and most respected law offices on Music Row; has several highly regarded specialists in copyright law in the firm.

J. David Wykoff, Esq.
1700 Hayes Street
Nashville, TN 37203
Tel. (615) 963-9940
Represents popular alternative rock and alternative country artists.

#4—About Live Auditions

Once the record label has heard your demo and met with you and your support team, it will probably request an artist showcase. Usually, if the company has requested a showcase, it will pay for it. However, you should still have a very thorough knowledge of the different types of showcases there are and the one that will work best for you (see chapter 17). That way, when the label asks you for a showcase you can tell them how you prefer to do it.

If you have several labels showing some interest, but no one seems ready to give you a commitment, it might be a good idea to go ahead and put on your own artist's showcase. It's OK to invite all the record labels; that is a very common practice in Nashville. If the label you are interested in knows that another label is interested in you, then most likely they will all show up! It puts you in the driver's seat. However, if you haven't been able to impress any of the labels, publishers, managers, or attorneys with your artist's package, better wait before putting on a show. First, get a buzz going, then have a showcase.

Photo by Kay Williams

INDUSTRY INTERVIEW WITH ANTHONY SMITH

Successful producer and country/ pop writer Anthony Smith has taken two new country acts to Nashville record labels and gotten them a deal. Here is how he did it:

SouthSixtyFive—Atlantic Records

"Delious Kennedy had discovered these five great young guys called SouthSixtyFive; nineteen- to twenty-two-year-olds—only one of them is over twenty-two. They have a great pop sound. He took them to Rick Blackburn and Al Cooley at Atlantic Records, and they were curious to see what SouthSixtyFive would sound like in the studio. Rick wanted a producer with a background in country and pop, so he called me in on the project. I liked the idea that the label was so excited about them, so I set up a time to meet with Delious. He was thinking about giving it a month to produce some sides. I thought it would take at least six months, so we compromised and set aside three months to see what we came up with.

"They came into the studio and I asked them to sing a cappella. Several of them had never even been in the studio before. They had boundless energy at midnight! The wonderful thing was that they were so fun. It's great to get someone right at the beginning, with all of the fresh energy.

"We had a great project on tape, but I knew it was too pop to get played on country radio; so I asked Delious to give me some time and let me do the final mix. I cut the one side that got them their deal. They recently did Fan Fair, and the Oak Ridge Boys came and sang with them on stage. They all sang 'Bobby Sue'—it was the old and the new together. It was so exciting."

Trini Triggs—Curb Records

"John Earl Roe and Herbert Graham of Graham Central Station (a popular five-story multi-genre dance club in several cities including Nashville), came to see me about Trini Triggs, a hot young singer that was getting a lot of attention in Louisiana. From the time they first came to talk to me about Trini and the time they finally talked me into working with him, a year and a half had passed.

"Charles Smith introduced me to Roe and Graham. Charles lives in Louisiana and made lots of trips up here to Nashville. I said I would meet Trini for breakfast. I had meant to spend one hour with him, but I liked him so much I spent the whole day with him! He had a demo tape he had done in Charles's Louisiana studio, but I wasn't able to shop it.

"He just kept at it. A year and a half later he came back with another tape that was produced by a well-known Nashville producer, but I still didn't hear anything I thought I could pitch. So we went into the studio. The secretaries started hanging around, hanging out in the studio; there was a buzz going. We knew something special was taking place. After a year and a half, all of a sudden, things happened really fast—three weeks, three hours, three labels! We were in the studio three weeks, and when we were through we started pitching the tape to labels. Within three hours we had three labels courting him—Decca, Asylum, and Curb. They were all blown away by the production.

"I was going through a Leadership Music class at the time (an in-depth study of all facets of the Nashville music industry for top industry executives), and Mark Wright of Decca Records kept following me around. 'I've gotta have him, man. You're going to give him to me, aren't you? We're Leadership Music buddies, right?' Mark kept goading. But I didn't want to have anything with the deal. I didn't expect a deal to come through anyway. You usually don't get that right away. Then Curb did a deal memo and that cinched it.

Getting Started

"How did I get started? I was finishing college, getting ready for grad school—I had a scholarship which covered half of my tuition, so I thought I'd go to Nashville and 'sell some songs' to get money for the other half. *[Anthony uses the amateur term 'sell songs' to reveal how green he was at that time.—S.B.]* I stopped by Muscle Shoals on my way, but the recording studios wouldn't see me. So I went to Fame Music Publishing, pushed the intercom on the door and said, 'I'm an arranger from the West Coast,' and they let me right in. They liked my songs, and a group called the Muscle Shoals Horns recorded one of them with Fred Foster producing.

"Fred brought me up to Nashville and introduced me to Bob Beckham; I became a staff writer for Combine Music. I started having more fun than I ever thought about having. I never intended to stay, thought I would just check it out. I was at Combine from 1982 to 1987. Then they sold the catalog. Nobody renewed their publishing deals because we didn't know what was going on, so we all left. I had friends I was writing with over at Famous Music, so I went there until 1992.

"Susan Burns at Famous made writing appointments for me in Los Angeles and New York. When you live in Nashville and you go to Los Angeles or New York, you have priority time—studios that were booked will work around your schedule when you are from out of town. The same works in reverse. I would make as many as ten trips a year, writing songs and producing demos. When I would go out to places, they didn't know I was from Nashville. I've often heard, 'You don't look like you are from Nashville!' Then, in 1989, I met Donna Summer. Famous could get you into places you just couldn't crack on your own.

"In Los Angeles, everyone has their own 'camp,' ten or twelve writers that they cowrite with. They won't work with other writers and other studios. But being from Nashville, I can go from camp to camp. They can't do that or don't want to do that because, in their own camp, they are the Generals! Los Angeles writers are in and tied to major things; they can have as many people as they want around. They have their own little world.

"Nashville is such a songwriting center, everything revolves around the song. Los Angeles comes from a 'track' standpoint; it's a completely different process. They lay down tracks and get the whole thing rocking that way. Nashville is very structured; everyone works on a 10-2-6 schedule. Los Angeles works by the week, ten days, two weeks, in an unstructured manner. You sleep, then when you get up, no matter what time it is, you just resume working on the same project. In Nashville, you go to one project at 10:00, another at 2:00, another at 6:00! My favorite two things about Nashville are one, leaving; and two, coming back!

"So many of my friends started moving here, Nashville became 'Big Business.' Prior to that it wasn't perceived as 'Big Business' at all. But with all the consolidations it has really changed. For a while Music Row did not embrace people coming here—it's gotten a lot better in the last five to seven years.

"Relationships are crucial in getting your songs cut. If you are writing really good songs, and they are getting heard, you will get some cuts. A great song goes right past the brain straight to the heart—you are just reacting to it. A smash is something different, it really stands out. Everybody hits the floor. What you have in Nashville is a lot of excellent songs—lots of outstanding songs to choose from. You just have to narrow down the ones that fit that artist.

"Anything that you do and get done requires a lot of work, and while we support the project in theory, we might not want to do the work. For example, I'm working with an aspiring artist right now. She was introduced to me by EMI Music Publishing. She had met people at different places, and they really liked her, but nothing was happening. It always takes longer than you initially think. I'll be working for six months at least. You need to put a lot of time into a project.

"For me, what I figured out is, a record tells it all—it answers all the questions. It becomes a product the record companies can sell. When it comes right down to it, that's what they do, they sell records. This is the record business—you've got to have a record. I can make a record—I don't need to put on a showcase for someone to see my act. The producer and the record label need to work together. If you make something they can 'sell,' then you've got a deal. I hate that word, but basically, it comes right down to that. You don't ever want to compromise, but you can use techniques that suit the label best—there is a lot of room in there. When you are trying to make your project the best it can be, it will be a lot better.

"I also don't put on showcases, or even go to see an artist's showcase. If the label wants a showcase, they will fund it. After you have something in your hand, then you can showcase. But if you are not well-funded, you can get substandard product that way.

"Just because someone says 'I want you on this label' doesn't mean you have a record deal. Even labels that I have relationships with might not be the right labels for an artist. You have to ask yourself, who gets the most excited about this artist? No artist is right for every label.

"I've always produced my own song demos, and that's how I got started. You have to be careful not to try to reinvent the wheel, and then bring it through this little bitty gate of industry standards; but you'll try that in the beginning. I'm either writing or in the studio for one reason or the other. There are also lots of meetings to do with production, endless business things that take a lot of your time.

"I like to do community work. I'm going to Memphis next week to sit on an ASCAP panel for NSAI, along with Ralph Murphy and Roger Cook. The title of the panel is 'So You Think You're Something!' Everyone thinks they are going to take the town by storm. It just doesn't happen that way. So you give your time to helping educate people; and give something of yourself back to the community. I used to have the 'save the world' mentality and tried to help people; but then you discover they don't want to be helped. They will go ahead and do exactly what you tell them not to do. Now I just give them the information they need and hope for the best for them.

"You don't do anything in this town without friends. Energy, drive, hard work are not enough—you can't do it without friends."

ANTHONY SMITH, a versatile songwriter, producer, and arranger, has achieved success in pop, R&B, country, and jazz. He has written with and/or had songs recorded by Donna Summer, Regina Belle, Kirk Whalum, Suzy Bogguss, Lonestar, John & Audrey Wiggins, Clinton Gregory, Clay Walker, Kenny Rogers, Neal McCoy, and many others.

Anthony cowrote ten of the twelve songs on Donna Summer's critically acclaimed *Mistaken Identity* album. This success garnered five singles in Europe and the Top Twenty hit, "When Love Cries." Anthony also has credits in such feature films as *Earth Force, Almost an Angel,* and Stephen King's *Graveyard Shift.*

A graduate of Leadership Music, Anthony has his own publishing companies: Notes to Music (ASCAP) copublished with Maverick Music, and Words to Music (BMI) copublished with Notewrite Music.

7

A Basic Understanding of Working as a Musician in Nashville

A musician's life in Nashville is much different from that of a song-writer or an aspiring artist. There are no doors to knock on, no materials to prepare, and no one to help represent you. It's just you and your instrument.

NASHVILLE'S MUSICIANS

For the aspiring musician, all there is to do is network, hang out, network, hang out. There are lots and lots of live music venues of every size in Nashville, but they don't hire musicians. The people who play in the clubs put together their own bands. These are the people you need to network with.

To start out, you will have to volunteer your services. Offer to do demo sessions for free, offer to sit in if someone doesn't show up, offer to do just about anything to get the opportunity to be heard. Most of the people performing in clubs are songwriters trying out their songs on an audience. Usually songwriters are not the greatest instrumentalists. Offer to back them up, help them out.

Many musicians put bands together and spend a lot of time rehearsing in someone's garage. That's OK, too, if the band starts playing live sometime soon. But you don't want to spend too much time in that garage! You want to be in the clubs playing as much as you can, even if it's not your band and even if it's not a cool gig. Just get up on stage and play as soon and as much as you possibly can.

There are two very important things you need to know about being a musician in Nashville:

1. Nashville is on a 10-2-6 schedule.
2. All musicians are expected to be experts at the Nashville Number System.

10-2-6

All recording sessions in every recording studio are booked from 10:00 A.M. to 2:00 P.M.; from 2:00 to 6:00 P.M.; and from 6:00 to 10:00 P.M.; no exceptions. That's just the way it's done. Not only do the recording studios operate that way, but everybody else including songwriters and publishers are loosely on that schedule as well. That doesn't mean that you can't get an appointment on Music Row at 9:00 or 11:00 A.M., but if you have a 10:00 A.M. writing appointment, don't be surprised if your cowriter has to leave for a 2:00 P.M. appointment with another writer. It's best to think in terms of 10-2-6, because there is a lot of activity going on in town that is on that time schedule, and everybody else works around it.

THE NASHVILLE NUMBER SYSTEM

The Nashville Number System is a method of transcribing music to paper so that a song can be understood on the basis of chord relationships rather than notations in a fixed key. Nashville musicians do not think or write A-B-C-D-E-F-G. They think and write 1-2-3-4-5-6-7. This method works really well when someone wants to change key. The chart doesn't have to be rewritten, because it's still 1-2-3-4-5-6-7 no matter what key you are in. If you want to succeed as a musician in Nashville, you *must* learn the Nashville Number System. The best way to learn is to buy Chas Williams's book, *The Nashville Number System*. (You can order it through the Internet at *http://nashville.net/~troppo/nns.htm*.)

Here are some excerpts from Chas's book:

> Nashville charts substitute numbers for the chord letter symbols found in traditional music notation. Rhythmic and dynamic notations, as well as chord voicing symbols from formal music are used with the chord numbers. Since the Middle Ages, musicians have substituted Roman numerals for chord letters. However, around 1957, Neal Matthews, a member of the Jordanaires, originated the idea of substituting numbers for notes. Neal was familiar with the system of shape notes used by gospel quartets in the '30s and '40s, which used a different shape for

each note of the major scale. He began writing vocal charts substituting numbers for the shape notes and developed his own system of writing music with numbers.

In the early '60s, Harold Bradley (the music industry's most recorded musician), Charlie McCoy, Wayne Moss and David Briggs noticed the unique approach that Neal and the Jordanaires used to map out a song on paper. Each of them began to devise his own number system, and the idea quickly spread among other session players in Nashville.

Musicians use the number system to chart out an entire song on paper while hearing a demo of the tune for the first time. This innovative system has become the standard method of music notation in Nashville and will remain so as long as records are produced in this town. One of the benefits of a number chart is that it can be played in any key, without transposing or rewriting the chart into a different key. The numbers represent the same relationship for a song's chord changes, regardless of the key.

Oddly enough, there is no one definitive version of the Nashville Number System. Many musicians use different symbols and notations to express the same musical idea. Everyone seems to have a system of notation that works best for him. Of course, a lot depends on whether you are writing a chart for your own purposes or for a band that has never heard your material or read your charts before. There are a wide variety of notational symbols acceptable in Nashville, so use the ones that work best for you.

The number system is the common language for communicating music in Nashville. If you are a songwriter it is a valuable tool to help you express your ideas so other musicians can understand and translate them effectively. If you are paying for a demo of your song, a well-prepared chart of the tune will save time and communicate your musical ideas precisely.

If you are a musician looking for work in Nashville, you will be presented with the task of reading or composing a number chart almost immediately. You'll be glad you had the opportunity to prepare ahead of time. The Nashville Number System is a musical shorthand that is simple, logical, and magical. If you learn it now, you'll be one step ahead of the game.

How the System Works

Numbers assigned to each note of the major scale represent chords as well as single notes. In the key of A, we have the major scale, A, B, C#, D, E, F# and G#. These become chords 1 through 7 in the key of A. It may seem too simple, but this is the method of assigning numbers to chords, which is the basis of the Nashville Number System. In the key of B, B becomes 1, etc. In the key of C, C is 1, etc. And so on for other keys.

A Sneak Peek at Harold Bradley's Notebook

Here are some basic rules, taken from the lecture notes of legendary session guitarist Harold Bradley.

1. All chords are major chords unless otherwise indicated, such as:

   Minor (-); Major 7th (Δ); Diminished (0); Augmented (+)

2. Use common time signatures. A number will hold for all beats within a section unless otherwise indicated. In 4/4 time, with each set of parentheses representing one measure:

$$ (1\ \ ),(1\ 4\ \ ),(1\ \ 4) $$

   Add notations if you wish to indicate which beat corresponds to the chord change:

$$ (14\ \ )(1\ \ 4) $$

3. If desired, you can use numbers for each beat or note:

$$ (1444),(1114) $$

4. Bass notes can be indicated under the chords as follows:

$$ 1\ \frac{54}{76}\ 5 $$

5. Some prefer to write the number groupings down the page, others across the page:

   1144
   5511 or 1144 5511 1144 1515
   1144
   1515

There are many other symbols that can help you notate important areas of interpretation on your charts. A little study will add special notation for pickup notes, modulation, walkups and walkdowns, dynamics, feel and style, etc. Whether you are a songwriter or serious musician, a quick review of the Nashville Number System is well worth your time.

A Typical Nashville Session
Although there are no hard-and-fast rules, basic rhythm tracks are normally put down first, then, at different times, the vocals are done and various instruments are overdubbed. The basic rhythm tracks consist of drums (the most important to lay the foundation), rhythm guitar, lead guitar, bass, and usually keyboards. One of the musicians is named leader, which means many times he is responsible for hiring the other musicians, either choosing the musicians himself or helping the producer choose the musicians. He also helps with musical interpretations and files the paperwork for the rest of the musicians. He is paid double scale for his duties.

The producer starts by playing a demo of the song to be record-ed, and the musicians write their number charts from the demo. Once in a while the songwriter is asked to come in and perform his song live, instead of using a demo tape. This allows for more interpretation on the part of the musicians. Often a master session will turn out exactly like the demo, especially if the demo was done by Nashville's top session players.

Once the number charts are finished, the musicians will run through the song a few times, each working out his own contribution to the song. It is not unusual for Nashville's experienced session musi-cians to get a great basic rhythm track on just a few takes.

It is not difficult to get to know Nashville's top session players. They are often found sitting in at one of the showcases around town. Study the label credits on country albums; you'll see the same names on many different record labels. Then check the *Tennessean* and *Nashville Scene* for the clubs around town. There's a good chance some of the ses-sion players will be performing live, especially if there is a showcase for a major label artist or songwriter. Part of being successful in Nashville is getting to know the people who are already at the top.

Don't feel as though you have to get into the top recording stu-dios to see what's going on in Nashville. Much of the activity is taking place in all of the various studios around town. Everyone is working on a project of some sort—a song, an artist project, a new studio. Get involved! You'll be surprised at how receptive others are to your fresh ideas.

Excerpted from *The Nashville Number System,* © 1988, 1997 by Chas Williams. Available from the Nashville Number System, 1424 Robert E. Lee Lane, Dept. B, Brentwood, TN 37027 ($12.95 + $2.50 postage and handling—or check your local music store).

FOR MUSICIANS ONLY

There are two very important publications released in June each year in Nashville, which focus primarily on musicians. June is Musician's Month in Nashville in honor of the city's ultimate guitar picker, Chet Atkins. Chet traveled to France one summer and discovered the most wonderful tribute to musicians. For one full month, the streets of France are filled with musi-cians of every craft and style, playing and entertaining the passersby. Restaurants and merchants join in the festival by making their wares avail-able on the streets as well. Chet was deeply moved by the experience and felt that since Nashville housed the best and greatest musicians, the ultimate tribute to musicians should take place in Music City. He met with various organizations over several years, hoping to make his dream a reality.

Then, an enterprising businessman by the name of Tom Morales of TomKats catering and special events, who was not afraid of a massive undertaking, took the challenge. He established the Chet Atkins' Musician

Days, and for one week in June filled the city with outdoor stages free to the public and offered a guitar clinic and a star-studded concert to benefit music education. The festival was produced two years' running in June, then was moved to the fall for better student attendance and cooler weather. But Chet Atkins' Musician Days had already made its mark on the month of June. There are two important publications during the month of June that highlight musicians. They are:

The Nashville Scene "Musicians' Directory"

This is an insert into the publication's weekly newspaper the first week in June. It offers a listing of all the different bands that play around town, and a brief description of each. The listing is free; you just have to send in your name and details about your band. There is a nominal charge to run a picture or logo. The editors will make an announcement in the newspaper when they are compiling information for next June's issue, and you can just send in your bio and picture. To give you a clear idea of what the directory contains, here's how they describe themselves:

> Another night on the town, another frantic scan through the weekly listings. Who are all these bands, anyway? Whadda they look like? Would any of 'em be willing to play a wedding in July for 100 bucks?
>
> Or maybe you're a band in search of a drummer. Hell, maybe you're a drummer in search of a band. Either way, whatever your question, the answer's here in the *Nashville Scene*'s "Musicians' Directory"— your guide to the city's wealth of musical talent.
>
> See, the idea is, you can't possibly keep up with all the music and musicians in town—not without help. So pull this section out and hold onto it. 'Cause you never know. Someday, you just might *need* a four-piece metal polka band.

Music Row Publications—Annual Music Row Awards Edition

Published the last week in May to be on the newsstands in June, this edition of *Music Row* honors the editors' and critics' picks of the best of the best. Their awards for Song of the Year, Producer of the Year, Marketing Achievement, Best Video, and Breakthrough Songwriter are picked solely at their own discretion, and not based on any formula, like chart position or number of records sold. In their own words, ". . . honorees were chosen by a consensus of Music Row critics and editors. And there were no injuries at the critics' powwow."

However, the musician awards, which are the majority of awards given, follow a very strict formula. They take the top fifty albums that appeared in the top ten of the *Billboard* Top Country Albums chart for a one-year period, and then they analyze the label copy of each album. Then they simply make a list of the musicians who played on these albums; categories are keyboards, engineer, bass guitar, guitar, drums, fiddle, steel guitar, and background vocals. These musicians are known as the "A" players and there are only one hundred of them—one hundred musicians and background vocalists combined play on the top albums coming out of Nashville.

All of these guys—and they are all guys except eight gals listed in the background vocal category—know each other really well, work together very well, and are used mainly because of the remarkable way they seem to read each others' minds. If you have hopes of one day becoming a studio musician in Nashville, then you will have to find a way to get to know these people. Some of them play out in the clubs at night. You might get lucky and find their name listed in the club listing in the *Tennessean* or *Nashville Scene*.

Industry Interview with Dave Dunseath, Drummer for Dan Seals, T. Graham Brown, Billy Dean, and Lee Ann Womack

"I've been interested in drumming ever since I can remember—got my first drum kit when I was eight years old. It was the 'Ringo' kit; a Black Diamond Pearl just like Ringo's—boy, what a beautiful set! I wish I still had it! I didn't really start playing in earnest until I graduated from college. I loved music, but I didn't want to teach music for a living so I majored in marketing and advertising at the University of Arkansas. Once I had my degree I decided just to go ahead and jump out and learn about the music business by playing. I played Top Forty and rock for about three years, going from St. Louis to Atlanta and surrounding areas. Then I picked up and moved to Nashville on one phone call.

"My former minister had moved to Nashville and was managing his sons. He told me they were getting out of gospel music and moving into secular music, and asked me if I could live on $1,000 per week! 'Gotta have you in three days,' he said. I was working with a band in Florida at the time, and I left the band in a lurch to hurry to Nashville for what I thought would be the opportunity of a lifetime!

"We wound up working at a Holiday Inn in Minnesota, playing for a lot less than a grand a week. It was all a sham. Nashville is full of dreams; if it weren't, none of this would be going on anyway! I wound up staying in Nashville, and decided to make my home here—just get down in the dirt and get to work.

"Musicians have a series of jobs; there's no such thing as a career—no retirement plan! I started doing small demo work. Everyone has a demo studio in his basement in Nashville. I did as much networking as I could,

hanging out, sitting in occasionally for friends. Then I started being recommended for jobs.

"I heard about this great group of players who were looking for a
drummer for the Starlight Lounge on Dickerson Road. I thought,
'Audition in a dive? Oh no!' But the players were Bob Regan (hit songwriter and session player) and two members of Reba's band. Here in this
little dive bar were these great players! Actually, everyone should at least
stop in once at the Starlight—it's a Nashville landmark.

"I got the gig but little did I know that these guys were going to leave
the band. They all left, and there I was, on Dickerson Road. That led to
another gig that turned out to be a great job working at Dad's Place (a popular dance club for the over-forty jet set) at the Ramada Inn. I played there
six nights a week for two years—tequila and beer helped me through it.
The customers became like family, sending drinks to the band and showing lots of enthusiasm for our music—they were great.

"You can count on one hand the number of house bands there are in
Nashville. There are pluses and minuses to paid work—it was the consistent paying job I was so hungry for, but it was also very hard work. Within
three months of getting this job I also started doing carded (Union) sessions. Other players recommended me. Even though I was working late
nights, I never turned down a daytime session—I played for anyone who
needed any help. You never know who's going to be on that session. You
should want to take everything that comes along—hence the phrase 'paying your dues.'

"If you want to succeed in the arts at all, what are you willing to put
up with? Rejection, low pay, bad treatment, not being paid at all—these are
all part of the picture. If you can stay the course, you'll make it.
Perseverance is the key!

"Dan Seals was putting a band together, and a friend that I met in one
of these sessions recommended me for the drumming slot. The audition
was the performance. I didn't even meet Dan until thirty minutes before
we went on stage. I got that gig and subbed-out the Ramada Inn job when
we went on the road. So I was working two jobs for two years. I learned
an amazing thing about people's point of view outside of the music business. I made twice the money with Dan Seals and the gig was closer to my
career goals, but when I went to buy a house they were more impressed
with the Ramada Inn job.

"The best comments I've heard about drummers were from non-
drummers. Duke Ellington said, 'Drummers are in the driver's seat . . . we
are just along for the ride.' Being a musician is all about people skills. Being
a good player, that's just expected. How do you get along with folks? . . .
that's the question. The artist, the way we travel together, the personality of

the band—it all kind of plays in. Most players are just as nice as they can be; don't have a chip on their shoulder, don't have an attitude—the ones that tend to are not successful.

"I like to compare music to acting. Great actors don't necessarily succeed. John Wayne and Clint Eastwood are not the greatest actors in the world, but we love them! There are tremendous vocalists out there that only receive demo work—they don't make it to the top.

"Dan Seals started doing an acoustic unplugged set, went down to a trio, and didn't need a drummer. About the same time T. Graham Brown was looking for a drummer. He's one of the truly great singers in the industry. Every time a slot comes open in Nashville, everyone in the band has at least one friend to recommend. A friend of mine called to tell me about the gig and said it was mine if I wanted it. When I got there, there were at least ten other drummers auditioning for the gig. Actually, I prefer that, because the artist has a better disposition when he can compare you to others. They gave me a tape of T. Graham songs and had me work up two or three. The audition is just as important as a jam. I was hired, but, truthfully, I think it comes down to personal taste. A handful of drummers could do any one of these jobs. There is just a little something the artist is looking for. I've been to auditions with some great drummers, but they didn't always get the job.

"I left the Ramada Inn and went on tour with T. Graham for a year—then I got a call from a company that was putting together auditions for a band for Billy Dean. I said 'no' at the time, and they auditioned fifteen guys but didn't hire one. Then I got another call. They said Billy would be opening for Reba on her tour. I knew this was a golden opportunity, but I just didn't want to leave T. Graham. I went to the audition, and as I pulled up, the drummer for Jefferson Starship was just getting out of a cab. We both auditioned and I got the gig . . . it just goes to show you—he is a tremendous drummer!

"T. Graham is a drummer's dream job—funk, R&B—a blue-eyed soul boy and a great guy. I didn't know what to do. I called Lyle Lovett's drummer, a great friend, and told him I felt like I was losing all innocence—all the love of drumming I was trading in for money. He said that I knew in my heart I would have to make this career move, and he was right. I was three years with Billy, until he went unplugged.

"There is no such thing as a career as a sideman. It's just a job after another job after another job. There are no parting gifts; no going away party. It's just pretty much good-bye, don't come back. Billy's road manager said, 'Boys, you've all seen the schedule.' It's just 10-2-6, every day.

"I hope I've helped some musicians figure out Nashville a little bit. The other thing I'll say is, learn the Nashville Number System. Remember my very first gig? The $1,000-a-week job? The first thing that happened when I sat down to play was that someone explained it to me. I was lucky. We also had a steel player who had just moved to town. He kept making mistakes. We would stop, try to help him work things out, and then he'd make more mistakes. Finally someone asked him if he had a chart. 'Someone gave me this weird math problem,' he said, 'but I haven't solved it yet!' It's expected that you know it, and it's so simple to know and use, you are crazy not to.

"I tell everyone I meet there is always room for other players here. More songwriters too. There's no reason not to give it a try. The key to success is hanging out, subbing, networking period. That's how the bulk of the work comes down. As a musician, you really can't make up a demo, then go knock on studio doors or label doors. You've just got to get out there! It's like pulling teeth to go out to the clubs sometimes. But I've never driven home thinking it was a waste of my time.

"Now I am able to stay home and write, then go out on the road for a while. I treat writing seriously, like a business. Some writers just write when they are inspired; others write every day. I just started getting interested in writing—it's a new challenge and a new goal."

8

A Basic Understanding of Nashville's Songwriters Organizations

There are three songwriters associations in Nashville, and the best advice for someone who is just getting acquainted with Nashville is to join all three. You never know where the next step to a successful writing career might lead. They are all very different and vary greatly in the benefits you will receive from each one. Here is a very brief analysis of why you should join as soon as possible. A more comprehensive list of services follows.

NASHVILLE'S THREE SONGWRITERS ASSOCIATIONS

NSAI is the largest and most respected organization, with national and international recognition. They have over a hundred chapters across the United States, so the chances are there is one close to you. If you belong to one of these regional chapters, then you can perform at a writers' night at the Bluebird Cafe (you don't have to be a member to perform at open mic). And, you can also get your songs critiqued by an NSAI panel of experts. The NSAI board of directors consists of Nashville's hottest hit songwriters. SGA is a national organization that focuses very intently on protecting songwriters' rights and assists in negotiations with publishers. TSAI is a grassroots organization, with a small group of passionate members.

Each of these organizations have a myriad of services designed to assist you in your songwriting efforts at various stages of development. In planning your trip to Nashville, it would be ideal to plan it around one of the programs they offer. I would highly recommend the NSAI Spring Symposium and Tin Pan South as don't-miss events. Attending one of these events and the other events offered every week will give you maximum exposure to the songwriting community. Although you are guaranteed to learn a lot about songwriting and the Nashville music industry, the most valuable benefit will be meeting publishers, A&R reps, Nashville's hit songwriters, and potential cowriting partners.

NASHVILLE SONGWRITERS ASSOCIATION INTERNATIONAL (NSAI)

1701 West End Avenue, Third Floor
Nashville, TN 37203
Tel. (615) 256-3354, (800) 321-6008
Fax (615) 256-0034
Web site: *www.nashvillesongwriters.com*

Weekly Workshops:
The following formats alternate every Thursday night:
• Critique: Your songs evaluated by the best in the business.
• Publisher Night: A chance to attract a publisher to your songs.
• Pro Teaching: The pros share how they did it.

Yearly Events:
• Spring Symposium: A two-day intensive program on songcrafting, including the opportunity to have songs critiqued and an excellent opportunity to meet key executives in Nashville.
• Tin Pan South: The nation's largest festival spotlighting the songwriters and the song, the festival is a week-long event featuring all genres of music in all of Nashville's popular music venues. Also includes a golf tournament and Legendary Songwriters Concert.
• Song Camp: An intense, three-day retreat with six pro writers; large and small group sessions, with individual song evaluations by one pro writer.

Other Services:
• Office Facilities & Writers' Rooms: Telephones, typewriters, fax machine, computers, photocopier, single-tape dubbing decks, reference library, industry publications, bulletin board, copyright forms, phone message service—wow! Your Nashville office!
• 800 Number: Members are given a toll-free number to call with questions regarding Nashville and your upcoming trip.
• Newsletter: *NSAI Newswire* is a bimonthly newsletter on NSAI happenings.

- Song Evaluation Service: Members can mail one song at a time to NSAI for evaluation.
- Online Workshops: Can't be there? Jump online!
- Counseling: The NSAI staff is available to answer questions.
- Books and Merchandise: Discount rates for members.
- Insurance Plans: Major medical, disability, accident and life.
- Pro-Writer Category: NSAI offers special services for member songwriters who have had their songs recorded by major recording artists, such as regular informal meetings with label heads.
- Regional Workshops: NSAI may have a workshop near you, or will help you set up a workshop in your own hometown.
- Active Legislation Involvement: Fights for songwriter rights on a national level through a legislative committee and various songwriting coalitions.

INDUSTRY INTERVIEW WITH BARTON HERBISON, EXECUTIVE DIRECTOR, NSAI

Photo by Larry DiRosa

"If you are going to make it as a songwriter in Nashville, there are certain things you have to do. I do know the formula—it is:

"Number One: Talent. If your songs aren't great, forget it. Even the most gifted writers need to hone the craft, but you've got to have the gift to begin with. A lot of people just don't.

"Number Two: Hard work and persistence. Just as if you were starting as a professional athlete. You've got to give it all the physical energy you've got.

"Number Three: Luck. I believe you have to have luck to a large degree. The more opportunities you make for yourself, the more luck will come your way.

"Number Four: Desire. Songwriting is not an incident, it's a pursuit.

"You may have the best song ever written, but you've got to work at the business of the industry to get that song into the right hands.

"Hit songwriters all have one thing in common: It's something they do every day of their life. A lot of people come up here and get someone to listen to their songs, then they think they are done. But it's just the beginning. The most common thing I hear from the great writers is, 'I had to do it. I didn't have any choice.' Great songwriters never question why they do it.

"NSAI is a reality check. We want to foster the dreams and shatter the myths. It breaks my heart when I hear that a writer/artist had given someone $30,000 to produce a record or spent $5,000 to get their songs demo'd. Come see us before you spend that kind of money.

"What do you get from (membership in) NSAI? . . . nothing, except opportunity and resources. We don't make it happen for you. We give you the information you need. We try to shoot straight. If you are a songwriter, it's good to hang out at NSAI. We have three writers' rooms, and there is a great energy among the staff. There is magic in the building.

"And you've got to hang out at those writers' nights around town. Why?

"One, to build relationships. You'll meet someone influential who likes your songs and will make calls on your behalf. Two, to get feedback on your songs. And three, to perform, for those that can; your performing helps you with your songs.

"Songwriting is a calling, not an incident."

For the past decade BARTON HERBISON served as Chief Administrative Officer for U.S. Congressman Bob Clement of Nashville. In that capacity he joined NSAI in fighting battles to protect writers' intellectual property rights. Prior to that he worked as a reporter and spent fourteen years in country radio. Bart grew up in the rural west Tennessee town of Paris.

SONGWRITERS GUILD OF AMERICA ("THE GUILD" OR SGA)

1222 16th Avenue South, Suite 25
Nashville, TN 37212
Tel. (615) 329-1782
Fax (615) 329-2623
E-mail: *SGANash@aol.com*
Web site: *www.songwriters.org*
Los Angeles: (323) 462-1108; e-mail *LASGA@aol.com*
New York: (212) 768-7902; e-mail *SongNews@aol.com*
New Jersey: (201) 867-7603; e-mail *KLStrnad@aol.com*

Weekly Meetings:

- Ask-A-Pro: An informal monthly meeting with top industry professionals; i.e. producers, A&R execs, publishers, managers, lawyers, etc.—anyone and everyone you need to meet.
- SongCritique: An industry professional listens to your demo and gives you honest input.

- Hit Song Analysis: A hit songwriter reveals the behind-the-scenes story on his latest chart single.
- Songmania: Writers' night at one of Nashville's popular venues.

Other Services:

- Songwriting Workshops: Periodic workshops with top songwriters, publishers, and other industry professionals. Usually last two or three full days, and include panel discussions on important topics, writers-in-the-round, keynote speaker, and lots of networking time. Try to plan your trip to Nashville around one of these workshops.
- The Guild Contract: The Guild has the best songwriters' contract in the business. It contains important items that a "standard" songwriters' agreement might not have, the most important being a reversion clause and the written right to audit a publisher's books. Guild members *are not required* to use a Guild contract, one of the biggest misconceptions about membership in the Guild.
- Contract Review: The Guild will review a publisher's contract and give you the information you need to bargain for a better deal.
- Royalty Collection: The Guild has a royalty collection plan which insures that you collect royalties from all sources. They also keep a copy of your contract on file in case of an emergency. Guild members *are not required* to use this plan, another misconception about Guild membership.
- Publisher Audits: The Guild has an ongoing program of audits of music publishers.
- Catalog Administration Plan (CAP): For writers who control 25 percent or more of the publishing rights to their recorded and published works, the Guild offers the CAP at very low rates as compared to other catalog administrators.
- Copyright Renewal and Termination: All Guild members are given a one-year advance notice when their songs are due to be renewed or reclaimed from publishers.
- Catalog Evaluation: Financial evaluation of a catalog for tax or estate planning, catalog sale, or negotiation for renewal or termination rights.
- Group Medical and Life Insurance.
- Newsletters: Local and national periodic publications.
- Legal/Legislative Work: Constantly seeks to strengthen your rights and increase your royalties through appropriate action directed at publishers, industry groups, the courts, or Congress.

Photo by Allan L. Mayor

INDUSTRY INTERVIEW WITH RUNDI REAM, REGIONAL DIRECTOR, SONGWRITERS GUILD OF AMERICA

"The Guild was founded in 1931 by three hit songwriters that wanted to help others. They called themselves the Songwriters Protective Association. Our mission is to provide songwriters with the services and activities they need to succeed in the business of music, and that includes the creative, administrative, and financial aspects of the industry.

"We are the only songwriters' asssociation that is allowed to go before Congress. The Guild is the organization that sets royalty rates along with the Recording Industry Association of America (RIAA) and the National Music Publishers Association (NMPA). These three organizations went before Congress and changed the rates, which have gradually been increasing over a ten-year period.

"There are big differences between our organization and the others—we are the most business-oriented. Actually most of our programs are so different, we wind up referring writers to each other. We are not overly competitive, and complement each other.

"The one thing we like to do is keep our programs small and intimate. That gives everyone a chance to get meet one-on-one with workshop speakers. When they're just starting out, songwriters should go everywhere and do everything that they can to learn about the business and meet as many people as possible. It's a good idea to belong to both organizations.

"Working for an organization that has a great songwriters' contract, it's hard to see writers settle for something less. I really want to protect writers from signing a bad contract. Most writers want a contract so bad they don't care what it says. Even writers who should know better will sign a bad contract. It's hard to stand by and watch that happen.

"I hope that writers will use the Guild to help negotiate their contract. Don't negotiate until the Guild has looked it over. We'll tell them how their contract varies from a Guild contract, and what is necessary in a contract to protect the rights of a writer. We have ten basic points that a contract should include, and at a minimum, every writer should know what these ten basic points are. Don't be so quick to jump into a contract.

"A few of those points are:

"1. Work for Hire: Make sure nothing in the contract says 'work for hire' or 'employment for hire.'
"2. A Reversion Clause: The contract should include a provision that, if the publisher does not secure a release of a commercial sound recording within a specified time, the contract can be terminated by you. Be flexible about the number of years, maybe, but don't sign a contract that doesn't have a reversion clause.
"3. Being Paid on Gross Revenues Instead of Net: Some publishers deduct the entire Harry Fox Agency fee from the writer; the Guild contract allows only half of that fee to be deducted. (See chapter 2 for more on the Harry Fox Agency).
"4. Audit Capability: Your contract really should include a provision for you to be able to audit a publisher's books. Most contracts don't contain that provision.

"I don't think there is one set way to make it in this town. It's different for each person. It's not going to come from any one source. Do what you do. Do what feels right. Don't try and force something that's not you.

"We have a lot of fun at the Guild. I'm constantly amazed by the willingness of music publishers to help writers. I call and ask them, 'Can you do a critique workshop?'—they say, 'When?,' again, and again, and again. They see it as what they do. It's funny, because you can't get in their door, but they'll make themselves available through us. That's one of the reasons we keep our things so small. Tim DuBois (head of Arista Records) was here and met with thirty writers. He could look everyone in the eye, and everyone got to meet him and talk to him.

"We had a Horror Song Night on Halloween. Hit songwriters Rick Carnes, Casey Kelly, Kendal Franceschi wore masks and told horror stories of the industry. I think all the different jobs I did before I came to the Guild have helped me in my job. Planning student activities, special events, working in artist management, doing publicity—all the things I did before are now rolled into one. I love my job!"

RUNDI REAM is currently the southern regional director for the Songwriters Guild of America. She has increased visibility of the organization through constant publicity and special events efforts, such as the hilarious Songmania shows, the annual SGA Building A Songwriting Career Seminar, Ask-A-Pro sessions and numerous benefit shows for the Nashville Humane Association, tornado relief, etc. In addition, she maintains the Web site for the entire association.

While attending Watertown (Wisconsin) Senior High School, Rundi Ream formed the Bar-ettes, a girls' barbershop quartet. Although she never realized her dreams of promoting the quartet to the top of the record charts and having a Bar-ettes float in the Watertown Fourth of July parade, she did put together one heck of a senior recital. And so a music publicity and marketing career was born.

Prior to taking the helm of the Nashville division of SGA, Rundi was the radio/media liaison for Rick Alter Management, where she worked with Blackhawk and Nicolette Larson. She spent eight years as a publicist, promoting such events as the Music City News Awards, WSIX Parade of Pennies concert, and the Stars Come Out For Christmas benefit for the Children's Miracle Network. Before moving to Nashville, Rundi worked as the assistant director for campus entertainment at the University of Wisconsin and was a booking agent at entertainment firms in Wichita, Kansas and Cincinnati, Ohio.

A 1985 graduate of the University of Wisconsin/Oshkosh, Rundi earned a journalism degree with an emphasis on public relations/advertising.

TENNESSEE SONGWRITERS ASSOCIATION INTERNATIONAL (TSAI)

P.O. Box 2664
Hendersonville, TN 37077-2664
Tel. (615) 969-5967
Fax (615) 822-2048
E-mail: *ASKTSAI@aol.com*
Web site: *www.clubnashville.com/tsai.htm*

The Tennessee Songwriters Association International is a "hands-on" organization. Its members are encouraged to actively participate in the growth and development of the association. TSAI welcomes your ideas and energy and encourages your participation.

Weekly Meetings:

The following formats alternate every Wednesday night:

- TSAI Workshop: Deals with all phases of the music industry that will help you better understand the business and those who operate it.
- Critique Night: A chance to have your song critiqued by your peers and get the feedback to make it a better song.
- Pitch-A-Pro Night: An opportunity to pitch your songs directly to someone looking for hit songs, including producers, A&R reps, publishers, and artists.

- Pro-Rap Night: A chance to ask questions of a top-notch guest speaker from the music industry.
- Legends Night. A chance to meet stars of the Grand Ole Opry and listen to them share their stories.

Other Services:

Monthly Newsletter: packed with information, tip sheet on who's looking for songs, interviews, ideas, songwriting updates, and other useful articles.

INDUSTRY INTERVIEW WITH JIM SYLVIS, EXECUTIVE DIRECTOR, TENNESSEE SONGWRITERS ASSOCIATION INTERNATIONAL

"The biggest problem I see all the time is that people come into town and have no concept of what is going on here. They are still writing songs in the genre of Faron Young or Ray Price or the like. They have the wrong concept of what country music is today. Aspiring songwriters need to come into town a couple of times and find out what's going on—just hang out and get a feel for the place.

"They need to listen to the radio stations that are playing current country music, not the golden oldies or classic country. And it would be a really good idea to join a songwriters' organization in your own home town, get your feet wet in networking with other songwriters, something that is essential in Nashville.

"Also it's important to get some feedback on your demos before you start pitching them around. Usually when new writers come into town, their demos are not anywhere near Nashville standards. So I would advise writers to spend enough time in Nashville to get to hear some Nashville demos and compare their own demos to those. Chances are, they will have to redemo their songs in Nashville in order to get the right sound.

"I've been in the business a long time, running our songwriters' organization for seventeen years, and I've seen the same thing over and over. People come here completely unprepared. So my advice for everyone is to learn as much as you possibly can before you come here; and make at least a couple of trips to Nashville just to learn how things are done before you start pitching your songs. Certainly you would want to make a couple of separate trips here before you pack your bags and move. Nashville might not be at all what you are expecting."

9

A Basic Understanding of Nashville's Performing Rights Organizations (PROs)

Many songwriters do not realize that each of the performing rights organizations, ASCAP, BMI, and SESAC, can help them get started, even though it isn't necessary to affiliate with one of them until you actually have a song recorded. They are in the song business and are constantly on the lookout for great songwriters. If, in their opinion, your songs can become hits, they will be quick to help you find a publisher you can work with. If all three organizations tell you your songs need work, it might be wise to reconsider your songwriting goals. Although anyone's opinion is just that, an opinion, the performing rights organizations have a very good idea of what has commercial appeal, and their opinion carries a lot of weight. They tend to be very conservative and don't discourage writers unless they are sure there is little possibility of future success.

ABOUT NASHVILLE'S PROS

The main function of PROs is to collect performance money on your behalf, and they have several different departments to guide that process. Each PRO has a writers' representative department that spends its time looking for new songwriters, helping them find a publisher or record deal, helping place songs with artists, and generally servicing accounts. Your decision of which organization to choose usually depends on the personal relationships you have made in the company. Getting to know the people at each of the PROs is an important step in the song process.

Try to get your songs reviewed by each of the PROs before you come to Nashville. That may be very difficult to do, as these organizations receive as many tapes in the mail as publishers. At a minimum, try to get an appointment with a writers' representative as close to your arrival time as possible. These three organizations will be your most helpful contacts during your trip.

The three organizations have the same purpose, but are very different in the way they operate. Their purpose is to collect money from radio broadcasters, live concert auditoriums and clubs, restaurants, television, cable, and the Internet, and distribute the money they collect to their affiliates (writers and publishers). These collections are based on a percentage of advertising income and broadcast capacity of radio and TV stations, and the size of live concert venues. They differ greatly in the way they monitor the songs being played or performed, and also in the way they distribute the money.

ASCAP collects the most money, as they are the oldest organization and represent many standard songs. BMI is a close second in collections. SESAC collects considerably less money than the other two, but has proportionately fewer affiliates to whom they distribute the money. Check out all three, then concentrate on developing a close relationship with the one organization you feel most comfortable with. Don't rush to sign with a PRO. Since their main function is to collect for the performance of a song, there really is no need to sign up until your song has been recorded.

Although the letters in ASCAP, BMI, and SESAC stand for something (of course), they always go by letters only. So there is no need to remember what they stand for. It's included here just so you'll know.

ASCAP
(American Society of Composers, Authors and Publishers)

Headquarters:
One Lincoln Plaza
New York, NY 10023
Tel. (212) 621-6000
Fax (212) 724-9064

Los Angeles:
7920 West Sunset Boulevard, Suite 300
Los Angeles, CA 90046
Tel. (323) 883-1000
Fax (323) 883-1049

Nashville:
2 Music Square West
Nashville, TN 37203
Tel. (615) 742-5000
Fax (615) 742-5020

Atlanta:
541-400 10th Street NW
Atlanta, GA 30318
Tel. (404) 635-1758
Fax (404) 627-2404

Chicago:
1608 West Belmont Avenue, Suite 200
Chicago, IL 60657
Tel. (773) 472-1157
Fax (773) 472-1158

Miami:
844 Alton Road, Suite One
Miami Beach, FL 33139
Tel. (305) 673-3446
Fax (305) 673-2446

London:
8 Cork Street
London, UK W1X 1PB
Tel. (011-44-171) 439-0909
Fax (011-44-171) 434-0073

Puerto Rico:
(800) 244-3087

Web site: *www.ascap.com*

How They Determine Who Gets Paid

ASCAP uses two methods, census survey (a complete count) and sample survey. Two hundred thousand hours of radio are sampled in a one-year period by the actual taping of radio shows and the use of data from program logs and the number of spins reported by BDS. The use of music on the Internet is monitored by EZ-Eagle, an Internet antipiracy and music licensing application.

How They Pay

Every performance generates a certain number of credits. Each credit is worth a certain dollar value ($4.64 in 1998). Performance credits depend on several factors, including medium, type, station weight, time of day, and allocation applied to broadcast feature performances. In addition, ASCAP members can apply for special awards. Application forms are sent to every ASCAP member.

Special Writer Services

- Straight Talk—once a week at 10:00 A.M.: overview of ASCAP; how to approach Music Row and market your songs
- Monthly writers' night at the Bluebird
- 8-track/ADAT recording studio—available to members
- Pop Workshop—four-week workshop in fall
- Country Workshop—six-week workshop in spring
- Workshops taught by top writers like Gretchen Peters, Kix Brooks, Steve Seskin
- Open to all writers
- Health plan
- Credit union
- Toll-free phone number
- Legislative representation
- Member discounts

Photo by Alan L. Mayor

INDUSTRY INTERVIEW WITH JOHN BRIGGS, ASSISTANT VICE PRESIDENT, ASCAP

"What I like about ASCAP the most is that we are the only performing rights organization in the United States created and controlled by songwriters and publishers—there are twelve songwriters and twelve publishers on the board of directors, who are elected from the membership and serve for two years. ASCAP is very transparent. Everything is open. In fact, we have a membership meeting once a year in Nashville, New York, and Los Angeles, and all board of directors and decision makers for the organization are in the room. No one can leave. They have to answer songwriter's questions. When you think about it, I've got 85,000 bosses (members of ASCAP).

"Also we have a writer/publisher advisory committee. It's a good exchange of information between writers and publishers and the board of directors. Hit songwriter Wayland Holyfield chairs the advisory committee and has a good understanding of the system. Wayland was elected to the board, and when he was there he made big changes in our payment structure which will take place this year. Members really make a big difference in our organization.

"Our CEO, John LoFrumento, was with American Express before he came to ASCAP, and he's gotten our overhead down to 16 percent. Our payment system has to be approved by the Department of Justice and sometimes by the U.S. Federal Court. Once it is set, it can't be changed; so we can't make arbitrary payments, short-term special deals, or management favoritism. Money that comes from country radio is paid out to country writers. We can't manipulate figures—what we survey is what we pay on.

"We collect on two hundred thousand hours of radio airplay. Sixty thousand hours equals 1 percent of radio. The ones we sample we pay on. We use computerized logs, BDS, and tapes. We tape radio shows in six-hour increments and then we compare radio logs supplied to us with music we actually tape. We find the logs to be about 30 percent inaccurate! Now that new technology is starting to change our industry, we are finding ways to expand survey sources. For example, we recently announced a pilot project with ARIS/MusicCode, to establish the International Standard Work Code (ISWC) as the standard numbering system for audio watermarking for ASCAP members. This arrangement is nonexclusive, as we want to be able to work with all watermarking systems. There are several in the industry right now.

"Also, ASCAP just licensed MP3.com. Everyone has been so concerned about the free use and downloading of music on the Internet, with MP3.com, especially; but we were able to license this Web site. It's a pretty big deal because they were considered the big pirates of music.

"Another thing we are actively doing is centralizing our backroom operations with other performing rights organizations to create a shared service center to handle music rights processing in the digital age. ASCAP (United States), Buma•Stemra (Netherlands), and MCPS-PRS (United Kingdom) have formed this joint project, yet to be named. It's just a step forward in the global marketplace.

"I'm guilty of being passionate about my job. I love working with the true creators of music. My brother, David Briggs, feels the same way. He wrote two Number One hits for Brenda Lee, and that's his biggest pleasure. He loves playing on hit records, loved playing on sessions and being on the road with Elvis; but he feels it all goes back to the writer. I learned a lot from him and the other writers at Wishbone Music in Muscle Shoals. I started out playing in a band like most kids. I play most brass instruments, plus keyboards. I thought I was a writer until I met Mac McAnally, Tommy Brasfield, Robert Byrne, and Donny Lowry. It was a good experience, listening to that catalog!

"The staff at ASCAP is very involved with the writers. When Bob Doyle (who discovered Garth Brooks) was at ASCAP, he started the first country workshop and the first country writers' showcases. Now his son Mike is at ASCAP doing showcases on college campuses—at Belmont, Middle Tennessee State University, Tennessee State University, Fisk, and University of North Alabama. There is still a great music scene in Alabama.

"Ralph Murphy publishes Murphy's Laws, which is a tip sheet on our Web site. He knows international publishing really well, goes to MIDEM every year and helps writers and artists make great deals there. We help young writers get established. One thing we do at ASCAP is a writers' pitch, targeted to publishers that are looking for writers. We do different kinds of music, like gospel, rock, and country.

"Our job at ASCAP is to help writers figure out the business side of things; it's such a huge benefit to understand Music Row. Ninety-nine percent of the time, the writers who come through my door need to go to NSAI. I can count on one hand the number of writers who have walked through my door ready to be signed to a publishing deal in my entire fourteen years at ASCAP. Songwriting is a craft that's developed, and you learn that craft from the greats."

JOHN BRIGGS grew up in Killen, Alabama, near the famed Muscle Shoals music scene. Aside from signing new members from all genres of music, John is responsible for assisting writers with royalty and distribution questions. He has helped writers to obtain publishing and record deals over the years. He has been with ASCAP since 1985. He has been involved in bringing the Backstreet Boys, Dixie Chicks, ZZ Top, Little Texas, the Cranberries, Brother Crane, Alan Jackson, Deana Carter, Clint Black, Suzy Bogguss, Brian McKnight, Mutt Lange, and various other acts to ASCAP.

Dedicated to the advancement of music, John serves on many music industry boards and committees. In 1997, John received the Alabama Governor's Award for his involvement in the entertainment industry. Interested in the music business both as a songwriter and a musician from an early age, John received a degree from the University of North Alabama in commercial music with a minor in business administration.

BMI
(Broadcast Music, Inc.)

Headquarters:
320 West 57th Street
New York, NY 10019
Tel. (212) 586-2000
Fax (212) 245-8986

Los Angeles:
8730 Sunset Boulevard, 3rd Floor West
West Hollywood, CA 90069
Tel. (310) 659-9109
Fax (310) 657-6947

Nashville:
Ten Music Square East
Nashville, TN 37203
Tel. (615) 401-2000
Fax (615) 401-2707

Miami:
5201 Blue Lagoon Drive, Suite 310
Miami, FL 33126
Tel. (305) 266-3636
Fax (305) 255-2442

Atlanta:
3636 Habersham Road, Suite 1103
Atlanta, GA 30305
Tel. (404) 261-5151

London:
84 Harley House
Marylebone Road
London, England NW1 5HN
Tel. (011-44-171) 486-2036
Fax (011-44-171) 224-1046

Web site: *www.bmi.com*

How They Determine Who Gets Paid

BMI tracks radio performances by using the daily logs of radio stations. They track every song a station has played over a three-day period, collecting logs for 600,000 hours in a one-year period. Music performed on network TV, cable TV, and local TV stations is reported to BMI on music cue sheets, which list all music performed on a program. The use of music on the Internet is monitored by "MusicBot," a web robot designed also to gather market information and music trends.

How They Pay

Each station is stratified by musical genre and market size, and each performance is multiplied by a factor which reflects the ratio of the number of stations logged to the number licensed. For every three thousand radio performances logged, the writer is paid $1,000. As performances increase, so do writers' royalties. BMI has midlevel, upper level, and super bonus–level rates for songs that reach the 50,000 to one million performance plateau. A Number One song has the potential to earn $200,000 a year.

Special Writer Services
- BMI Roundtable—monthly: history of BMI and of Music Row. Gives good fundamental guidelines to a beginning songwriter
- BMI Songwriters' Workshop—monthly. If you have been to a BMI roundtable, you can attend a songwriting workshop taught by award-winning songwriter Jason Blume.
- BMI Demo Derby with Jason Blume—monthly. For BMI members only. Professional feedback and constructive critiques of songs within a small, supportive group.
- BMI Music Connection Showcase—twice a month in New York, Los Angeles, Nashville, Atlanta, and Miami. An artist showcase, including all genres of music.
- Screening room, writers' rooms
- Affiliate loan program
- Direct deposit
- Insurance—equipment, health, dental, life
- Legislative representation

INDUSTRY INTERVIEW WITH DAVID PRESTON, DIRECTOR OF WRITER/PUBLISHER RELATIONS, BMI

"We have an open-door policy here at BMI. We will always make an appointment to see writers if they make the effort to call in advance. It's not necessary for a writer to have anything published in order to sign a two-year contract with us, and there are a lot of advantages to joining BMI. For example, we have a lot of great workshops for beginning songwriters, including BMI Roundtable, BMI Writers Workshop with Jason Blume, and BMI Demo Derby with Jason Blume. Jason is a great songwriter and instructor, and has helped a lot of writers in various stages of development.

Photo by Richard Crichton

"BMI was formed because country and R&B writers of the early 1900s were not being recognized as viable creators of music. Only standards by writers like Irving Berlin and John Philip Sousa were licensed to be played on the radio. Stations weren't allowed to play other songs unless they had permission from the songwriters, which individually was impossible to do. So a group of 425 radio broadcasters got together in 1940 and started BMI. In 1958 Frances Preston opened a Nashville office in support of the growing country music industry. For this reason BMI has always been considered the home of rock 'n' roll, country, and R&B.

"BMI's real strength is that we log more music than anyone, with over 3 million song titles, including music from the Top Ten motion pictures of all time. We monitor over 500,000 hours of music annually, using both the radio station program logs and BDS reports on the country charts. We have also launched a new technology program called the BMI Horizon Project, which has twelve new major advances aimed at transforming and greatly enhancing BMI's service to its songwriters and publishers. One new service is that writers will be able to receive royalty information via e-mail, and can have payments sent directly to their bank account. Similarly, licensees, or the companies that use our music, can file reports of use directly online, completely eliminating the use of paper reports, or airplay logging.

"The coolest new technology is BMI MusicBot Reports, which is a series of studies about the use of music on the Web. Each report compiles information about music trends like MP3 and supplies that information to the managers of international copyright organizations. Also, we've begun to do field trials of leading music watermarking technologies like ARIS, Cognicity, Blue Spike, and Liquid Audio.

"BMI has also taken a leadership role in the development of a global copyright information system to create a 'virtual database' of musical works.

We are working with CISAC Common Information System on a prototype so that performing rights organizations can exchange information directly among their mainframe computers.

"BMI actively looks for new writers and writer/artists. We have ten college reps in all of the hot music centers: Austin, Athens, Seattle, Chicago, Washington D.C., Boston, Raleigh-Durham, Gainesville, Phoenix, and Boulder. There are scouts on each of these cities' college campuses looking for talent and organizing showcases, one every semester. We do not accept unsolicited material in the mail or dropped off at the front desk. You must call in advance and get permission to send in material, or make an appointment to come in.

"The atmosphere in Nashville right now is highly competitive; there are approximately 250 artists signed to major and independent labels in this town, and approximately 50,000 songwriters in Davidson County alone! A lot of artists write their own material, and they produce only one CD a year—twelve songs. That's not very many chances to get songs recorded.

"It's very important that songwriters realize there are a lot of people out there trying to get their songs heard. The number one rule is: *Have a professional and courteous approach.* It's important to be persistent but polite. Doing your homework before you come is very beneficial. Know the names of the producers and publishers, writers and artists. That's a huge help. Having an artist in mind, an idea of who you think can cut your material, is very important. Read *Billboard* and study their charts, and read the label copy on CDs. Study all about the artists, the publishers, the producers. I meet with a lot of people who are really out of touch with the industry and aren't familiar with the current country artists. It's frustrating!

"If you move to Nashville today and you are a great songwriter, then you are looking at least at five years before you start having some success; the average is ten years. Even great songwriters have to work very hard to write a great song. Songwriters who work hard at the craft of songwriting will make major improvements over time. With developing writers, I always say, 'Come see me again in six months.' If they come back with the same songs, no changes, I'll realize that they aren't serious about it.

"This is especially true with artists. Once they start getting better, at some point they will get *a lot* better. That's when Nashville starts paying attention."

DAVID PRESTON is a native Nashvillian and son of BMI president and CEO, Frances W. Preston. Mr. Preston graduated from Peabody Demonstration School and studied Mass Communication at Denver University. Prior to joining BMI, Preston was national sales manager with Premier Marketing Group. Mr. Preston is currently a director of writer/publisher relations in BMI's Nashville office. Mr. Preston is on the board of directors of the Tennessee State Museum and served as chairman for the NeA Extravaganza for 1996 and 1997. He is the entertainment chairman of the Nashville Zoo and was most recently awarded the Nashville Hit Award from the Nashville Area Chamber of Commerce as the Art and Music Volunteer of the Year. Mr. Preston is married and has three children. Some of his favorite hobbies include traveling, snow skiing, jet skiing, scuba diving, four-wheeling, and coaching soccer.

SESAC, INC.

Headquarters:
55 Music Square East
Nashville, TN 37203
Tel. (615) 320-0055
Fax (615) 329-9627

New York:
421 West 54th Street
New York, NY 10019
Tel. (212) 586-3450
Fax (212) 489-5699

United Kingdom:
Gresham House
53 Clarendon Road
Watford, Hertfordshire, UK WD1 1LA
Phone (011-44-1923) 228-870
Fax (011-44-1923) 228-872

Web site: *www.sesac.com*

How They Determine Who Gets Paid

SESAC began using BDS (Broadcast Data Systems) in 1994 with its SESAC Latina division. Because of its success with SESAC Latina, the company expanded its usage to all mainstream commercial radio formats in 1996. BDS is the same system used by *Billboard Magazine* to compile its music charts, a standard for the music industry. With BDS, SESAC monitors more than 8 million hours of radio programming annually. In 1998, SESAC became the first performing rights organization in the world to sign an agreement with Aris Technologies Inc. to use its MusiCode "watermark" technology to track musical performances. With MusiCode, SESAC will comprehensively track performances generated by film, TV, cable, Internet, and music libraries.

How They Pay

SESAC uses BDS and MusiCode tracking data to make royalty distributions for all mainstream commercial formats, including Top Forty, country, Latin, R&B, adult contemporary, and AAA. For all noncommercial formats, SESAC uses a payment system that uses chart position to determine royalty payment.

Special Writer Services

Writer/artist showcases at high-profile music conferences

Photo by Kay Williams

INDUSTRY INTERVIEW WITH PAT ROGERS, SENIOR VICE PRESIDENT, WRITER/PUBLISHER RELATIONS, SESAC

"Founded in 1930, SESAC is a private, for-profit corporation with a strong emphasis on new technologies. SESAC first emerged as a technological leader in 1994, when the company's SESAC Latina division utilized BDS for performance tracking and royalty distribution. Because of the success with BDS for SESAC Latina, SESAC began using the 'digital fingerprint' technology to monitor all of its mainstream commercial formats. As a result of BDS, SESAC actually monitors more than 8 million hours of airplay, as compared with 800,000 hours at ASCAP and BMI, combined.

"SESAC has two offices in the United States, with our international office in England. In Nashville and New York, our writer/publisher relations staff consists of music industry professionals with backgrounds in virtually every musical genre. Every member of our staff works with a variety of songwriters. Of course, the Nashville office handles the majority of our country songwriters, while most of our urban, R&B, and jazz affiliates are handled through the New York office.

"SESAC is, by design, a small company. Because of our size, we are very selective. Our smaller size also enables us to act quickly when necessary, without getting bogged down with a lot of bureaucracy. For example, SESAC is totally committed to being the technological leader in performing rights. If a new technology comes along and we need to change the way we do business to use it, then we'll do that. We've already demonstrated our commitment to new technologies and our flexibility by moving way ahead of our competition with the use of BDS and MusiCode. SESAC will continue that business strategy.

"In order for a songwriter to be considered for affiliation, he or she must be referred by someone in the industry or another SESAC publisher or writer affiliate. Unsolicited tapes will be returned to the writer. When appointments are made to meet with songwriters, we try to learn as much as we can about them. We do a thorough analysis of everything a songwriter is doing. For example, we consider how serious the writer is about his or her career. The process can take as little as a week or up to six weeks, depending on the writer and what he or she has going on. At times, SESAC actually operates like a publisher or A&R department. We listen to the music and have to feel that the music is viable and ready for the marketplace. If we meet with the writer and believe that the potential is there, then we usually will sign.

"SESAC prides itself on its relationship with its affiliates. We work closely with them, being as much a member of their creative team as possible. If I feel a writer is ready for a publishing deal, I will refer that person. The same is true if I feel a songwriter is ready for an artist deal; I will refer him or her to a producer or record label. We may even help the writer do a showcase if it's warranted. All of this, of course, depends on the individual and where he is in his career, and is done on a case-by-case basis. The point is, because of its size, SESAC is able to step in when we think we can do something for the writer.

"One thing that has changed since I've been in Nashville is that the industry has moved into corporate/vertical ownership. Aspiring writers and artists no longer get the nurturing they need. You have to walk in with the goods. That's the reality of today's business world. Because of this business climate, songwriters have to go where they can to get that nurturing: NSAI, PROs, and other writers. Another reality is that publishers are downsizing their writing staff. It's getting tougher. Therefore, writers must be part creative and part business savvy. Young writers today must know what's in a contract. Naivete must go by the wayside.

"I would like to stress that writing is not like any other occupation; the more you put in it, the more chance you will have to succeed. It is a dream. There are no magic ways. Songwriting takes a lot of time, a lot of dedication and a lot of hard work. Don't think you can just come to town and things will start happening; most great writers have starved to do it.

"Nashville is still the place, more than any other, for a songwriter's dream to come true. That's the cool thing about this town."

PAT ROGERS directs all of SESAC's writer/publisher relations efforts throughout the United States and Canada. She plays a key role in developing strategic initiatives for the company as well as facilitating writer and catalog affiliation. The Anderson, South Carolina native holds a master of music degree from Manhattan School of Music and has many years of experience in music publishing, music education, and musical theater. Rogers began her career in Nashville as a staff songwriter at Sony/ATV Tree Music Publishing and served as assistant to the senior VP/Creative and as the professional manager of Tree's creative department. During the early 1980s, Rogers left the music industry to single-handedly reestablish the Middle Tennessee chapter of United Cerebral Palsy, raising more than $2 million for the chapter. Prior to joining SESAC in 1996, Rogers served as executive director of the Nashville Songwriters Association International. During her tenure, NSAI became the largest and strongest association for songwriters in the United States, doubling membership to almost five thousand aspiring and professional songwriters, developing a national and international presence, and raising more than $4 million in revenues for the organization. Throughout her career, Rogers has served on many boards in the fields of mental health, home health care, entertainment, and music, and is the founding board member of the Nashville chapter of Gilda's Club, a national support organization for people living with cancer.

10

A Basic Understanding of Nashville's Networking System

Nashville runs on a 10-2-6 schedule, but people are pretty much in their offices by 8:30 A.M. or so. They don't leave until late, and when they do, it's usually to go to a writers' night, artist showcase, or . . . a party.

PARTY, PARTY, PARTY

There are a zillion parties in Nashville for everything under the sun. Every time a single goes Number One on the Country Chart, the publisher throws a party for the writer. There are usually more than one publisher and writer involved, so there might be more than one party. Also, the PRO might throw a party for the writers and the publishers. The publisher will make up a banner for the occasion and hang it outside on his building. You will see these banners all over Music Row.

Record labels throw a party for an artist when his album sells Gold, and another when it goes Platinum. Sometimes these parties can be very elaborate, and everyone on Music Row is invited. Other times it's a small gathering at the record label offices. Sometimes the label will have a listening party when an album project is completed. These parties are usually held at the recording studio.

It's not too difficult to crash most of these parties, but it's best to tag along with someone who was invited or knows plenty of the people who are going to be there. Don't be surprised if you find yourself at one of these parties, but be sure to be on your best behavior! There is lots of great food and drink and many celebrities, so it's easy to get carried away with the ambiance.

The reason they give these parties is because of the importance of networking. It takes place on every level. Everyone wants to stay in touch with all the different people who worked on a project. Hopefully they will be back to contribute to another project in some way and make valuable contacts which will lead to future creative ventures. While you are in Nashville, be aware of these opportunities and take advantage of them if you can.

EAT, DRINK, AND BE MERRY

Music Row restaurants are not just for eating. Since hanging around publishers' offices is a very difficult task, hanging around Nashville's restaurants can be the reward for a job well done! And you'll probably have more success meeting people in the restaurants than at the writers' nights and publishers' offices combined. If you are uncomfortable going to a restaurant by yourself, all the better. You will be forced to ask that new writer you met at the Bluebird last night to join you. Lunch and happy hour are the best times to run into people—dinner would be more of a long shot. But don't skip these networking opportunities . . . you could hit the jackpot! Seriously, everyone you are trying to meet or get an appointment with is in one of the following restaurants:

Breakfast

The Pancake Pantry
1796 21st Avenue South
Tel. (615) 383-9333

This restaurant used to be in a tiny room next door to the current location, and there was a table right next to the kitchen that was reserved for Chet Atkins, Harold Shedd (producer, Alabama), Ray Stevens, and all of their friends. They ate there every morning. Alas, progress changes everything. Even the "Cake" is upscale now, bigger and better, and Chet doesn't drop by much anymore, but most of the diners are someone in the industry.

Lunch

Sunset Grill
2001 Belcourt Avenue
Tel. (615) 386-3663

Without a doubt, *the* place where the industry hangs out, especially songwriters. Often seen: Pat Alger, Richard Leigh, Ralph Murphy. Start at the bar, then have lunch in one of the dining rooms, then drift to the outside patio for dessert and watch Music Row parade by. Or get there early and get a table on the patio, where you have a ringside seat to watch everyone who comes in and out.

Midtown Café
102 19th Avenue South
Tel. (615) 320-7176
Recently purchased by Sunset Grill, but retained its original menu.

Sammy Bs
26 Music Square East
Tel. (615) 320-5438
The maitre d' used to head up the promotion department at Sony Music (when it was CBS Records). Now he serves them lunch! You'll find a bunch of Sony Music employees among the other industry diners, plus some Sony artists as well. It's so convenient!

Noshville Delicatessen
1918 Broadway
Tel. (615) 329-6674
Fashioned after a New York deli. Industry execs like it because it reminds them of home! Popular for breakfast too.

Granite Falls
2000 Broadway
Tel. (615) 327-9250
Industry execs, plus Marty Stuart and his clothier extraordinaire, Manuel (his elegant shop is next door), are seen here frequently. Friday night happy hour is a favorite among industry A&R execs and song pluggers.

The LongHorn
110 Lyle Avenue
Tel. (615) 329-9195
Popular writers' hangout.

Happy Hour

Sammy Bs and Sunset Grill

The Trace
2000 Belcourt Avenue
Tel. (615) 385-2200
A big, upscale happy hour crowd. You'll find music industry mixed with Nashville's upper crust.

Dinner

Sunset Grill, the Trace, and, if you are someone else's expense account:

Morton's of Chicago
625 Church Street
Tel. (615) 259-4558
Music industry executives like to entertain their clients at the downtown Morton's because it also reminds them of New York. A be-seen type of place; not the best for socializing, except with your dinner guests, of course.

THE ACKLEN STATION POST OFFICE

No kidding! Everyone has a post office box at the Acklen Station behind Sunset Grill on Acklen Avenue. You never know who you'll run into there, but you will be sure to run into someone important in the music industry. Faith Hill used to drop by every day to pick up mail for Reba McEntire! You might want to stop by there when you are in the vicinity. You could get lucky and stumble into just the person with whom you were trying to get an appointment.

GOLFING, FISHING, AND PLAYING TENNIS

Highly recommended for great networking opportunities. Music Row professionals are really into golf, and there is a tournament almost every week during the summer. Top record executives, producers, publishers, and songwriters all participate, mix and mingle, and compete on the course. The most popular music industry tournaments are The Vinnie, HoriPro, T.J. Martell during CMA Week, and NSAI during Tin Pan South. For tennis players, the Music City Tennis Invitational is held the last weekend in April and the first weekend in May.

Songwriters love to go bass fishing. Many a great song has been written on the water, including the recent classic "Wind Beneath My Wings."

PROFESSIONAL ORGANIZATIONS

There are three very important professional organizations which you will want to know about: the National Academy of Recording Arts and

Sciences (NARAS), the Country Music Association (CMA), and the Country Radio Broadcasters (CRB). Also known as the Recording Academy, NARAS produces the Grammys; the CMA produces the CMA Awards Show. Both network TV shows are extremely important to the country music industry, and greatly affect an artist's career. An appearance on one of these shows is a guarantee of significant album sales in the immediate days following the broadcast. Membership in all three organizations is limited to persons who derive a significant amount of income from the music industry, and new members have to go through an interview process in order to be accepted. You may not be interested in joining these organizations, but you will definitely want to check with them before coming to Nashville. They host several different special events throughout the year that are open to nonmembers as well as members.

Country Music Association (CMA)
1 Music Circle South
Nashville, TN 37203
Tel. (615) 244-2840
Fax (615) 726-0314
Web site: *www.CMAworld.com*

- Fan Fair. Second week in June. A weeklong opportunity to meet all of the top-name country recording artists at their fair booth, and/or onstage at their record label showcase.
- CMA Awards Show. Last Wednesday in September—subject to change at network discretion.
- MINT. An in-depth workshop and industry trade show on computer and Internet technology
- CMA Marketing Conference. A two-day conference on attracting and working with corporate sponsorships to market country music.
- *CMA Close-Up.* An outstanding magazine dedicated to country music, available to CMA members only.

National Academy of Recording Arts and Sciences (NARAS or the Recording Academy)
1904 Wedgewood Avenue
Nashville, TN 37212
Tel. (615) 327-8030
Fax (615) 321-3101
E-mail: *nashville@grammy.com*
Web site: *www.grammy.com*

- Grammy Awards Show. Held each February, this annual awards presentation on national television highlights the best of the best in many different genres of music. Winners are selected by a jury of their peers—members of NARAS.
- Educational Seminars. The Nashville chapter of NARAS hosts a variety of seminars, panel discussions, and events that are sometimes open to the public. Check with NARAS for time and place.
- MusiCares. The Nashville chapter of NARAS also hosts a variety of fund-raising events, such as the Governors Awards Dinner, which is open to the public in support of Musicians' Aid. Check with NARAS for time and place.

Country Radio Broadcasters, Inc. (CRB or CRS)
819 18th Avenue South
Nashville, TN 37203
Tel. (615) 327-4487
Fax (615) 329-4492
Web site: *www.crb.org*

Country Radio Seminar. Formerly known as the DJ Convention, CRS is an annual weeklong event the primary purpose of which is to introduce artists, radio personalities, and programmers to one another. There are lots of seminars, dinners, showcases, and record label parties which maximize opportunities.

BACK TO SCHOOL: RECORD INDUSTRY COURSES

Many of the people who work on Music Row are graduates of a recording industry program at either Belmont University or Middle Tennessee State University (MTSU). Both colleges have a great curriculum aimed directly at getting a job in the Nashville music industry. The biggest advantage offered by both of these universities is their internship program, which places students directly in the offices of Music Row businesses. They also have state-of-the-art recording studios and film and video production facilities, and prominent Music Row professionals teach courses at both universities. If you are seriously considering a career in the country music business, then you would benefit greatly from attending either of these colleges. Both are very well integrated into the Music Row community, but they are quite different in structure.

Belmont University (Belmont)
1900 Belmont Boulevard
Nashville, TN 37212
Tel. (615) 460-5504

Fax (615) 460-5516
Web site: *www.belmont.edu*
Program: Mike Curb School of Music Business

Belmont is a private university with a religious base. It requires some attendance at religious seminars and has some basic religious restrictions. Its close proximity to Music Row enables the students to closely interact with Music Row businesses. Belmont offers an extension program in Los Angeles and a music business MBA degree from their Massey Graduate School.

Middle Tennessee State University (MTSU)
P.O. Box 21
Murfreesboro, TN 37132
Tel. (615) 898-2578
Fax (615) 898-5682
Web site: *www.mtsu.edu/~record*
Program: MTSU Recording Industry Department

MTSU is a state university and, as such, offers affordable enrollment. It is the country's largest recording program with over 1,400 different majors. Music Row works equally with both MTSU and Belmont, but the greatest hardship is on the MTSU students who have to travel back and forth between Nashville and Murfreesboro, a forty-five–minute drive.

OTHER IMPORTANT RESOURCES

American Songwriter Magazine
1009 17th Avenue South
Nashville, TN 37212
Tel. (615) 321-6096
Fax (615) 321-6097
Web site: *www.songnet.com/asongmag/*

Owner/publisher Jim Sharp is a Music Row veteran, having been in key positions at CBS and Monument Records and heading the Nashville office of *CashBox* magazine. Highly respected in the country music industry, he has been helping songwriters through *American Songwriter* for over thirteen years. The magazine is very affordable at $25 per year, and contains lots of detailed information about Music Row and great interviews with Nashville songwriters, providing valuable insight into the challenges of the profession. Be sure to stop by their offices when you are in town, as they have many valuable services for visiting writers.

Nashville Chamber of Commerce
161 4th Avenue North
Nashville, TN 37219
Tel. (615) 259-4755
Fax (615) 256-3074
Web site: *www.nashvillechamber.com*

The Nashville Chamber is inundated with calls from people wanting to know how to get started in the music business. They are also very concerned about the great number of aspiring artists and songwriters who travel to the city with very few resources, expecting to become an overnight sensation, who wind up seeking assistance to get back home. Although the city does not have a large homeless population, a notable number are people who thought they could make it big as country singers or songwriters.

For this reason, the Nashville Chamber put together a very comprehensive music industry package designed to help people gain a realistic view of Music Row. Their music industry package is only $25 and contains information not found anywhere else. For example, the package includes a list of hit songwriters and their phone numbers, so you can talk directly to the pros. It also has a fact sheet about the business side of the industry, such as how much money it generates for the city, and articles on some of the top companies. They have their own guide to the recording industry, hints on cowriting, and another list of DO's and DON'Ts for aspiring writers and artists.

ABOUT MUSIC CONFERENCES

Approximately twenty years ago some very enterprising people realized there was a treasure trove of talent in Austin, Texas, just waiting to be discovered. The college town of Austin is rich with live music clubs, mainly situated in one area on Sixth Street. College students hop from club to club searching for new and different music, and the bands thrive on this appreciative audience. Organizers put together a music conference and invited top music executives from Los Angeles, Nashville, and New York to come and hear these bands. In another stroke of genius, they planned their conference during spring break, so that students from other campuses across the country could attend as well.

The conference is called South By SouthWest (SXSW), and has grown to gigantic proportions. Originally, it was designed to showcase new emerging talent for the record industry, but the record companies were so receptive to the idea, they began to hold their own showcases of their hot new acts. Today, SXSW is a huge event attended by aspiring songwriters and artists, music industry executives, and journalists. SXSW now includes a film festival as well, and conference attendees are likely to meet some of Hollywood's top stars.

It didn't take long for other cities to recognize the impact a music conference would make on their own city, and music conferences began to spread like wildfire across the country and Europe. There is at least one a month in some city somewhere in the United States. Organizers are careful to pick dates that don't interfere with other conferences in the hopes of attracting large crowds of music industry executives. SXSW organizers produce many of these conferences themselves, with NXNE in Toronto, Canada, and NXNW in Portland, Oregon.

Besides showcases of both signed and unsigned talent, conferences include panel discussions on just about every topic under the sun, including songwriting, getting a job in the industry, and getting a record deal. They also have great networking opportunities including cocktail parties, golf tournaments, and riverboat rides.

Trying to find a music conference near you might take a little bit of detective work. Music magazines like *Spin* and *Rolling Stone* will have articles and, more likely, advertisements on various conferences. Some, like the Atlantis Music Conference in Atlanta, Georgia, have links to other conferences. Try *www.atlantismusic.com* to get started. You can also call the chambers of commerce in the biggest cities near you. It will be worth the effort to track them down, as you will benefit greatly from these conferences no matter what level your stage of development, no matter how advanced your aspirations are.

11

Packaging
Your Product

I n Nashville, you will be expected to have your music on a CD or cassette tape. Lead sheets with the music written out are absolutely never used in Nashville. You cannot go into anyone's office with your guitar and sing a few songs—it is simply not done anymore. No one has that kind of time, and it's not the norm. Nashville has a strict way of doing things, and the song demo is at the top of the list.

THE SONGWRITER'S DEMO
Not too long ago a songwriter could take his guitar into a publisher's office and perform his songs live. Songwriters and publishers with a close working relationship may share new songs in this manner, particularly in the developmental stages of a song, but publishers require a work tape to be made for each song so they can listen to it at their own convenience. The difference between a demo and a work tape is the production. A work tape is the best way to pitch songs to publishers, but work tapes are never pitched to producers and A&R executives. Their ears are used to hearing full-blown demos which have the entire production already in place. One of the most important functions of Nashville publishers is knowing how the producers and A&R reps like songs to be presented. Publishers produce their demos according to these preferences.

JOHNNY BOND
PUBLICATIONS

To: John Van Meter
From: Betsy Meryl Hammer

Songwriter demo
"Tomorrow Never Comes"
"Your Old Love Letters"
"Love Gone Cold"
P.O. Box 158029 • Nashville, TN 37215-8029
(615) 297-7320

Example: J-Card insert
Songwriter's Cassette Demo
Sample of a three- to five-song demo to be pitched to a specific person at publishing company.

THE WORK TAPE

A work tape is a very simple guitar/vocal or piano/vocal. If done correctly, that is all that is needed to shop songs to publishers in Nashville. It is perfectly acceptable for you to record your songs yourself, but the tape quality and sound should be very good—no tape hiss or background noises—and the vocalist must be excellent. The song needs to be delivered in a straightforward manner, with not too much inflection in the voice. The vocalist has to do a good job of following the melody accurately. The lyrics must be crystal clear.

It is important not to spend a lot of money on demos. Remember that it is a publisher's job to demo material, and they have their own ideas about how a song should be presented. Your goal is to make an excellent work tape to present to a publisher, who will then put his own money into a professional demo. If you spend a lot of money on a demo yourself, then you will have a major investment in the song which may in turn change your focus. You might spend too much time on one song when you need to move on to something else, or you might become inflexible regarding rewrites or the need to redemo. Be very conservative with your demo budget.

Don't hire someone to write music to your lyrics. If you are a lyricist only and do not write music or play an instrument, then you need to find a cowriter—someone who is as involved in your lyrics as you are and whose music is a perfect interpretation of your words. This cannot be purchased at any price.

THE FULL-BLOWN DEMO

The majority of songwriters get so carried away with how great their songs are, they want to go straight to the artist with their song. They can't imagine even needing a publisher, except for their contacts and connections. So they go ahead, skip the work tape process, and go straight to demoing their songs. They are hoping that once the publisher hears it, he will take it directly to the artist.

A full-blown demo can represent a song more accurately, but a demo can make or break a song. A poor demo can ruin a great song, so great care should be taken in producing your demos. An overproduced demo is the biggest danger—you don't want your listeners to get distracted by the production. Also, Nashville demos have a certain sound that is similar to what is played on contemporary country radio, so your demos should be close to that quality. Also make sure that the vocals are turned up in the mix; in a Nashville demo, vocals take precedence over the music.

Nashville producers and A&R reps continually say that they like to hear guitar/vocals because they want to be free to think of their own production ideas. However, they are rarely pitched guitar/vocals, or work tapes, by Nashville publishers. These publishers have their own demo studios, and spend a lot of money and time producing demos that sound like a master recording. This intense competition is what you are up against when pitching to A&R, producers, and artist managers. That's why you want to first play your demos for publishers, the songwriters' organizations, and all three PROs before pitching them to the rest of the music industry. You will learn a great deal about your songs, your demos, and the way the Nashville music industry thinks in the process.

To: Wilbur Rimes   For: LeAnn Rimes
"Your Old Love Letters"
(Johnny Bond)

©
1998

JOHNNY BOND PUBLICATIONS
(615) 297-7320

Example: Cassette label
Publisher's Cassette Demo
Sample of a one- or two-song cassette pitched to a producer or A&R rep.

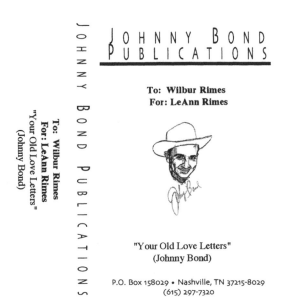

JOHNNY BOND PUBLICATIONS

To: Wilbur Rimes
For: LeAnn Rimes

"Your Old Love Letters"
(Johnny Bond)

P.O. Box 158029 • Nashville, TN 37215-8029
(615) 297-7320

**Example: J-Card insert
Publisher's Cassette Demo**
Sample of a one- or two-song cassette to be pitched to a specific producer or A&R rep, for a specific artist. Never pitch more than three songs—one is preferable. Lyric sheet is folded to the size of the cassette, placed underneath, and then attached by rubber band.

As you can well imagine, there are lots of great demo studios in Nashville. It would be a good idea to have your songs demo'd in Nashville, as opposed to a studio in your own hometown, because it will be one more opportunity to get to know people in Nashville. Also, you will have a greater chance of getting a Nashville sound production, more like the demos producers are used to hearing. Following is a list of some popular demo studios:

NASHVILLE'S TOP DEMO STUDIOS

Bobby Angello
526 East Iris
Nashville, TN 37204
Tel. (615) 383-0888
Bobby has been producing songwriter demos for many years.

Beaird Music Group
107 Music City Circle, #314
Nashville, TN 37214
Tel. (615) 889-0138
Fax (615) 883-7278
Larry Beaird has been producing songwriter demos for many years. He works well with songwriters who are new to the process and do not live in Nashville.

Arvl Ellis Bird
Brush Hill Studios
1421 Tempany Court
Nashville, TN 37207
Tel. (615) 870-1221
Fax (615) 870-0416
Web site: *www.bhstudios.com*
Producer/Engineer Arvl can do everything for the beginning song-writer, from guitar and vocals to full-band album projects.

Country Q
P.O. Box 40228
Nashville, TN 37204
Tel. (615) 298-1434
Country Q is the most popular song demo studio in Nashville.

Dave Pomeroy
Earwave Productions
P.O. Box 40857
Nashville, TN 37204
Tel. (615) 298-3504
Web site: *www.davepomeroy.com*
Bassist Dave Pomeroy is a very popular session guitarist, session leader, producer, and live performer. He hosts a regular syndicated radio show featuring Nashville artists for National Public Radio (NPR).

Durrett Productions
50 Music Square West, #700C
Nashville, TN 37203
Tel. (615) 320-0007
Keyboardist Rick Durrett is a very popular session keyboardist, session leader, and producer.

Jim Hoke
Tel. (615) 292-4507
Jim is a very popular band leader in Nashville.

Juke Box Recording Studio
646 W. Iris Drive
Nashville, TN 37214
Tel. (615) 297-9100

Engineer Howard Toole has been producing songwriter demos for over twenty years. He ran the House of Gold demo studio and produced hits like "Wind Beneath My Wings."

Malloy Boys
1216 17th Avenue South
Nashville, TN 37212
Tel. (615) 327-4735

Production company and studio of Jim and David Malloy, accomplished Nashville producers.

Michael Morris Music Service
812 Shenandoah Drive
Nashville, TN 37027
Tel. (615) 661-9992

Michael specializes in jazz and arrangements for all types of music.

Music Makers
3000 Hillsboro Road, #11
Nashville, TN 37215
Tel. (615) 292-2140

Keyboardist, songwriter, and arranger Al DeLory was the producer of Glen Campbell's early hits.

Larry Rogers
Studio 19
821 19th Avenue South
Nashville, TN 37203
Tel. (615) 327-4927
Fax (615) 327-0858

Larry owns several studios in Nashville and Memphis, and has produced songs for many hit artists over the years.

The Song Cellar Production Service
P.O. Box 121234
Nashville, TN 37212
Tel. (615) 383-7222

Jackie Cook established his performing, writing, and recording career in Memphis before coming to Nashville to sing and play guitar for the legendary Roy Orbison. In 1984 Jackie started the Song Cellar in the basement of NSAI. Since then he has been involved in the production of over four thousand songs. Some have won Grammys, others have made it to Number One on the charts. The Song Cellar offers a variety of packages, from simple guitar/vocals to full-blown master quality demos.

Top Tracks
113 17th Avenue South
Nashville, TN 37203
Tel. (615) 742-1555

Owner/producer Tom Pallardy has been producing demos on Music Row for many years.

BEWARE OF SONG SHARKS
A "song shark" is anyone who will publish your songs for a fee. The most notorious song sharks offer a contract that says they will record your song, put it on an album with nine or so other songs, and present them to radio stations and/or record labels. There is nothing illegal about this practice—it just doesn't have anything to do with the music industry. Radio stations and record labels throw this product in the trash. You do not want your songs to be associated with these companies. Be very wary of anyone who wants to charge you a fee for publishing your songs.

You have to be equally careful when looking for a producer. There are a lot out there that have some pretty impressive credentials, but really aren't as connected as they used to be. Or even worse, they are still connected, but will produce some "vanity" projects for a little extra income. A vanity project is a CD produced for someone who really doesn't have a clue about the music industry. He is just content to see himself on an album cover, and doesn't really understand the big picture. If you ask the right questions, you should be able to weed out the song sharks.

The catch-22 is that it will probably take some output of money on your part to get things accomplished; professional song demos and/or an artist's package are expensive. Just make sure that if you need to hire a professional to assist you in this process, you hire someone who is well connected on Music Row.

PUBLISHER FEES
Publishers do not charge anything at all for their services. However, publishing is an expensive business, with the financial return greatly delayed. It can take up to two years to start collecting for a song that is currently on the singles charts. Some small publishers may need help with demo costs, and while this is not the most ideal situation for a songwriter, it is not unethical for publishers to ask for assistance in producing a demo of the

material. If you have paid for your own song demos, and a publisher wants to start pitching your demo, then you have the right to ask for half of the publishing. If the publisher objects (which he will), offer to let him administer the rights for your publishing company and tell him that you would be willing to give up your share of the publishing in the event that some publishing has to be given away in order to get the song recorded (not as common a practice as is rumored). At a minimum, if you sign over all the publishing on a song that you paid to be demo'd, get your demo money reimbursed.

THE SONGWRITER'S DEMO PACKAGE

The demo package consists of a CD or cassette tape and a lyric sheet attached. Every song that is pitched in Nashville has a certain look to it, and yours should look exactly the same. In some kind of reverse logic, tapes that stand out from the others are most likely to wind up in the round file (trash can).

The CD and DAT

CD is the best way to pitch songs, because of the superior sound quality. DAT is quickly phasing out because of its poor shelf life. If you have invested heavily in DAT equipment, then continue to use it. Everyone on Music Row has CD and DAT machine capability as well as a cassette tape deck.

Betsy Meryl Hammer • Songwriter demo
"Tomorrow Never Comes" • "Your Old Love Letters"
"Love Gone Cold"

©
1998

JOHNNY BOND PUBLICATIONS
(615) 297-7320

Example: Cassette label
Songwriter's Cassette Demo
Sample of a three- to five-song demo to be pitched to a publisher.

The Cassette Tape

Cassettes are still the most common method used to pitch songs. You don't have to invest in CD or DAT equipment—cassettes will do just fine. You should be aware that cassette tapes come in lengths under thirty minutes. The best tape is twenty minutes, ten minutes on each side, and you should put songs on *one side only.* No one turns the tape over and listens to the other side.

Put no more than three songs on a twenty-minute cassette tape. Put your best song first, a novelty song (if you are pitching one) last. Your cassette label should look something like the one shown below. Put a copyright notice on your cassette label, even if you have not registered your songs with the copyright office. If you have registered your songs and they all were registered in different years, use the most recent year for your cassette notice.

Needless to say, putting the song titles and your name, address, and phone number on each cassette is very, very important. Also on the J-card, lyric sheet, letter, note, memo, fax, e-mail—each and every printed or electronically produced item pertaining to your songs. It is mind-boggling how many people forget to include some way to reach them on the cassette itself, relying on a lyric sheet or business card to contain that information. Cassettes often get separated from the rest of a song's package, so all important information should be included on the cassette itself.

The cassette is best protected by a case. Use the clear, hard plastic case, the kind you get when you buy a cassette in the stores. The soft plastic cases are difficult to open and do not display as well. The publisher may circle a song title or make notes on the cassette itself. These notes are easier to read through the clear plastic. Also, you will want to use a J-card, that little card that fits inside the cassette case. Lots more information about you and your songs can fit on that card.

The Lyric Sheet

Don't ever pitch a song without a lyric sheet. Important things to include are:

- Your name, address, and phone number.
- Copyright notice at the bottom of the first page (there should only be one page).
- An indentation for the chorus, bridge, and tag. Many people do not look at the lyrics when they are listening to a song, but will glance at them occasionally. Your lyric sheet needs to be laid out so that whoever's glancing at it can find his place easily.
- Do not use a lead sheet (melody line and chords printed out). Lead sheets are hard to read and are no longer necessary due to the change in copyright law which allows copyright registration with a cassette tape instead of a lead sheet.

The Bio

Biographical information is completely unnecessary and should be avoided, unless you really have something important to say, i.e., songs you have had recorded or awards you have won. Publishers don't need to know where you went to high school or college and what bands you've played in, etc.

Miscellany

- Business Cards. A card with your picture on it is very effective and helps a publisher remember you. Have lots of cards handy for all the people you are going to meet at writers' nights, restaurants, and publishers' offices.
- Manila Envelopes. Some songwriters and publishers prefer to enclose their tape in a manila envelope, especially if they are pitching CDs. If you use this method, be sure you use a small size (6″ × 9″) and have professional, typed labels on the front. Do not seal the envelope; make it easy to get inside.

Example: J-Card insert Artist's Cassette Demo
A professional artist's demo should be on a CD, not cassette. However, you may want to make up some cassette copies for wider distribution. Here is an example of an artist's cassette with photo.

A Nashville Song Demo Package

If you make your way into a publisher's or producer's office, you will see that the desk will be covered with cassette tapes, stacked on top of each other in neat little piles. Each cassette tape will be in a hard plastic case, and the lyrics to the songs will be neatly folded to the size of the cassette case, placed on the bottom and secured with a rubber band. You will see these neat little piles of tapes everywhere, including the receptionist's desk and little bins next to the receptionist desk put there to collect tapes for producers and A&R reps. Your songs should be packaged like all the others.

Cassette labels, J-cards, lyric sheets, and business cards should be professionally done with a word processor. This is very inexpensive to do these days. If you don't have your own PC and printer, any of the quick copy stores can design something for you for practically nothing. Then you can either type in song titles on ready-made cassette labels and J-cards, or you can have them do it for you. You will probably be pitching the same songs to lots of different people, so you can get them made in bulk. Do not ever submit anything that is handwritten. It will not get listened to.

Betsy Meryl Hammer

Example: Artist's CD Demo
The possibilities are endless for graphics and information contained on a CD insert. Here is one idea for a simple basic design.

THE ARTIST'S DEMO

Your artist demo must be the best that you can possibly afford. The final demo will have to be produced on a CD—cassettes won't do for an artist's demo. You are going to need a professionally produced CD of master quality. If you are a really great writer and artist, you should try to get a producer or publisher to put up money to produce you in exchange for the publishing on your songs. That would be the most ideal situation. The next best thing would be to spend your money (or your investor's money) on the best producer you can afford. Following is a list of some of Nashville's best.

NASHVILLE'S TOP PRODUCERS

Brown Bannister
RBI Productions
P.O. Box 1569
Goodlettsville, TN 37070
Tel. (615) 327-1245
Fax (615) 859-7284
E-mail: *dugout56@aol.com*
        Credits: Steven Curtis Chapman, Amy Grant.

Barry Beckett
BTM Records
33 Music Square West, #106A
Nashville, TN 37203
Tel. (615) 742-0900
Fax (615) 742-4803
E-mail: *btmrecords@aol.com*
    Credits: Lynyrd Skynyrd, Etta James, Vern Gosdin, Neal McCoy.

David Briggs
House of David Recording Studio
1203 16th Avenue South
Nashville, TN 37212
Tel. (615) 320-7323
Fax (615) 329-1304
    Writer, arranger, producer, and musician—played keyboards for Elvis.

Tony Brown
MCA Nashville (Universal)
60 Music Square East
Nashville, TN 37203
Tel. (615) 244-8944
Fax (615) 880-7447
    Entertainment Weekly named him one of the one hundred most powerful people in entertainment.

Steve Buckingham
Vanguard Records
P.O. Box 159159
Nashville, TN 37215
Tel. (615) 297-2588
Fax (615) 297-2510
    Two-time Grammy winner.

Buddy Cannon
Bud Ro Productions
1706 Grand Avenue
Nashville, TN 37212
Tel. (615) 320-4880
Fax (615) 320-4883
E-mail: *bud_ro@hotmail.com*

Producer, songwriter, publisher, background vocalist, band member, and six-year label executive for Mercury Records.

Buzz Cason
Southern Writers Group Creative Workshop
2804 Azalea Place
Nashville, TN 37204
Tel. (615) 383-8682
Fax (615) 838-8696
E-mail: *bcason@musicnashville.com*
Songwriter and producer; recent releases include artists U2, Gloria Estefan, River Road, and Gary Allen.

Don Cook
DKC Music/Sony/ATV Tree
8 Music Square West
Nashville, TN 37203
Tel. (615) 726-8300
Fax (615) 244-6387
Web site: *www.treepublishing.com*
Produces Brooks & Dunn, Alabama, Joe Diffie, and The Mavericks, to name just a few.

Dino Elefante
The Sound Kitchen
112 Seaboard Lane
Franklin, TN 37067
Tel. (615) 370-5773
Fax (615) 370-1712
Dino Elefante owns the Sound Kitchen recording studio and produces Petra.

Garth Fundis
Sound Emporium
3100 Belmont Boulevard
Nashville, TN 37212
Tel. (615) 383-1982
Fax (615) 383-1919
Web site: *www.members.aol.com/semporium*
Fundis owns Sound Emporium recording studio and has produced Trisha Yearwood and Don Williams, among many others.

Byron Gallimore
Song Garden Publishing
25 Music Square East
Nashville, TN 37203
Tel. (615) 244-8950
Fax (615) 244-4711
    Publisher and producer of Tim McGraw, Faith Hill, and many other top recording artists.

Emory Gordy, Jr.
Independent Producer
Tel. (615) 646-9731
    Songwriter and producer of several country artists, including his wife, Patty Loveless.

Scott Hendricks
Virgin Records Nashville
48 Music Square East
Nashville, TN 37203
Tel. (615) 251-1100
Fax (615) 313-3700
    Scott Hendricks formed Virgin Records Nashville for EMI; has produced over forty Number One records and over a dozen platinum-plus albums.

Chuck Howard
Kinetic Diamond Music
E-mail: *vistario@home.com*
    Chuck Howard is publisher and producer for LeAnn Rimes, Hank Williams, Jr., and Trini Triggs.

Dann Huff
Independent Producer
Tel. (615) 377-8028
    Top session guitarist and producer for Faith Hill, Bryan White, and other top country artists.

Doug Johnson
Giant Records Nashville
1514 South Street
Nashville, TN 37212
Tel. (615) 256-3110
Fax (615) 256-9395
    Johnson is president of Giant Records and producer of numerous hit artists.

Kyle Lehning

Independent Producer
Tel. (615) 269-9559
Fax (615) 269-4901

Produces Bryan White, Dan Seals, and Randy Travis, to name a few.

Josh Leo

Warner Chappell Music
21 Music Square East
Nashville, TN 37203
Tel. (615) 254-8777
Fax (615) 726-1353

Leo is a songwriter, guitarist, producer, and former label executive with RCA.

Brent Maher

Moraine Music Group
2803 Bransford Avenue
Nashville, TN 37204
Tel. (615) 383-0400
Fax (615) 383-2375

Maher is a songwriter, publisher, and producer of many artists, including the Judds.

David Malloy

Starstruck Entertainment
40 Music Square West
Nashville, TN 37212
Tel. (615) 259-0001
Fax (615) 259-5298

Malloy is VP, A&R, and producer for Starstruck Entertainment, Reba McEntire's multifaceted company.

Patrick A. McMakin

Sony/ATV Tree
8 Music Square West
Nashville, TN 37203
Tel. (615) 726-8300
Fax (615) 244-6387
E-mail: *Pat-McMakin@sonymusic.com*

McMakin is in charge of artist development at Sony/ATV Tree, and helped launch the careers of Aaron Tippin and David Kersh.

Jozef Nuyens
The Castle Recording Studios
1393 Old Hillsboro Road
Franklin, TN 37069
Tel. (615) 791-0810
Fax (615) 791-1324
    Nuyens is the owner of Castle Recording Studios and produces rock, pop, R&B, and country acts BR5-49 and Jason and the Scorchers.

Michael Omartian
Omartian Productions
P.O. Box 3608
Brentwood, TN 37024
Tel. (615) 371-1254
Fax (615) 377-8422
    Produces Vince Gill, Donna Summer, and many others.

Warren Peterson
Javelina Recording Studio
P.O. Box 120662
Nashville, TN 37212
Tel. (615) 242-3493
Fax (615) 777-3496
    Warren Peterson is publisher, producer, and owner of Javelina Recording Studios.

Allen Reynolds
Jack's Tracks Recording Studio
1308 16th Avenue South
Nashville, TN 37212
Tel. (615) 385-2555
Fax (615) 385-2611
    Reynolds owns Jack's Tracks and produces Garth Brooks.

Randy Scruggs
McLachlan-Scruggs International
2821 Bransford Avenue
Nashville, TN 37204
Tel. (615) 292-0099
Fax (615) 385-4013
    Scruggs is an artist, writer, musician, and producer. He produced the late great Keith Whitley, among others.

Ed Seay
The Money Pit Recording Studio
622 Hamilton Avenue
Nashville, TN 37203
Tel. (615) 256-0311
    Seay is the engineer for the Money Pit, and produces several country artists, including Sherrié Austin.

Anthony Smith
Notes to Music/Words to Music
118 16th Avenue South, Suite #268
Nashville, TN 37203
Tel. (615) 255-0360
Fax (615) 758-7786
    Smith coproduces Trini Triggs and SouthSixtyFive; also hit songwriter and arranger.

Keith Stegall
Mercury Nashville
66 Music Square West
Nashville, TN 37203
Tel. (615) 320-0110
Fax (615) 320-9442
Web site: *www.songnet.com/stegall/*
    Stegall is an artist, songwriter, and producer. Producing credits include George Jones, Alan Jackson, Billy Ray Cyrus, and many other hit recording artists.

James Stroud
DreamWorks Records Nashville
1516 16th Avenue South
Nashville, TN 37212
Tel. (615) 463-4600
Fax (615) 463-4615
    Stroud is the head of DreamWorks Records Nashville and produces Clint Black, Tim McGraw, and Randy Travis.

Billy Joe Walker, Jr.
Billy Joe Walker, Jr. Productions
914 18th Avenue South
Nashville, TN 37212
Tel. (615) 321-0902
Fax (615) 327-3395
    Top session guitarist and producer of Tracy Byrd, Travis Tritt, and others.

Norro Wilson
Bud Ro Productions
1706 Grand Avenue
Nashville, TN 37212
Tel. (615) 320-4880
Fax (615) 320-4883
E-mail: *bud_ro@hotmail.com*
    Wilson has won thirty-nine BMI awards as a writer, and twenty-seven Number One awards as a producer, for acts like John Anderson, Gary Morris, and Mickey Gilley.

Paul Worley
Independent Producer
1108 16th Avenue South
Nashville, TN 37212
Tel. (615) 255-7033
Fax (615) 255-7544
    Noted Nashville producer, former head of Sony Music. Currently produces the Dixie Chicks.

Mark Wright
MCA Nashville (Universal)
60 Music Square East
Nashville, TN 37203
Tel. (615) 244-8944
Fax (615) 880-7447
Web site: *www.mcanashville.com*
    Wright is a hit songwriter and producer and Senior VP of A&R for MCA Nashville.

THE ARTIST'S PACKAGE

An artist's package consists of a CD, 8″ × 10″ glossy, and bio. The more simply these materials are put together, the better. Record label reps and producers will be looking for the quality of these items, not the packaging. The very best presentation is all three inserted in a 9″ × 12″ envelope. The envelope should have a label with the same graphic design as the CD and bio. A consistent, professional look to everything is very important.

    Realistically, those three items will be easily separated, so the next best package is a folder with a slot on both sides. When opened, your CD will be on one side and the bio and photo on the other. There is usually a little slot to put a business card as well. This folder will then fit into a 10″ × 13″ envelope with matching label. You don't have to print fancy folders or have anything written on the folder itself. Remember that simplicity is the key.

Stay away from fancy and expensive plastic folders. There are all kinds of packages with a little slot for a cassette or video, or whatever. You are better off not using this kind of package. The professionals don't use them, so neither should you.

12

Establishing Contact Before Your Trip

Besides learning as much as you possibly can about the music industry in general, there is a lot you can do to learn as much about the Nashville music industry in particular. The more you learn before your trip, the more successful your trip will be. It is very important to do your homework *before* you go to Nashville. Although your first trip should be regarded as a learning experience, Nashville is *not* the place to learn about the music industry. You don't want to waste a publisher's time (and your own) asking him what he does, how you are going to earn money for your songs, etc. Likewise, a producer and record company executive do not want to waste their time with someone they have to educate. That is the music industry's biggest pet peeve. They especially get upset if you come in pitching a song for someone who doesn't even have a record deal anymore, or even worse, has passed away! Don't laugh, it happens all the time. Prepare yourself ahead of time.

SUBSCRIBE TO MUSIC ROW PUBLICATIONS

If you haven't done so already as recommended in chapter 2, subscribe to *Music Row* magazine. The bible of the Nashville music industry, this publication contains information about everything that's going on in minute detail. In addition to news about Nashville, this biweekly also includes in its issues several comprehensive directories on various topics. These are very important directories that will provide an update to the listings in the back of this book. As you can imagine, people move around frequently in this business, and *Music Row* magazine will be the best and most economical way to keep current. For example:

- **June** issue contains the "Annual Music Row Awards," which analyze the Top Fifty country albums in a one-year period, and tell you the names of the session musicians who played on these albums.
- **July** issue is the "Studio Report," which lists the top studios and tells you a little about their equipment and the artists who record there.
- **September** issue publishes the "Artist Roster Report," which lists the A&R, management, booking and publicity contacts for Nashville artists.
- **November** issue lists music publishers in its "Publisher Special."
- **April** issue—the most important issue—is "In Charge," which is a listing of Nashville's top decision makers. It includes a picture and brief bio of the person, along with a contact address and phone and fax numbers. Since "In Charge" comes out in April, and you may subscribe to *Music Row* magazine after that and won't receive this issue for some time, go ahead and request a copy in addition to your subscription. It will cost extra, but is well worth the money.

As was mentioned in chapter 6, *Music Row* also publishes a tip sheet called *Row Fax,* which is a gossip column that tells you every little thing that happened on Music Row in a one-week period. If you did nothing else but start your own personal database with the people who are mentioned in *Row Fax* each week, you would soon have a very comprehensive directory of Music Row decision makers. *Row Fax* may be more than you need to know, and more than you need to spend right now, but you might want to go ahead and subscribe for three months or so just to get a feeling for what goes on in Nashville. Everyone on Music Row subscribes to *Row Fax,* and everyone discusses its contents in their staff meeting on Monday morning. There are no secrets in Nashville, by the way. That's one reason your music is sure to be discovered if you are truly a great writer, artist, or musician.

About Demo Critiques

It is imperative that you have a Music Row professional critique your songs before you come to Nashville. There are only a couple of options available for this purpose; the performing rights organizations and the songwriters organizations. This is a review of information covered in previous chapters, but just in case you missed it, here it is.

Performing Rights Organizations

BMI will probably be the most open to accepting your demo tape through the mail. It has what it calls "an open-door policy," which means that BMI will make an appointment with you if you call in advance, and someone will listen to your tape. The challenge for you will be in getting through to an individual, and not just BMI in general. You've got to glean some information out of the receptionist. Ask to talk to a writers' representative, and be sure to get his or her name so if your call doesn't get through the first time, you can ask by name the next time you call.

ASCAP prefers to have writers go to its weekly "Straight Talk" session before they start making appointments and listening to demos. But you might get lucky and get to talk with a writers' representative. It's definitely worth spending some time to try to get someone to say "yes, send that tape!" SESAC needs a referral from a writer or publisher affiliate, or some other professional in the industry.

NSAI has a song critique service, but you have to be a member to be able to use it. You really should go ahead and join, and plan your trip to Nashville around one of NSAI's seminars or events. It has several during the year. The critique you receive from NSAI will be right on target. You can trust what the staff tells you. SGA staff doesn't critique songs. TSAI might, if you can talk them into it. They have a volunteer staff, so their time is limited.

Before you go to Nashville publishers, you will want to have had your demo critiqued by as many other professionals as possible. You really don't want a critique from a publisher—you want a song contract! Unfortunately, if a publisher agrees to listen to your song, he gets to give you his opinion of your song. Once you start playing your songs for publishers, you will get a myriad of differing opinions. That's why it's best to get as many professional opinions from nonpublishers as you can before you start playing your songs for publishers.

STUDY THE TRADES

The "Trades" are three weekly magazines that chart the progress of country song singles. They are *Billboard's Country Airplay Monitor, Radio & Records (R&R),* and *Gavin. R&R* was the preferred chart for the Nashville record labels for the past decade, but BDS technology finally won out, and the industry shifted over to *Billboard,* which uses the BDS watermarking system. *Gavin* is used by the industry to chart Americana and alternative country music. When someone says to you, "study the trades," what he really means is that you need to know who the current artists are, what label they are on, and what their current single is. You certainly should be familiar with all the Number One songs for the past year or so. The trades are the easiest place to find this information all in one place. The trades will tell you who the Top One Hundred recording artists are. *Billboard* goes even further and tells you who wrote their current single, who produced it, and who publishes it.

The reason it is imperative for you to have this information is that Music Row thinks in terms of what's hot right now. Nashville songwriters write songs specifically for current country artists—songs that are similar to the artist's other hit singles. The country music industry is constantly criticized for producing product that all sounds the same. It is this method of doing things that causes this phenomenon. Although the labels and producers talk about the need to make some big changes, change will come slowly if at all. There are a lot of people involved in this process who will have to make the same changes.

There are a lot of great country artists that aren't on a major label, artists like Vern Gosdin, Gene Watson, John Anderson, Earl Thomas Conley, Johnny Cash, Loretta Lynn. If you have written a song that fits one of these artists, then you need to know where to take it, and it won't be to a major record label or producer. There is no such thing as writing a great country song and playing it for everyone and letting them decide who should record it. Songs are written for specific artists and pitched to the specific people who work with that artist, only at the specific time they are looking for songs. It's a highly specialized process, which you will learn a little bit about from the trades and tip sheets.

STUDY CD LABEL COPY

What you *really* need to do is buy the CDs of the current country artists and study them inside and out. The label copy, everything written about a CD, will give you lots of valuable information. There is a connection between everyone mentioned in the label copy, so you need to know who all these people are, especially the songwriters, publishers, and producer(s). It is a sad fact, but your songs need to sound like the songs on these CDs. The challenge is to write something just like these songs, only original! Somehow the top Nashville songwriters are able to do that.

The most important information on the CD label copy is the publishers listed. That's where you are going to get the information you need to call a Nashville publisher and get an appointment with him. Now you know some very specific information about each of the publishers listed: what writers they represent, what songs they publish, and which artists they have a close personal relationship with. You can use this information to your advantage when you call to get an appointment. You can also use this information to add to your own personal database directory. Now you not only know who the top decision makers are in Nashville, you also know how you relate to the product they are marketing. You probably won't be crazy about all of the songs on the album—you may have written songs that are better. But you now have a reference point to work from.

About Making Appointments

Your very first appointments should be with the PROs. It won't be necessary to make appointments with the songwriters organizations. Their weekly workshops are open to everyone, so you just have to show up. You can drop in anytime at NSAI; someone is always available to help you. Plus, they have lots of office facilities at your disposal, so you can make some phone calls while you are there.

You might have a hard time making an appointment with a writers' representative at ASCAP, because they provide a weekly "Straight Talk" session for new writers, which they will refer you to on your first trip to Nashville. BMI will make an appointment; you just have to ask. They also have a monthly BMI Roundtable. You may want to schedule your trip around this workshop, because it is the first in a series of workshops you can attend. SESAC requires a referral, but you still might stop by their offices when you are in town. It's worth a try.

Once you've had your songs evaluated by a writers' rep at one or more of the PROs, and/or some other Music Row professional, and they've given you some pretty positive feedback, then you are ready to contact the publishers. Here's your target list:

- **Publishers you've researched from the trades and CD label copy.** You now know a lot about these publishers now. Remember: There are a lot of staff members at these companies—professional manager, creative director, and song pluggers. You can get their names out of "In Charge" and the *Music Row* "Publisher Special."
- **Nashville's Independent Music Publishers.** In chapter 5, there is some information about Nashville's independent music publishers. There is more information about them in "In Charge." Research as much as you can before you call. Tell them where you are from and that you will only be in town one week—this is your only chance to see them. It might work, as they are always looking for writers outside of Nashville. Also, be sure and drop the names of the people who critiqued your demo. That will help to get an appointment.

That should be enough to keep you busy for months trying to get an appointment with a publisher. This might be easier than you think, and is very, very important. The key to success in Nashville for songwriters and aspiring artists lies with the publishers. It is a little-known fact that publishers are the most important link in the chain. Publishers have direct contact with the artists, record companies, producers, and artist managers—as well as all other publishers and their staff songwriters. They know when an artist is recording and what kind of material he is looking for, and they relay this information to their staff writers. So, while evenings should be spent at writers' nights (meeting other writers, hopefully), days should be spent in publishers' offices—or trying to get in to see a publisher.

Since you have carefully prepared for your trip, you have with you a target list of publishers to call on. You know some of the songs they publish, a little of the history of the company, and you have a vague idea what they look like (you saw them in a magazine or at a writers' night). Now you are ready to hang out on Music Row.

The sign at the publisher's door says "No Unsolicited Material." That's OK. Go on in. Chat with the receptionist, get her name, tell her who you are, stall, stall, stall. You are basically just hanging around as long as you can in the hopes you will run into someone you recognize. The chances of running into someone you saw or met at a writers' night is very good. Plan on it . . . be prepared. Have a cassette tape or CD ready to give to someone you can make a personal contact with. People are not taken aback when you hand them a tape or CD. It's almost expected. Everyone does it. That's what Nashville is all about. There are tapes and CDs everywhere. You might even be able to leave one on the receptionist's desk, or maybe you can talk her into taking it.

Publishers do not accept unsolicited material for many good reasons. The one they emphasize the most is the fear of unwarranted lawsuits, songwriters who think their idea was stolen. Ideas and song titles are not protected by copyright. The truth is, publishers are bombarded with enough material from the people they know and do business with on a daily basis. They don't need outside material. And ninety-nine percent of unsolicited material is really poor quality. So, even if there is a gem in there somewhere, it's not worth taking the time to look for it.

Finding a Nashville publisher to represent your songs should be your first priority, way before pitching to record companies, producers, or artist managers. Nashville publishers are the pulse of the Nashville music industry. They are closely associated with the record companies, have their own artist production companies, and work closely with artist management. Publishers can also advance a musician's career, through songwriter demos and artist development projects. Careful study of Nashville publishers will be well worth the effort. The more you know about a publisher, the better your chances of getting an appointment.

13

When To Go:
Important Industry
Events Month by Month

ere is a month-by-month guide to what's happening in Nashville. Once upon a time you could set your calendar by events on Music Row. That's no longer the case. If you want to attend any of the cool events described below, be sure to call first and check on the dates.

January
It would probably be a good idea to avoid this month altogether. The industry pretty much shuts down during the holidays, so people are just getting back from a long vacation. It's also a time when songwriters have made a new determination to get their songs heard, so publishers and producers get an exceptional number of calls this month.

February
By now most songwriters have forgotten about their New Year's resolutions and have quit blitzing publishers with calls—the publishers are concentrating on songs because the artists are in the studios. This is a high-activity time. Producers and artists are looking for material to take into the studio, and publishers are pitching songs and looking for new songs also. The only drawback for both January and February is the weather. It only snows occasionally in Nashville, but when it does, the town shuts down. The city has limited snow removal equipment, so businesses usually close when the weather report even hints at snow. Music Row, known to be efficient, punctual, and reliable, suddenly becomes undependable. However, if you

are comfortable maneuvering in the snow and can be flexible about finding something else to do with your time if your schedule gets disrupted, February is an excellent month to get things accomplished.

There is a very special event in February called the Nashville Music Awards. Everyone in town attends, and many celebrated guests from out of town as well. It is an awards show honoring artists, musicians, and writers who reside in Nashville. Recipients are nominated by their peers and voted in by the community. The show features several live performances from all genres of music. Only a small portion of the show and awards presentations is dedicated to country music.

The Grammy Awards Show also takes place in February, usually in the second week. Since the Grammys are usually held in Los Angeles or New York, the entire Nashville music industry will be out of town for a week during the awards, which also hosts many nightly industry events. Check to see when it is before you plan your trip to Nashville.

March

A great month to come to Nashville including ideal weather. There are two major events you should plan to attend, according to your own interests: the Country Radio Seminar (CRS) and Tin Pan South. CRS was formerly called DJ Week and was held during the week of the CMA Awards Show. All the artists attend the event to meet with visiting radio air personalities and programmers, and to record radio spots ("Hi, this is Reba McEntire, and my favorite radio station is . . . "). During the day, there are in-depth panel discussions on every topic deemed important to country music, and at night, there are label shows in the clubs downtown. There is a New Faces Show for the labels to introduce their hot new artists, and a Super Faces Show showcasing one of the industry's superstars.

Named after New York's songwriting district, Tin Pan Alley, Tin Pan South is a weeklong celebration of Nashville's most important citizen—the songwriter. There are seminars and panel discussions connected to the event, as well as a golf tournament and a Legendary Songwriter Show. No songwriter should miss it.

April

Great month to come to Nashville. February, March, September, and October are the busiest months, when artists and producers are in the studios recording their next album projects. Publishers are hustling to get songs to them at the last minute, and that is very often the time new songs are picked up. Although it's good to be involved in this activity, you are not likely to get much personal attention during those months. April and May are the ideal months for songwriters to approach publishers. There is still a lot of recording activity going on; publishers have exhausted their catalogs and are receptive to new material; everyone has more time available.

Tennis, anyone? Music Row hosts a tennis tournament the last weekend of April and first weekend of May. The purpose of the tournament is to provide networking opportunities for writers and industry executives and to raise a little money for Vanderbilt Children's Hospital. It's lots of fun and so popular many players come from out of state year after year. If interested, call (615) 322-7450.

May

Another great month to visit, but check first to see when the Academy of Country Music (ACM) Awards Show is held in Los Angeles. The show is on a Wednesday night, but you don't want to plan a trip to Nashville during that entire week, because everybody will be in Los Angeles! The HoriPro Golf Tournament takes place the Monday and Tuesday after Mother's Day—the golf course is literally strewn with every top music industry professional from Music Row, including Bob Beckham himself, president of HoriPro Entertainment Group.

June

By June, recording activity has really wound down, as the artists go out on tours. June is a great time to come to town to meet with publishers, except for Fan Fair Week. Fan Fair is a huge country music festival produced by the CMA, which gives 25,000 fans the opportunity to meet and have their "picture made" (as they say in the South) with their favorite stars. Each label gives a great show featuring several artists from their roster. It's a good opportunity for you to meet the new artists and get a real feel for what they are like, but you won't be able to pitch them any songs. They have reserved this time for their fans, not songwriters. Pitching a song would be out of place. It's also not a good time to try to set up appointments, because everyone, including publishers and the staff of PROs and the songwriting organizations, is at Fan Fair all day long. Record company executives work twenty-four–hour days during this week, planning their record label show, escorting and entertaining artists who are in town for the event, and trying to keep up with their regular duties. Don't even think about calling a record label this week!

July and August

A good time to concentrate on developing a relationship with publishers. Artists are on the road, recording schedules are very light, and there is very little pressure on anybody. No one moves too fast during these months. Temperatures are in the high nineties, with the humidity the same. Frequent summer showers are welcome to cool things off. Vince Gill's very popular golf tournament, the Vinnie, takes place during the first week of August. Check it out at *www.thevinnie.com*.

September

Things start to get serious after Labor Day. Artists are back in the studio, producers are looking for material, and publishers are hustling to get songs recorded and to sign new songs. It's a great month to come to Nashville. Towards the end of the month, CMA Week completely dominates the industry. It is a weeklong celebration of country music centering around the nationally televised CMA Awards Show. There are five black tie events, where the men wear the same tuxedo every night, and the women wear five different spectacular evening gowns. Starting Sunday night, it's the NSAI Songwriters Awards Dinner, followed by nightly awards banquets hosted by ASCAP, BMI, and SESAC. The PROs honor their songwriter and publisher affiliates and members who had the most radio airplay during a one-year period. The CMA Awards Show is centered in the middle, on Wednesday night.

That's just the beginning. Every night after the awards banquets, several publishers have private parties to honor their writers. After the CMA Awards Show, all of the record labels have private parties in honor of their artists who won awards or were performers on the show. And since all of these parties are by invitation only, the T.J. Martell Foundation sponsors events which you can attend simply by buying a ticket. Since so many people in the industry are not on the banquet guest lists (for award winners only), there are lots of folks who want to have fun, too. T.J. Martell offers a tennis tournament, golf tournament, bowling tournament, silent auction, and celebrity concert. Proceeds go to cancer and AIDS research. You might want to come to town during this time and join in the fun, but chances of getting much work done are slim.

October and November

Heavy studio months. It's a great time to come to Nashville—there is a lot of activity going on with writer showcases, parties, events. Everyone is focused on work and getting lots accomplished.

December

After Thanksgiving things really begin to slow down. There are holiday parties and many other distractions that start interfering with the song process. The business turns to year-end budgets and other housekeeping duties. Most record companies are closed for at least two weeks or more, and many publishers follow suit. Although some publishers may stay in town to get things done, finding someone to take an appointment may be difficult. Best to wait until next year.

14

The Logistics
of Your Visit

fter you have recorded your work tape, picked your travel dates, and decided what your goals are, you still have to work out the practical details of your trip. Once you make up your mind to go to Nashville, you won't want to be thwarted because you inadvertently brought the wrong clothes, or booked a hotel room in the middle of nowhere.

WHAT TO BRING

- Guitar. If you compose songs using a guitar, then you will certainly want to have yours with you. As you will see when you attend your first open mic night, songwriters perform at all stages of ability. If you can perform your own songs with a certain agility, then you don't have to have a great voice or be able to hit all the high notes.
- Boom Box
- *Music Row*'s "In Charge" and this book (of course!). You'll want to have "In Charge" with you to refer to constantly. You will run into people who will mention someone you are not familiar with. You can look them up.
- Personalized stationery and envelopes, lots of business cards, post-cards with your picture or logo on one side, blank on the other, and stamps. You never know when you might need to confirm some business agreement in writing, so bring stationery and envelopes

just in case. Hopefully, you will be able to book yourself at a song-writers' night or open mic night with enough notice to send out invitations. Use your postcards for that. You can handwrite a few to key Music Row executives (get addresses from "In Charge"), or you could get a

- Set of mailing labels. You might get booked on a really great show, and you will then want to do a big mass mailing to the industry. You can get your blank postcards printed while you wait, stick on the labels and drop them in the mail. The industry people will get them the next day, and yes, they do pay attention to this type of invitation. It can be a simple invitation on an $8\frac{1}{2}'' \times 11''$ piece of paper, folded once or twice, if you didn't make up postcards. But don't stick an invitation to a showcase inside an envelope. Chances are slim it would be opened.

- Portable PC. Are you proficient with e-mail? At the printing of this book, e-mail is just catching on in Nashville, and most top executives, producers, and A&R reps don't communicate through e-mail, except internally in their company. Don't plan to use this means of communication as your primary source, only as a backup and to create intrigue for your showcase. Make sure any e-mail invitation to your showcase looks like personal correspondence, and not spam. Fax communication is very popular in Nashville; publicists usually send out a day-of reminder for showcases and parties. But that's hard to do on a portable PC, unless you are staying someplace that has a direct line out.

- Umbrella. It rains a lot in Nashville, and you'll be glad of it in the summertime, when the humidity is one hundred percent!

- Antihistamine and allergy medicine. Nashville is hard on those who suffer from allergies, and even might bother some who don't usually react to pollen. There are lots of beautiful things growing here that generate fuzzy and airborne by-products.

WHAT TO WEAR

Every day is casual day on Music Row. Even the top executives wear jeans with a nice dress shirt and sport coat. It's OK to go without a tie. The best advice is to dress in your favorite clothes, the ones that make you feel and look great. Stay away from Western gear unless that's your regular clothes and the ones you are most comfortable in. You won't see many cowboy hats on Music Row, except for the aspiring artists hoping to attract attention, but you will see people wearing cowboy boots or tennis shoes.

You'll need an overcoat mid-October through mid-March; temperatures hover near 30° during the winter. In the summer, temperatures stay around 80° to 90°, but the humidity makes it feel like 180! You'll be grateful every time you step into an air-conditioned room. Spring and fall only last for a minute or two.

You'll be doing a lot of walking, so bring some really comfortable shoes. Save pretty heels or dress shoes for writers' nights and you might get lucky and get invited to one of the many Music Row parties. You can spiff up then with some special accessory. But don't plan on anything too dressy.

TRANSPORTATION

Almost everything on Music Row is located in a small area, and there are medium-priced hotels and motels nearby. Unfortunately, nothing is really within walking distance; the Row itself is fairly stretched out, with long blocks and long distances between companies. Plan to rent a car; then plan to park that car a good distance away from where you want to go. You'll probably stay within a few miles of the Row, drive to the Row and park your car, then walk to many of the places you want to go to. There is no public transportation to speak of, and taxis are more or less used to get to the airport and back, and that's about it.

If you absolutely can't drive or rent a car, you will still be able to stay fairly close to the Row and walk to most of the places you need to go to. Just be prepared to have to deal with the weather. If this is your only option, then plan your visit for April or October, towards the first of the month. That's the prettiest time in Nashville anyway, and the most pleasant weather. You just can't count on the nice weather lasting very long.

Even if you do rent a car, you won't have to do much driving. You will probably get by with less than a tank of gas, so rent accordingly.

WHERE TO STAY

It's not going to cost an arm and a leg to stay a week in Nashville, if you are not picky about your accommodations. There are even places listed in the Classified section of the *Tennessean* for $55 per week! Sounds too good to be true and probably is, but even the range of $100 to $150 is pretty reasonable. Occasionally something in that range becomes available right on Music Row. As soon as you know when you'll be coming, get a copy of the *Tennessean* from a bookstore that carries out-of-state newspapers, or contact the *Tennessean* at *www.tennessean.com*. Most accommodations in this price range will be in the airport, Dickerson Road, Madison, or Gallatin areas. These areas are not near Music Row. With traffic, they are probably thirty to forty-five minutes away, with the airport area being the closest.

There are very nice medium-priced hotels and motels almost within walking distance from Music Row, but not quite—depending on your stamina and the weather.

Shoney's Inn
I-40 & Demonbreun
Tel. (615) 255-9977/(800) 222-2222
$79 per night—no weekly rates
Shoney's is a chain of motels and restaurants—this one is just a few blocks from Music Row.

Courtyard by Marriott
19th Avenue South & West End Boulevard
Nashville, TN
(800) 321-2211
$92 per night—no weekly rates
Very close to Music Row.

Guesthouse Inn & Suites/Medcenter
1909 Hayes Street
Nashville, TN
Tel. (615) 329-1000
$72 per night—no weekly rates
Guesthouse has special rates for people in town for outpatient medical treatment. It is a little off the beaten path but not too far away—and has a free shuttle to Music Row.

Days Inn-Vanderbilt-Music Row
1800 West End Avenue
Nashville, TN
Tel. (615) 327-0922
$59.95 per night—no weekly rates

Quality Inn Hall of Fame
1407 Division Street
Nashville, TN
Tel. (615) 242-1631/(800) 451-9202
$44.95 for a minimum of 7 nights—$59.95 per night
The closest motel to Music Row; also the oldest.

The Spence Manor
11 Music Square East
Nashville, TN
Tel. (615) 259-4400
$450 for 7 days; $1,650 per month; negotiable

Built on Music Row expressly for the privacy of the music industry—has a guitar-shaped swimming pool and large apartment suites.

Loews Vanderbilt Plaza Hotel
2100 West End Avenue
Nashville, TN
Tel. (615) 320-1700
$199 per night—does have special rates around Holidays and other occasions for around $100 per night

The Vanderbilt Plaza, as it is known, is where all the music industry executives stay when they come to town. It's down the street at 21st Avenue South and West End Avenue. It's not necessary to stay here to impress anyone or, hopefully, run into anyone.

Other Less Expensive Areas

You might save a little money if you stay further out from Music Row and Downtown Nashville; stick to the airport area, Murfreesboro Road area, or Nolensville Road–Harding Mall area. They are each about twenty minutes away from Music Row and aren't bad neighborhoods. The EconoLodge on Murfreesboro Road has weekly rates of $150 for a seven-night minimum, or $40 per day during the week and $45 per day during the weekend—call (615) 361-6830.

You can search Nashville Yellow Pages for other motels in these areas online at *www.yp.bellsouth.com*.

15

Your One-Week Itinerary

The following is an *imaginary* one-week schedule. Actually, one week would be a pretty long time. If you need to narrow it down, the best time would be to arrive Monday afternoon, work hard Tuesday, Wednesday, and Thursday, and then leave Friday afternoon. The most important songwriters' showcases, the ones featuring hit Nashville songwriters, are on Wednesday or Thursday nights. There's not much happening on weekends, except for the Bluebird Cafe Sunday night shows.

GENERAL GUIDELINES

This is a general guideline, and it's not recommended that you strictly adhere to this schedule. You might meet a great writer and wind up doing nothing else but writing a hit song on your trip. This itinerary is simply to give you an idea of some of the things you might consider doing while you are in Nashville—the primary purpose of this schedule is to get you out of your hotel room and on Music Row where you will get more accomplished!

It really doesn't matter whether you arrive on Sunday or Wednesday or whenever. But some of the things included on this one-week itinerary are very important. They are:

- **Obtain a copy of the *Nashville Scene* and the *Tennessean.*** The *Nashville Scene (www.nashvillescene.com)* is a weekly alternative newspaper which is available free at area restaurants and stores. It comes out on Thursdays, so if you arrive on Sunday or Monday, you may have trouble finding a copy. You can always get one at their office, 2120 8th Avenue South, Nashville, TN 37204-2204. If you are seriously considering a move to Nashville, you may want to subscribe to the *Scene.* It will give you an in-depth view of current issues affecting the city. The *Nashville Scene* has a comprehensive music section and lists the addresses and phone numbers for all the music clubs, providing detailed information about open mic nights, writers' nights, and showcases. There is very little coverage on country music since it is not a part of the live music scene in Nashville, but you should check out all the clubs for songwriters' nights and you will need the addresses as well. The *Nashville Scene* will be very helpful to you.

  While you are in Nashville, you will also want to get a copy of the daily newspaper, the *Tennessean (www.tennessean.com)*. They have regular feature articles on country artists, the Music Row business community, anything and everything affecting the country music industry in Nashville. They also have a daily preview of what's happening on the live music scene that evening, with recommendations of what to see. Like the *Nashville Scene,* the *Tennessean* publishes a list of clubs with addresses and phone numbers on Thursdays, in their "Weekend" section. But you'll want to pick up a copy of the *Tennessean* every day, to read their previews of what's happening that night.

  In addition, on Wednesdays, the *Tennessean* publishes a free guide to what's going on through the next ten days, available wherever you can find the *Scene.* "OnNashville" contains reprints of feature articles from their regular newspaper, plus more.
- **Attend a writers' night every night.** And try to get to more than one if possible. Some start at 6 P.M., and others start at 9:30 P.M.— so you can go to two per night.
- **Perform at as many open mic nights as possible.** It's the best exposure you can give your songs. As soon as you know what clubs you'll be playing, make up invitations. If you have made postcards with your picture or a striking logo on one side, you can handwrite information on the other side (the only time handwritten materials are permitted!), or have a set run off at one of the instant copier places.
- **Attend the workshops at NSAI, SGA, TSAI, ASCAP, and BMI.** If you do nothing else but attend these workshops, you will make very valuable contacts.

- **Spend at least one day just stopping by the publishing companies, dropping off tapes.** Don't expect to get to see anyone in particular, but get a feel for the offices, get to know the receptionist, try to find out names of the people who work there. Then, when you are back home calling on the phone trying to get permission to send another tape, you'll have a good idea how that office works. Each one is different. Not every company is right for you. Be selective about the companies you approach. Have your tape or CD handy to give to someone if the occasion arises (plus invitations to any open mic nights or writers' nights you book). Don't hesitate to offer your tape to someone.
- **Hang out at area restaurants.** As I mentioned in chapter 10, the people at the bars in Sammy Bs, Sunset Grill, and, on Friday nights at Granite Falls, are all industry people. If you prefer not to drink, then have some juice or bottled water, and strike up a conversation with the folks around you. You may be dying to get a certain song to a specific producer or A&R rep; your chances of running into him at a nearby restaurant are very good. Don't go up to him when he is eating, but look for another opportunity.
- **Set appointment goals.** Try to get an appointment with all three of the PROs, and at least one publisher.
- **Set songwriting goals.** Try to get at least one song started with a cowriter while you are in Nashville. Then you'll have at least one good solid contact in town.

DAY-BY-DAY, HOUR-BY-HOUR SCHEDULE

This is an imaginary schedule, one to use only as a guideline, especially when you are not sure what to do next. The most important item on this itinerary is the open mic nights—that's where your direct competitors are hanging out, and you can get a firsthand look at what you are up against. Your first task will be to get comfortable in this environment. If you can impress this audience, chances are you will impress the rest of Music Row.

Sunday

Arrive in the afternoon; pick up a copy of the *Nashville Scene* and the *Tennessean*. Your hotel might have a copy, or they are found outside most restaurants and markets. Carefully look over all the open mic, writers' nights, and showcases and select the ones you plan to attend. Call and make arrangements to play as many open mic nights as you can. Take a walking tour around Music Row.

Sunday Night

Observe these two important showcases at the Bluebird Cafe

- **6:30 P.M.—Bluebird Cafe Sunday Spotlight.** This show is very special and very different from what you normally see at the Bluebird. This is a mini-artist showcase for qualifying writers and artists and the best opportunity to showcase for writers who are not backed by a Nashville publishing company. Worth checking out.
- **8:00 P.M.—Bluebird Cafe Writers' Night.** The ultimate writers' night. Writers who play this show have gone through a long audition process.

Monday

- **9 A.M.—Breakfast at the Pancake Pantry.** Many Music Row executives have their first meeting of the day at this popular breakfast spot. Afterwards, go around the corner and stop by the Acklen Post Office.
- **10 A.M.—ASCAP.** Sign up for ASCAP's "Straight Talk." See if you can meet with a writers' representative.
- **10:15 A.M.—BMI.** Find out when BMI Roundtable is being held, and sign up if you will still be in town. See if you can meet with a writers' representative. They also have a telephone in the lobby you can use for a limited number of calls.
- **11:00 A.M.—SESAC.** Check in and chat with the receptionist. Ask to speak to a writers' representative.
- **11:30 A.M.—SGA.** Introduce yourself and get SGA's schedule for the week. It may have a workshop this afternoon, or you might be just in time for the noon workshop! SGA has weekly workshops on Mondays, but the time varies between 12 noon, 5 P.M. or 5:30 P.M. Whatever it is this week, sign up!
- **12 noon—Lunch.** Sunset Grill (or SGA workshop)
- **2 to 3 P.M.—Appointments with publishers.** If you don't have any appointments, then just start walking down 17th Avenue, dropping in on the publishers that are on your list. Try to make an appointment but be prepared to leave your tape.
- **3:00 P.M.—Head out to the Bluebird Cafe (thirty minutes driving time).** Get in line to sign up to play the Bluebird Cafe. Sign-ups are from 5:30 to 5:45 P.M.—only fifteen minutes to sign up everybody. They can only take so many, so get there early. The earlier, the better. Take the *Scene* and the *Tennessean* with you; you can study the writers' nights while you are waiting, and discuss other writers' nights and open mic nights with the people in line.

- 6:00 to 9:00 P.M.—**Open Mic Night at the Bluebird Cafe.** (If you have to choose between the Bluebird Cafe Open Mic Night and the SGA workshop, go with SGA. You will have lots of open mic opportunities while you are in town.)

Tuesday
- 9 A.M.—**Breakfast at Noshville.** Another big favorite of Music Row executives.
- 10 A.M. to 12 noon—**Visit NSAI and SGA.** Staffers will take the time to answer your questions about Nashville and the music industry and give you any assistance you may need. Take the time to nurture a working relationship with people in the organization; they may become your very important link to Nashville.
- 12 noon—**Lunch at the Longhorn**
- 2 to 4 P.M.—**Stop by the publishing offices on 16th Avenue South.**
- 4:30 to 6 P.M.—**Happy hour at Sammy Bs**
- 8 P.M.–Douglas Corner Open Mic Night (check newspaper listings)
- 9:30 P.M.—**Attend a writers' night or showcase from the newspaper listings**

Wednesday
- 9 A.M.—**Breakfast at the Pancake Pantry.** Afterwards, stop by the Acklen Post Office again.
- 10 A.M. to 12 noon—**More appointments with PROs, songwriters organizations, and publishers.** Couldn't get any appointments? Then stop by ASCAP, BMI, or SESAC again and see if you can get an appointment with a writers' representative. Be persistent. Don't give up. Make it a goal to meet with someone at each of these companies this week and be sure to attend ASCAP Straight Talk and BMI Roundtable. Make a few calls to publishers from each of these locations.
- 12 noon—**Lunch at Sammy Bs.**
- 2 to 4 P.M.—**Stop by publishing offices and *American Songwriter* offices.**
- 5 to 6 P.M.—**Happy hour at Sunset Grill.**
- 6:30 P.M.—**TSAI Workshop at Belmont University.**
- 9 P.M.—**Songwriters' Night (Check listings).**

Thursday
- 9 A.M.—**Breakfast at Noshville.**
- 10 A.M.—**Call publishers for appointments.** By now you should have a pretty clear idea of whom you would like to meet with while

you are in Nashville. Try to get an appointment, but don't linger by the phone.

- **10:30 A.M. to 12 noon—Still no appointments?** Drop by the offices on 16th Avenue South (Music Square East).
- **12 noon—Lunch at the Longhorn.**
- **2 to 4 P.M.—Still no appointments?** Drop by the offices on 17th Avenue South (Music Square West).
- **5 to 6 P.M.—Happy hour at Sammy Bs**
- **6:30 P.M.—NSAI Workshop, Musicians Union (enter back door)**
- **9 P.M.—Songwriters' Night (check listings)**

Friday

- **10 A.M.—Time to get on the phone!** Spend Friday morning on the phone calling all the contacts you made, thanking them for their help, etc. Nashville is a genuinely friendly city that does business on a personal level. Let them know you appreciate their friendship and will be in touch.
- **12 noon—Leisurely lunch at Sunset Grill.** Music Row relaxes on Friday afternoons, most people taking off early. This would be a great time to cowrite with that new writer you met at an open mic night!
- **5 to 6 P.M.—Happy hour at Granite Falls.** Industry hangs out here on Friday nights.

Saturday

Finish that song. Plan your next trip. Relax and go visit Cheekwood, walk Radnor Lake, and enjoy the rest of Nashville.

16

Common Mistakes

Most people come to Nashville thinking they are going to set the town on fire and things will start happening for them right away. They fall into several different categories:

BIG FISH IN A SMALL POND

Good country singers, songwriters, and musicians who have a big following in their hometowns are surprised at the reaction they get when they come to Nashville. Their music is popular and widely received at home, and everyone is crazy about them! Everyone around them encourages them to take their music to Nashville. Once here, they are thrown into an environment rich with talent. No matter how great they are, they lack the advantage of having personal relationships in the recording studios and publishers' offices. Even though they may be outstanding, it will take a while for the people of Nashville to get to know them, trust them, and take a chance on substituting them for someone they already know can get the job done.

"HOLIER-THAN-THOU" ATTITUDE

People from a major music city such as Los Angeles or New York who have a great track record in other areas of music tend to think that gives them an edge in Nashville. It doesn't. Nashville is a separate entity in itself, and no matter what your success in other areas, everyone is on equal footing in

Nashville. Many songwriters make their move to Nashville when they have a single on the charts. Although that success may open a few doors, it still doesn't change things. It is going to take time for anyone new to Nashville to develop relationships.

DISPLAYING AN ATTITUDE

One of the toughest things about putting yourself on the line and exposing yourself to criticism is that you are going to get an awfully lot of differing opinions from strangers. It's a painful experience and one that doesn't make much sense. Everyone you meet is going to give you different advice. Keeping a cool head and remaining objective about this whole process is very challenging. Try to look upon your first trip as a learning experience. Don't go expecting to impress anyone. And try not to overreact or become defensive. Many a frustrated songwriter has left town in a huff under such duress.

TRYING TO BUY YOUR WAY IN

You would think that your life would be a whole lot easier if you had enough money to help make your dreams come true. But the truth is, lots of money doesn't really help that much, and more often than not it gets in the way. Nashville isn't really impressed with how much money you have, so if you are lucky enough to have a rich uncle or an investor, keep it a secret. There have been many wealthy businessmen who have come into town, set up lavish offices, even built new buildings on Music Row, only to quietly leave town a few years later. An investor's money should be used to hire the very best entertainment attorney as a spokesperson and contract negotiator, to produce a master quality demo (four songs only—a ten-song CD is not necessary) using a top Nashville producer and studio musicians, and to hire a top-notch publicist. An investor should not play a high-profile role in marketing an aspiring artist or musician, but rather remain behind the scenes. Talking about money detracts from the most important topic— your talent!

"SELL" SOME SONGS

"Selling songs" is a common term that is used by people that are not in the music industry and don't understand what a publisher really does. It is not possible to sell a song. When a publisher signs a song to a contract, no money transaction takes place. A publisher never "buys" a song. When you "sell" a song, it's like "selling" your smile or your personality. People can "buy into" your winning smile, but they don't pay for it; they just believe in it. Don't use this term under any circumstances.

SENDING TAPES THROUGH THE MAIL

Please don't take the address listings at the back of this book and mail everyone your CD project. It is a big waste of your time and money. Publishers, producers, and record companies receive hundreds of tapes and CDs in the mail each week. They have different ways of handling these tapes, but for the most part, they don't open the packages and they don't listen to the tapes for the following reasons:

- It is not cost-effective. It takes way too much time to sort through the bad tapes in the hope of finding one good song.
- They have their own source of songs.
- They are afraid of nuisance lawsuits by songwriters who feel their ideas have been stolen.

WRITING FOR PERMISSION TO SUBMIT A TAPE

This is almost as bad as sending in your tape without permission—a waste of time and money. Don't do this. One songwriter sent a clever questionnaire to all of the top music publishers in Nashville. It was very well-written, easy to fill out, and came with an SASE (self-addressed, stamped envelope). She simply wanted to know how they went about selecting songs for their catalog, and would they listen to one of her songs if submitted to their attention. Surprisingly enough, almost all the publishers took the time to fill out the questionnaire but all of them said "no," she couldn't submit material. Only one never answered. But what amazed her the most was that one publisher returned her envelope unopened with a rubber-stamped response on the front saying "No Unsolicited Material." How did they know what her envelope contained? she wondered. Easy. Publishers receive hundreds of letters asking permission to send material. Request letters are very easily spotted and receive negative or no response.

APPROACHING A PUBLISHER INCORRECTLY

Publishers receive a dozen calls a day that go something like this:

"Hello, I'm calling to see if you are accepting unsolicited material at this time."

"Hello, I'm a songwriter and . . ."

"Hello, I have a demo tape I'd like to send you."

"Hello, I'd like permission to send you a demo tape."

It's too easy to say "no" to those inquiries. Be much more specific. Find out as much as you possibly can about the company you are calling before you call. You can easily find that information in *Music Row Publications* and *American Songwriter* magazine. Between these two publications, you should have enough leads to make several calls a week. It will be the quality of contacts made, and not the quantity, that will determine your success. Use the same sales techniques you would for any other sales job. Perhaps a book or course on sales would be helpful when making cold calls to publishers.

PACKAGING PRODUCT INCORRECTLY

Incorrect packaging is the trademark of an amateur. You want to be very mindful of what your package should look like. Don't make the following very common errors:

Never, ever write by hand on a cassette label. The labels must be type-written. There are so many computer software programs to choose from, it is very inexpensive to produce a great-looking cassette label. If you'd rather not print your own labels, one of the many fast copy stores can do it for you at very little cost. Same for a J-card and lyric sheet. You need all three to have a uniform, professional look to them—nothing handwritten! CDs are a little different, in that you can burn your own individual CDs, one at a time. If you are using the type of CD that you can write on with a mark-er, then your own handwriting is acceptable. But the CD insert and lyric sheets will still need to be professionally done.

Don't send long personal letters and snapshots under any circum-stances. If your career goals go beyond songwriting, then you will need a pro-fessional bio and photo. See chapter 11 on how to prepare these materials.

Once you have identified the publisher you wish to contact, estab-lished a personal relationship with an individual in that company, and obtained her permission to send your tape or CD, following are some help-ful hints.

Write "Requested by _____" on the front of the envelope. Even with this notation on the front, sometimes a tape package won't get by the receptionist, because they are so used to rejecting this type of package. Lots of people use the notation "Requested Material" even when they haven't received permission to mail the tape, so you have to be more specific—who requested the tape and what's on it? Give as much information as possible on the front of your package.

If you don't have nice-looking professional labels with a nice business logo (which is not really necessary), then mail your package in a colored envelope. Use something other than manila or white. That way, when you make a follow-up call, you can tell the receptionist or publisher what your package looks like. It's probably sitting on their desk or in a box right next to it, under a pile of other tape packages.

Make a follow-up call around the time you think the package will arrive. If you wait a month, it will be too late. Find out what happened to each and every package you send out. And don't be surprised if you have to mail out another copy.

Don't ask for your tape or CD to be returned. Once you mail it, it's gone. Don't ever send your last copy, or only original copy.

NOT UNDERSTANDING THE INDUSTRY

Nothing frustrates an industry professional more than having to explain the basics of the industry—what a PRO does, why you need a publisher before approaching a producer or an A&R rep, etc. Do your homework thoroughly before you plan a trip to Nashville. If you wanted to design automobiles for a living, you wouldn't walk into General Motors without first having a degree in automotive engineering. The Nashville music industry is just as specialized, albeit a lot less technical! You have to know exactly who you are meeting with, what he does, what he can do for you, and specifically what you can do for him. What if he says "Yes"? You have to know what the next step is without him telling you, so you'll know if you are being treated fairly and getting what you deserve. Don't even think about coming to Nashville to pitch your songs or artist package before you have a thorough understanding of how everything works and the unique things you have to offer.

STAYING IN YOUR HOTEL ROOM WAITING FOR RETURN PHONE CALLS

This used to be more of a problem than it is now, since the widespread use of cell phones has changed the way we communicate. Now when you call, you can leave your cell phone number instead of your hotel number, and you won't have to worry about someone not being able to reach you. If you don't have a cell phone, it might be a good idea to rent one when you rent a car. That way, you'll be a lot more accessible and you won't have trouble making calls either. The main point is not to waste time waiting for someone to return your call. If you have a potential list of people you want to try to connect with (and you should have such a list), you can make calls first thing in the morning, then get out on Music Row. Get friendly with that person's assistant or receptionist, and stop by his office and introduce yourself to him when you are in his vicinity. Keep trying each day you are in Nashville, but don't make it a priority. You will get a lot more accomplished out on the Row than in your hotel room waiting for someone to call you back.

17

Planning Your Artist Showcase

The importance of careful planning cannot be emphasized enough in regard to showcasing in Nashville. Even though showcases are a common occurrence on the Row, they provide the highest visibility an artist can obtain. If you bomb, *everybody* knows about it. The news travels fast! Don't take a casual attitude regarding your own showcase—be prepared!

You should have a very specific purpose for presenting a showcase, the best reason being a request from a record company executive. Be aware of the artist roster of each record label, and how you may or may not fit in. Showcasing for publishers is a very good idea as well. Nashville publishers are very closely involved with artist development—many publishers have their own production companies and actively work with aspiring artists.

SHOWCASE GUIDELINES

Perform Original Material Only

Producers do not want to hear cover songs no matter how great your version of "Rocky Top." Don't be tempted to break this rule, because even if you have a very unusual arrangement of a well-known song and it's the best part of your act, there is a strong prejudice against performing cover songs in Nashville. People will think you aren't aware that this is a no-no, and that you don't know much about the Nashville music industry.

Make Sure Your Songs Are Awesome

Before you give an artist's showcase, get feedback on all of the songs you are planning to perform. Although you are looking for an artist's deal and not a songwriting deal, the songs you perform are still going to be the most important part of your showcase. That's just the way it is in Nashville, the ultimate song town. There are many aspiring artists in town who are great entertainers and have great voices. Unfortunately, they also think their songs are great when they aren't, and keep on performing them. It hurts their chances of ever getting a record deal.

Limit Your Show to Forty-Five Minutes

Actually, thirty minutes would be OK, too, if they include six great songs: two ballads, maybe one heartfelt acoustic number, two mid-tempo, and two rocking up-tempo. Music Row *loves* rocking up-tempo songs, and has a hard time finding great ones.

Start on Time

The best time for a showcase is 6 P.M., at a club conveniently located near Music Row, somewhere producers can stop by after work. Don't wait for the room to fill up; go ahead and start at the time advertised. It will be expected and appreciated by the people who are already there. Producers only need to hear a few songs to know if you are what they are looking for.

Schedule for Weekdays

Plan your showcase for Tuesday, Wednesday, or Thursday evening. Avoid weekends, as the industry folks are not out and about. Showcases are work for the music industry, not entertainment, and no one wants to work on a Friday or Saturday night, certainly not Sunday, with the exception of the Bluebird Cafe. The regular Bluebird Sunday night show does draw some industry people, especially if one of their friends, a well-known hit song-writer, is headlining the show.

Offer Free Food and Drinks

The music industry does not expect free food and drinks, except at places where it is not otherwise available, like soundstages. It's best to not offer food and drinks, even if you have an unlimited expense account. If you have personally invited certain executives, and you want to thank them for coming, you can make arrangements with the club to honor drink tickets. You can then give drink tickets to your special guests and settle with the bartender at the end of the evening.

Plan Seating

Plan reserved seating for record executives. These clubs are small and have limited seating. Usually a table in the back of the room is the best. Make up a table tent that says "Reserved," not "RCA Records" or the person's name, or they will be hounded to death. Hire a hostess who can recognize the people you have invited. Ideally, you will have hired a Nashville publicist. They know how to get people to your showcase, and they know all the people. The publicist or hostess will escort important guests to their reserved seats. If they don't show in the first fifteen minutes of your show, have the hostess pick up the reserved sign and let anyone sit down, particularly if it is crowded and the seats are needed. Industry execs don't mind fending for themselves.

Johnny Bond
Publications
presents...

Betsy Meryl Hammer

at the
Bluebird Cafe

Tuesday, July 23rd
6pm sharp!

For further information:
615.297.7320

Example: Artist Showcase Invitation
Picture postcard invitation. You can send a mass mailing of postcards to your entire database, then hand-deliver personal invitations accompanied with your CD to key industry executives.

Send Out Invitations

Make your invitations very simple and relatively inexpensive. Have your picture on the invitation—a picture postcard is perfect. Send them out a week or so ahead of time—two weeks maximum. If you send them too soon, you will be forgotten. If you are not going to do a picture postcard, then do a flyer or $5\frac{1}{2}'' \times 8\frac{1}{2}''$ heavy stock card that will go through the mail. Don't put an invitation in an envelope, because it might not be opened.

Make Follow-Up Phone Calls

You and your publicist, if you hired one, should start calling on Monday for your Tuesday, Wednesday, or Thursday show. If you have access to a fax machine, sending a reminder fax is a good idea, and you can reach a lot more people that way. An e-mail would be a personal touch, but don't use e-mail as your primary source for contacting people, just for a follow-up message.

Make a Quiet Trial Run

Do at least one showcase in Nashville, better two or three, before you invite the music industry. Don't send out invitations; don't invite people personally; don't spread the word. Simply book a date in one of the clubs. It will automatically show up in the *Tennessean* and the *Nashville Scene* club listings. Put on a great show, just as if you had invited the entire music industry (there will probably be some industry people there anyway). Have a professional there to evaluate your performance; maybe the publicist you are thinking about hiring, the people you have met at the performing rights organizations, or a publisher who has shown interest in your songs. This trial run will help you determine if you are ready for the real thing. It won't hurt to keep staging low-key trial runs until you are confident in your show. Just keep in mind that news travels fast on Music Row, and if you are really talented, the word will get out.

VARIOUS TYPES OF SHOWCASES: A GUIDE TO SHOWCASE CLUBS

The Most Common Showcase

A 6 P.M. show at a club close to Music Row (see below). These clubs have close, intimate, informal settings where producers can get in and out in a hurry. Producers and other industry professionals will probably not arrive on time or stay for the entire show. Two or three songs will tell them what they want to know. Again, you do not (and should not) provide complimentary food and drinks. Industry professionals do not expect it at these clubs. Your show will appear automatically in the *Tennessean* and the *Nashville Scene* club listings, and will be open to the public. This is the most inexpensive and the easiest way to put on your artist's showcase, as well as the most popular for the industry.

All live music venues are listed each week in the *Tennessean* Thursday "Weekend" section and the *Nashville Scene*. The *Scene* has an additional "Songwriters' Nights & Open Mics" listing, as well as a "Clubbing & Karaoke" listing. Listed below are the most popular clubs for showcase purposes.

3rd & Lindsley Bar & Grill

818 3rd Avenue South
Nashville, TN 37210
Tel. (615) 259-9891

Known mostly for blues and jazz, they don't host a writers' night and don't have many country acts perform here. But it's a great room. You might want to check it out!

12th & Porter Playroom

114 12th Avenue North
Nashville, TN 37203
Tel. (615) 254-7236

Popular showcase club with the largest stage of the clubs listed here. If you have a large band, you may want to perform here. Also, the Playroom is connected to a popular restaurant, 12th & Porter. If you provide complimentary hors d'oeuvres and put this information on your invitation, the industry will know that great food will be available!

Douglas Corner Café

2106-A Eighth Avenue South
Nashville, TN 37204
Tel. (615) 298-1688

Writers' hangout. Nashville's greatest writers perform here every night. You should spend a lot of time here on your trip to Nashville. It's a great place to showcase, too.

The Sutler

2608 Franklin Road
Nashville, TN 37204
Tel. (615) 297-9195

Lots of charm with great vibes. They don't have a writers' night, but they do feature all kinds of music. Check it out.

The Soundstage Showcase

A 6 P.M. show at a soundstage like The Castle Door, S.I.R., or SoundCheck. This showcase is in a formal setting and is by invitation only; no public will be in attendance. This showcase will not be listed in the *Tennessean* or *Nashville Scene*. Food and drinks must be catered, and will be expected. The sound quality and focus on the showcase will be superior to a local club. Careful consideration should be taken before choosing this format. If a specific producer or record company has requested a showcase, they might prefer this format. Do not use a soundstage unless you are assured attendance.

Your invitation should include a separate reception time, giving people a chance to mix and mingle and have refreshments. No matter how well the reception is going, start the showcase on time.

The Castle Door
115 16th Avenue South
Nashville, TN
Tel. (615) 255-2177
Great room, convenient location, lots of services including catering and video/audio taping capability.

Soundcheck
750 Cowan Street
Nashville, TN
Tel. (615) 726-1165
Soundcheck has one big room and a smaller room. It is off the beaten path in North Nashville, but everyone knows where it is and will go there to see a showcase.

Studio Instrument Rentals (S.I.R.)
1101 Cherry Avenue
Nashville, TN
Tel. (615) 255-4500
The sound gurus of Music Row. They have a small room for showcases with a "cool" factor attached to it. Or you can rehearse your showcase here before you perform for the industry. But even if you decide to showcase in one of the regular clubs listed above, you may still have to rent some sound equipment. S.I.R. and Soundcheck can take good care of you.

Late-Night Showcase

A 9:30 P.M. show—some artists prefer a later time, and the industry is pretty good at getting out for a late-night show. It is the music business, after all! This show is similar to the most common showcase, except that the public attendance will be larger and industry attendance smaller, unless you've done a great job at attracting some professional interest in your showcase. The same venues apply, plus one other very important club:

The Bluebird Cafe
4104 Hillsboro Road
Nashville, TN 37215
Tel. (615) 383-1461

Best room, best vibes, and best ambiance. There is no talking allowed during performances at the Bluebird, so you have a guaranteed attentive audience. You could consider a 6 P.M. show at the Bluebird, but traffic is a problem. Best to stick with a late-night show.

Other Showcase Venues

There are a few other live music venues that have a reputation for presenting exceptional music, and a showcase at one of these clubs might lend an aura of intrigue. You might attract some industry professionals just because it's something out of the ordinary. In Nashville, it's best to stick with the norm. The closer your showcase follows traditional patterns, the more professional you appear. That said, here are some nontraditional but attention-getting venues:

Exit/In
2208 Elliston Place
Nashville, TN 37203
Tel. (615) 321-4400

Once a famous club for showcasing cutting-edge alternative music, the Exit/In is rich in history. It has a huge stage and great layout for a showcase.

The Station Inn
402 12th Avenue South
Nashville, TN 37203
Tel. (615) 255-3307

If your music is grassroots country, bluegrass, Americana, alternative country, or traditional country—this is the place for you!

Broken Spoke
1412 Nolensville Pike
Nashville, TN 37222
Tel. (615) 226-3230

The Wildhorse Saloon
120 Second Avenue North
Nashville, TN 37304
Tel. (615) 902-8200

The Wildhorse is a huge country music dance hall owned by the Opryland Hotel. If you really have a grand show that gets people dancing, you might consider this venue. Make sure you have lots of friends to fill the dance floor, and that you and your band can handle the very large room. Everyone who attends your showcase will understand the challenges in playing that room and will be impressed if you can carry it off! Also keep in mind that a showcase at the Wildhorse will be a very expensive production.

The Clubs on "Lower Broad"

There is a cluster of honky-tonks on Broadway, between Fourth and Second Avenues, which play some pretty twangy country cover tunes. Clueless aspiring country artists, who don't know a thing about the music business, hang out here dreaming about getting discovered. You will spot them in an instant, both on- and offstage. This two-block area personifies the image of the Nashville music industry, not the reality. However, if you really want to have fun, forget the business for a minute and club hop on "Lower Broad." Locals and tourists alike dance, drink, and sing along to their favorite songs. Gibson's is a very classy coffeehouse with yummy desserts and a wide range of music; the rest offer diehard country classics. The Arista Records recording artists, BR5-49, were discovered at Robert's Western Wear, and it could happen again. Wolfy's presents all kinds of music, including swing. If you are a very traditional country artist, you might want to showcase in one of these clubs. But don't make the mistake of thinking that Lower Broad is what Nashville is all about. This is a tourist area and doesn't represent the Nashville music industry at all.

Gibson Café & Guitar Gallery
318 Broadway
Nashville, TN 37203
Tel. (615) 742-6343

Legends Corner
428 Broadway
Nashville, TN 37203
Tel. (615) 248-6334

Robert's Western Wear
416 Broadway
Nashville, TN 37203
Tel. (615) 256-7937

Tootsie's Orchid Lounge
422 Broadway
Nashville, TN 37203
Tel. (615) 726-0463

Wolfy's
425 Broadway
Nashville, TN 37203
Tel. (615) 251-1621

GETTING THE RIGHT PEOPLE TO YOUR SHOWCASE

Don't expect industry professionals to automatically show up just because you sent out invitations. They get a lot of invitations each week and don't attend unless they have a truly good reason to go. If they were a little curious about your showcase and didn't attend, they can easily find out how it went just from the street talk. If it was positive feedback, they'll make a mental note to go the next time. Yes, there probably will have to be a next time—even Garth Brooks wasn't signed on the basis of his first showcase! You will have to work *very hard* to get key industry executives to your showcase. *Here are some ideas on how to get help.*

NASHVILLE'S TOP PUBLICISTS

The publicists listed below are experts at getting the right people to attend an artist showcase. They know exactly whom to invite, what the invitation should look like, when it should be mailed, and what to say when they make follow-up calls. They know everyone in town and their schedules. They will know if there are any conflicts with your show and if it should be rescheduled. They know how to time press releases and how to get the best press coverage. Their calls will be taken or returned by the key decision makers. Just like Nashville's entertainment attorneys, a good publicist will be hard to find. Their reputation is on the line every time they invite industry leaders to a showcase. They cannot afford to waste anybody's time. So they will have very strict requirements which must be met before they agree to represent an aspiring artist. If all of the publicists listed below decline to represent you, that will be a sign that you aren't ready yet.

Alison Auerbach PR
1229 17th Avenue South
Nashville, TN 37212
Tel. (615) 329-0025 Fax (615) 329-0403
    Represents Vince Gill, among others.

AristoMedia
1620 16th Avenue South
Nashville, TN 37212
Tel. (615) 269-7071 Fax (615) 269-0131
    Represents Jo Dee Messina and many aspiring artists.

Betty Hofer
2121 Fairfax Avenue, #3
Nashville, TN 37203
Tel. (615) 269-9803 Fax (615) 292-7479
  Betty is a Music Row veteran.

Brokaw Company
1915 Church Street
Nashville, TN 37203
Tel. (615) 329-9360 Fax (615) 329-9647
  Represents Mark Chesnutt and others.

Dick McVey PR
24 Music Square West
Nashville, TN 37203
Tel. (615) 259-0708 Fax (615) 259-0701
  McVey is Nashville's musicians' guru.

Ellen Pryor
3811 Rolland Road
Nashville, TN 37205
Tel. (615) 292-8297 Fax (615) 292-8297
  Ellen is also a Music Row veteran.

FORCE
1505 16th Avenue South
Nashville, TN 37212
Tel. (615) 385-4646 Fax (615) 385-5840
Represents many major artists, including Trisha Yearwood and Alan Jackson.

Front Page Publicity
4149 Old Hillsboro Road
Franklin, TN 37064
Tel. (615) 383-0412 Fax (615) 383-0866
  Represents the Dixie Chicks and others.

Gangwisch & Associates
1706 Grand Avenue
Nashville, TN 37212
Tel. (615) 327-4000 Fax (615) 329-2445
  Represents Hank Williams, Jr., and other legends.

Gurley & Company
P.O. Box 150657
Nashville, TN 37203
Tel. (615) 269-0474 Fax (615) 385-2052
    Cathy Gurley is a former publicist for CMA.

Holley & Harman PR
3415 West End Avenue, #101G
Nashville, TN 37203
Tel. (615) 460-9550 Fax (615) 460-9553
E-mail: *beehive022@aol.com*
    Represents Wynonna and others; both Debbie Holley and Summer
Harman were with major labels at one time.

Hot Schatz Productions
1024 16th Avenue South, 2nd Floor
Nashville, TN 37212
Tel. (615) 782-0078 Fax (615) 782-0088
    Shatzi Hageman is a former publicist for Sony Music.

Joe's Garage
4405 Belmont Park Terrace
Nashville, TN 37215
Tel. (615) 269-3238 Fax (615) 297-7612
    Represents Emmylou Harris and others.

Network Ink
2021 21st Avenue South, #320
Nashville, TN 37212
Tel. (615) 297-0550 Fax (615) 383-2349
    Represents many major label artists.

PLA Media
1303 16th Avenue South
Nashville, TN 37212
Tel. (615) 327-0100 Fax (615) 320-1061
    Pam Lewis was Garth Brooks's first and only publicist—instrumental
in the development of his stellar career.

The Press Office
1229 17th Avenue South
Nashville, TN 37212
Tel. (615) 320-5153 Fax (615) 320-5738
    Represents John Anderson and Steve Wariner, among others.

Rubin Media
1227 17th Avenue South
Nashville, TN 37212
Tel. (615) 320-5000 Fax (615) 320-5551
Ronna Rubin is a former publicist for Warner/Reprise.

Schmidt Relations
209 19th Avenue South, #229
Nashville, TN 37203
Tel. (615) 846-3878 Fax (615) 846-4878
Represents a gazillion major artists.

So Much Moore
P.O. Box 120426
Nashville, TN 37212
Tel. (615) 298-1689 Fax (615) 298-1446
Martha Moore is a former publicist for Mercury Records.

Star Keeper PR
P.O. Box 128195
Nashville, TN 37212
Tel. (615) 329-0460 Fax (615) 329-0416
Represents Tracy Byrd and Mila Mason.

Turner & Company
1018 17th Avenue South, #6
Nashville, TN 37212
Tel. (615) 327-1274 Fax (615) 322-9462
Judd Turner is a former CMA publicist.

Whiting Promotions
1807 Grand Avenue, Suite Two
Nashville, TN 37212
Tel. (615) 327-9857 Fax (615) 327-2761
Chuck Whiting is the former publicist for the NASHVILLE *entertainment* ASSOCIATION.

Wortman Works
209 19th Avenue South, #311
Nashville, TN 37203
Tel. (615) 259-0035 Fax (615) 259-0250
Jules Wortman has worked for several major labels.

Other ways to attract industry attention to your showcase are:

Enlist the support of your attorney. Nashville entertainment attorneys will also be able to get the right people to your showcase, but they won't do the legwork for you—that is, you will have to mail out invitations and make most of the follow-up calls yourself. Your attorney will make a few phone calls to key targeted individuals at the record labels, as well as major producers and publishers. You really don't need an attorney until you already have some label interest and are close to getting a deal. An attorney can help speed up the process and create a buzz about you. If one label seems interested, they all will want to check you out. Attorneys are great at making that happen.

Send out invitations. You can produce your showcase on your own without a publicist or attorney—just be sure to follow the showcase guidelines very closely. Mail a postcard with your picture on it, plus time, place, etc., to everyone on the database listing at the end of this book. Get some friends to help make follow-up phone calls and call everyone on the list. Send a reminder fax and/or e-mail the morning of the showcase. There is a lot going on every night in Nashville, and people's decisions can be influenced at the last minute. If they have to be somewhere at 8 P.M., they might just stop by your showcase at 6 P.M. even if they don't have it on their schedule.

Once your showcase is in motion, relax and enjoy your time in the spotlight. It's your night, and you are giving it your all. Don't place all your hopes and expectations on this one night, thinking that it's your one big opportunity. Lots of things can interfere with success, the most common problem being scheduling conflicts. There might be some industry function you didn't know about, or someone else might be having a showcase at the same time. Even if the attendance isn't what you had hoped for, give a performance just as though the head of RCA Records was sitting in the front row. You never know, someone who works for him might be somewhere in the room.

18

Making the Decision to Move to Nashville

You can't go wrong if you pack up the moving van and head towards Nashville. It is a wonderful family community, with many of the attractions of a big city and all of the charm of a small town. Even if you move here for a few years only to return home later, you won't regret the time you spent here. Of course, we are talking about the quality of life, the wonderful southern hospitality, the beautiful historic architecture scattered throughout the city, and the relative ease of getting around town. We aren't really talking about your experience on Music Row and your chances of success.

SHOULD YOU OR SHOULDN'T YOU?

Most of the songwriters who move here get caught up in the comforts of the city. Nashville has an almost zero unemployment base and there is a wide diversity of jobs in print publishing, computer technology, hospitals, insurance, real estate, automotive, banking, and lots of jobs in the service industry. Writers will move here, get a great secure job, meet a beautiful southern belle or a Rhett Butler, get married, have children, and wonder where the time went. They came here to write songs and made some great contacts when they first started out, but somehow time slipped away and they lost sight of their initial goals. Come to think of it, what's so wrong with that?

The greatest danger in moving to Nashville is facing all the opportunities there are to distract you from your original purpose for moving here in the first place. With that in mind, your decision to move here and become a successful songwriter or artist should be based on your willingness to live a Spartan songwriter's existence, putting financial prosperity on the back burner for a few years. If it's money you are seeking, you shouldn't even be considering a career in the music business in the first place. Money is only a side benefit that may or may not ever materialize. The true reward is to be able to share your creative talent with an appreciative audience. Here are some great jobs for aspiring songwriters, artists, and musicians which will guarantee that you meet and chat with Nashville's top decision makers.

IDEAL JOBS

The Bluebird Cafe or Douglas Corner

The very best job you can possibly get is the one that is right in the apex of the songwriting community. The Bluebird Cafe should be the first stop on your job search. Amy needs waiters and waitresses, a bartender, a cook, a sound engineer, a maintenance person, and office workers. These jobs don't come open very often, but every once in a while they do, so stay tuned and ready to step in when the occasion arises.

Next stop, Douglas Corner. The same jobs are needed there, too, except they really don't need a cook. In Tennessee, establishments serving alcohol must also serve food, but that doesn't always mean cooked meals. You might consider applying at some of the other songwriter hangouts, but their customer base will not be as saturated with hit songwriters and industry executives as the Bluebird and Douglas Corner.

Some entrepreneurial writers come to town and start their own writers' night in a club or restaurant. That's a great idea because you can select the hit songwriters you want to meet and invite them to your writers' night, you get your name in the paper every week, and you meet just about every writer in town. But it's a lot of hard work, doesn't pay anything, and might distract you from the main reason you moved here—to write songs.

Music Row Restaurants

The next best jobs are waiting on tables at Music Row area restaurants. Sunset Grill, Sammy Bs, the Longhorn, Midtown Café, and Noshville would be the best places to meet people; but there are lots of restaurants in the vicinity, and music industry execs eat in all of them. Nashville restaurants have a very relaxed atmosphere, even the stuffy ones (actually, there aren't any stuffy ones!), and waiters can chat with customers. You'll get to know the people who dine in your restaurant. And everyone else working there is a writer or aspiring artist!

Randstad Staffing Services

Another ideal job is with a temp agency—*the* Music Row temp agency is Randstad Staffing Services. They even have an office on Music Row, at 1207 17th Avenue South, Suite 301, Nashville, TN 37212. Their phone number is (615) 321-9094; Web site *www.randstadstaffing.com*. Tell them you want only music industry jobs and that's where they'll send you. They can also get you a permanent job in the industry somewhere, but it's a good idea to temp for a little while to find out which companies you like the best. Also, you will have a chance to meet more people which may lead to a permanent job.

It's tough to get a full-time job in the Nashville music industry because of the local colleges' intern programs. Students at Belmont and MTSU recording industry programs get class credit for working for free at various entry-level positions in the music industry. So the businesses on Music Row don't have to hire anyone for these positions. They often have many interns from both colleges working for them. And then, as you would suspect, when a job does open on a higher level, interns are first on the list for that job. So the jobs rarely become available to someone outside the company.

It is not uncommon for nonstudents to offer to work for free also, in the hopes of ingratiating their way into the company. It's worked from time to time. Some companies have a very strict policy about working with interns and only accept qualified students; others are more lax. If you decide to go that route, it won't be hard to find out what the policies are.

Service Organizations

Jobs with the various nonprofit trade and service organizations are interesting, fun, and multifaceted. There are lots of different organizations and associations besides the ones mentioned in this book. Usually they operate on a streamlined budget and produce imaginative, challenging, and creative fundraising events. The entire Nashville music industry supports these various groups with corporate sponsorships and helps produce and manage some of their events. Industry execs also serve on lots of different committees in support of these organizations. So there is a great opportunity to work alongside a top industry executive who is volunteering his services for the organization and, ultimately, the Music Row community. The top choices would be NSAI, NARAS, CMA, CRB, and the Country Music Hall of Fame Museum.

Even if you don't get a job with one of these associations, it would be a good idea to volunteer your time to help out on one or two projects. It's a great way to meet people in the industry and, who knows, you may work your way into a job after all.

Catering and Special Events Companies

The Nashville music industry is big on parties, and there are lots of parties and special events every month. If you work for a catering company or special event company, chances are very good that you will be doing dinners and special events for the music industry. That includes the catering departments of area hotels. Included here is contact information for the most popular caterers and special event companies.

Event Managers

Events Unlimited
1114 17th Avenue South
Nashville, TN 37212
Tel. (615) 329-3091

Helen L. Moskovitz & Associates
95 White Bridge Road
Nashville, TN 37205
Tel. (615) 352-6900

Caterers

Kates Fine Catering, Inc.
619 W. Iris Drive
Nashville, TN 37204
Tel. (615) 298-5644

The Clean Plate Club
718 Thompson Lane
Nashville, TN 37204
Tel. (615) 292-2080

TomKats, Inc.
408 Broadway
Nashville, TN 37203
Tel. (615) 256-9596
Web site: *www.tomkats.com*

Hotels

Loews Vanderbilt Plaza Hotel
2100 West End Avenue
Nashville, TN 37203
Tel. (615) 320-1700

Utilizing Your College Degree

If you really can't imagine yourself in one of these "ideal" jobs, there are lots of great opportunities waiting for you in your field of expertise. Many major corporations have offices in Nashville: Dell Computers, Hewlett-Packard, Toshiba, Bank of America, BellSouth, Columbia/HCA (health care), Saturn, Nissan, Vanderbilt University and Medical Center, Gibson Guitars, to name but a few. The Nashville Area Chamber of Commerce has a JobsLink program on the Internet to help businesses find skilled employees with credentials outside of the city. You can contact them at *www.nashvillechamber.com*. They also sell an employment packet to assist with a job search. It contains the chamber's business directory plus a list of top employers, wage and salary information, and a list of executive search firms and personnel agencies. It's a little pricey at $45, but if you are serious about finding a job in Nashville, the packet and JobsLink Web page will be very helpful.

WHERE TO LIVE

Nashville has so many beautiful neighborhoods, it's hard to know where to start! Unfortunately, it also ranks as the eleventh most congested city in the nation, with longer traffic delays than Boston, New York, and Chicago. One problem is that the neighborhoods are not really near the jobs, so Nash-villians spend a lot of time in their cars. There is no transportation system to speak of.

It might be a good idea to get a job first, then pick a neighborhood with the easiest route to commute. There are lots of beautiful neighborhoods with unique qualities to choose from, so don't get your heart set on one before you find out where you are going to be working. BMI's President and CEO Frances W. Preston always tells every songwriter, "Get a job first, then move here."

Music Row

Music Row is right next to Vanderbilt University, so there is a lot of transient housing in this area. Vandy students tend to have a little bit of money to spend, so the area has some very nice condos and community living spaces that are frequently vacated corresponding to semesters. There are even some very nice condos and apartments right on Music Row. There are also some that are not as attractive but relatively inexpensive.

Music Row is a mix of businesses and residences. Horton Street is the dividing line. North of Horton is primarily businesses, many of them with offices in beautiful old houses. South of Horton is mostly residential, but many houses are being purchased by music industry companies and turned into offices. If you are into renovation projects, there are still a few run-down houses that could be saved, but they need a lot of work. Many of Nashville's most prominent executives live right on Music Row.

Belmont Area

Belmont University sits at the south end of Music Row, in a wonderful neighborhood. There are great small older houses that are still reasonably priced in the $100,000 range, lower or higher depending on the shape they are in. There is also a charming large apartment complex near the university. There are small croppings of specialty stores and restaurants sprinkled in with the homes, making it a very special neighborhood. The Belmont Area is right off of Music Row, close to downtown and to I-440 which connects to all of the other interstates that will take you to your job. Finding a house or apartment in this area would be ideal.

Fairfax Area

Just south of the Vanderbilt Campus, this housing area is built around a very special shopping area called Hillsboro Village. College students, music industry execs, and just about everybody else are attracted to the great restaurants and specialty shops in this two blocks deep and two blocks wide little area. The little village is bordered on one end by Wedgewood/Blakemore, and the other end by Fairfax Avenue. Fairfax ends at Hillsboro Village, and if you turn into the housing area on Fairfax, you will wind up in a beautiful neighborhood. It has a wonderful park nicknamed "Dragon Park" (in honor of the huge sculpture in the middle). The homes are a fairly nice size and in good condition, which gives the neighborhood real estate a median value of $250,000. The area has attracted investors who have renovated old apartment buildings and turned them into very nice living spaces. The Fairfax area keeps on going to West End Avenue on one side, and I-440 on the other.

West End Avenue

Sounds high-rent, doesn't it? It is, when you are on the boulevard. But keep going west and you will find smaller, charming houses that offer all kinds of possibilities. You can rent a house or a guest house, there are apartments mixed in with houses, or you can get a good deal on a house. The closer you are to West End, the higher the cost will be.

Sylvan Park

If you keep going southwest, you will eventually wind up in Sylvan Park. You can tell you are there because the streets are named after states for the most part. This area is filled with old houses that need a lot of fixing up. It is such a popular area, it's hard to find a good deal in Sylvan Park anymore. There are some great duplexes here that aren't much to look at, but the price is right ($400 per month) and they are very roomy. If you are a golfer (and you should be, if you are in the music industry), McCabe Public Golf Course is practically in your backyard. Also, there are two eateries that are very popular with the music industry, the McCabe Pub and Sylvan Park Restaurant—both serve delicious southern home cookin'.

Downtown

If you are into cool lofts over old warehouses or highrise apartments, you might find one downtown. There aren't many to choose from, but the Nashville Chamber of Commerce will be glad we mentioned it. A lot of effort has gone into the development of downtown and the prevention of urban sprawl in the city.

Edgefield Historic District

This is where you will find your best deals for a renovation project. Across the Cumberland River from downtown, the area has many historic homes, and they are protected by strict building codes. If you promise to renovate one of these homes according to their standards (if you buy one, you'll have to, anyway), you can get a great deal and get funding for practically nothing. There are just glorious homes here, many having been restored by loving hands. The residents are very proud of their district, and sponsor a tour of the homes once a year. They also have beautiful greenway park and a special neighborhood hangout called the Radio Café, with its own writers' night. Some very special writers and artists perform here regularly, particularly Edgefield residents.

Belle Meade • Green Hills • Forrest Hills • Oak Hill

The high-rent district. Belle Meade is the grandest neighborhood in Nashville, with some of the most beautiful homes you will ever see in our nation perched on acres of land. On your first visit to Nashville, be sure to drive through this neighborhood and gaze at the splendor. This is where you will find the old stone "slave walls," which were built by slaves around the plantations. Only parts of them still stand today. These neighborhoods are the most desirable living areas in the city. You can still find affordable housing in Green Hills, mostly huddled around Hillsboro Pike and I-440. The Villager is one of Nashville's most popular apartment complexes, because the price is right (starting at $500 per month). It's amazing that there are still apartments and condos for rent in this area, because it is probably the best geographic location in Nashville. You can get anywhere in fifteen minutes from this little area. Forrest Hills and Oak Hill are further south and are mostly very large homes and properties.

Farther on Out

If you really try hard and stick with it, you will probably find something you are looking for in one of the neighborhoods above. If you just don't have any luck at all, then here are some more options.

Harding Place

Not to be confused with Harding Road, which runs briefly through Belle Meade, Harding Place starts at Harding Road and runs across the southern part of the city. There are lots and lots of inexpensive apartments and condos for rent, some in nice areas, and others in not-so-nice areas. "Nice" refers to appearance more than anything else. If you wander off of Harding Road, north and south, you'll find many houses, but not neighborhoods, really.

Antioch • Bellevue • Rivergate

These are three areas that have grown up around mega–shopping malls. Antioch is in the southeast, Bellevue in the southwest, and Rivergate in the northeast. Lots of apartments, condos, houses—whatever you need. If you wind up working in one of these areas, then you might want to consider living there, too. But you'll be getting away from the mainstream. You'll probably find a writers' night somewhere in each of these areas, but you'll be driving into Nashville a lot in the evenings to go to the hot writers' nights and industry events.

This should be enough to help you in your search for a great place to live. If you are bringing your family, then you might want to go a little further out where you will find larger homes for less. A large percentage of music industry families live in Brentwood. Williamson County has a great school system (Nashville is in Davidson County), and you can probably get a big backyard and lots of kids in the neighborhood. Right now Cool Springs is a huge megamall, but huge homes are cropping up there as well.

Some people are taken with the history of Tennessee and wind up in historic Franklin, where a Civil War battle was brief and bloody. Others are interested in the vast farmland that is still available, and will settle on plots of land in Spring Hill or Fairview, or even farther out. There are lots of choices. One industry executive, the beloved Dale Franklin, lived in a barn! (An exquisite barn, that is.)

Before she passed away at too early an age, Dale founded three very important organizations: The NASHVILLE *entertainment* ASSOCIATION, Leadership Music, and SOURCE, a networking organization for top female music industry executives. If Dale could live in a barn, you can live wherever you want and still rise to the top. The more creative you are with your environment, perhaps the more creative you will be in your profession.

A ONE-YEAR GAME PLAN FOR SUCCESS ONCE YOU ARE SETTLED DOWN

This book has covered the ins and outs of Music Row from every conceivable angle. Now that you have made the commitment and actually moved here, it's time to get down to business. The first thing to do, if you haven't done this already, is get a day job. Some songwriters move here on a little nest egg they have put away, and plan to live on it for a year or two, expecting something to happen by that time. Even if you get a song put on hold tomorrow, it can take as long as two years before you ever see any money. The sales-to-collection-to-royalty payment process takes a long time. And, as was said previously, you don't want to put your own life on hold while you are pursuing your dream. Your dream *is* your life, living and working in Nashville and writing and creating great music at the same time.

Here is a list of milestones for a one-year period. "Every day" and "every week" doesn't necessarily mean weekends too! Take some time out to enjoy the wonderful perks of living in Nashville, like walking near Radnor Lake, attending outdoor concerts, and strolling through the many artisan fairs.

Every Day

- Keep a detailed journal. Write down every single thought and idea that pops in your head about the music industry, about songs, about almost anything. When you go out to the clubs at night or to a songwriters' workshop, write down whom you met and a little something about them to help you remember them later. Also, write down names you heard that someone else mentioned, and what they said about them. That name might not mean anything to you now, but it could turn out to be a very important person that you want to meet. You'll have a written record of a friend who could introduce you.
- Write a song, or work on a song that you started. The more you work on your songs, the finer tuned they will become. Even if you don't think that songwriting is your strong point and you probably won't pursue a career in songwriting, you might be invited to collaborate on a song as an artist or a musician. You might be better than you think, and at least you will have had some experience in the process.

- Practice playing your instrument. The better you are, the better you will get your song across.
- Listen to the country radio stations: WSM, WSIX, and possibly KDF (they keep changing their format). It is an absolute necessity, even if you get frustrated with what you hear. This is what the Nashville record labels like and spend their money to produce.
- Watch the cable channel CMT (Country Music Television) enough to make sure that you have seen all the current videos. Write down in your journal the artist, the song, the songwriters, the record label, and you might as well write down the video producer and production company too. They don't select the songs or sign artists and musicians, but they are an important part of Music Row.
- Stop by the Acklen Station Post Office. Hopefully, you were able to get a P.O. Box here, which is something you want even if you have most of your mail delivered to your residence. Everyone on Music Row has an Acklen Station P.O. Box and they will stop by every day to pick up their mail. So you need to stop by there, too. If you don't have a P.O. Box, then mail a letter to family or friends. They'll love to hear all about Nashville.

Every Week

- Browse through a record store. Bring your journal with you and take notes on which artists are being promoted and what their CD label copy says. Record labels pay big bucks to have their CDs placed in strategic locations, like the listening stations or the end of the aisle. Listen to all the country product in the listening stations. Soak up as much information as you can.
- Buy one CD per week and study it inside and out. If this is too expensive to do, maybe songwriter friends will join you in developing a current country music library.
- Read the trades. If you can't subscribe to *Billboard Country Airplay Monitor,* go to the library or sneak a peek at the bookstore. Read the *Music Row* magazine from cover to cover and take notes in your journal.
- On Monday, Wednesday, and Thursday attend the NSAI, SGA and TSAI workshops. Try for a minimum of one a week, but you really shouldn't miss one. There will always be an important somebody at each of these workshops that you will have a chance to meet face to face.
- Get out into the clubs and perform or observe as many open mics, writers' nights, and showcases as you possibly can. Make it a minimum of at least once a week (try to do more if you can).

- Collaborate on a song with a songwriter friend. This is a very important acquired skill and one you must develop! Don't skip this one!
- Make an appointment with an industry professional. Choose from PROs, publishers, and songwriter organization staff members. You will not be able to go back to the same people week after week, so you should have a long list of potentials. Once you meet with someone, plan to go back to see them in a month.
- Have lunch at a Music Row restaurant (see chapter 10). If they are too far away from your work, then stop by one of the hangouts after work on Tuesday (there's no songwriter workshop that night).
- For musicians only—browse through music equipment stores. Make sure your card is still on the bulletin board, or put another one back up there. Check out the other musicians who are listed there—make notes in your journal. You might have a good reason to call some of them and get to know them better. Remember that networking is the key to success, especially for musicians.

Every Month
- Review your journal. You'll be surprised to see that someone you wrote about a month ago is now a pretty good friend. Bring forward any names, ideas, or other important data that you want to be sure to remember. Some writers keep a separate song title or "hook" book. You can keep these ideas separate or in your journal—whatever works for you.
- Make a repeat appointment with someone you want to keep in close contact with.

Every Quarter
- Participate in an industry event. There are so many different industry events on Music Row, it would be wonderful to participate in every single one. But that would be very expensive and time consuming. Realistically, you probably aren't going to be able to do it all! So plan to do one per quarter, four per year.
- Invite key music industry professionals to your open mic, writers' night, or artist's showcase. Depending on where you are in your own stage of development, you may want to invite a few people just to get their feedback; or you may want to send invitations to your entire personal database listing. In any event, plan on four writers' nights/showcases per year, one per quarter.
- Record some work tapes on your songs. Please don't be tempted to do expensive full-blown demos until you really have something exciting happening with a song. Work tapes are relatively inexpensive and will help you discover your songs' strengths and weaknesses.

- Evaluate your progress. Be really easy on yourself. If you got a repeat appointment, that's great progress. If you made some key contacts, that's progress. If you finished a new song, that's really great progress. If you managed to do some of the things on this list, that's more than most newcomers to Nashville get done.
- Make some short-term goals for the next quarter. Whom would you like to get an appointment with? Where would you like to perform on a writers' night? Whom would you like to cowrite with?

Mid-Year Exam
- Have you established close relationships with someone at all three PROs?
- Have you met with all the publishers on your list of potentials?
- Have you identified your favorite open mic or writers' night hangout?
- Have you played a Sunday Writers' Night at the Bluebird Cafe? (This is a benchmark for writers who show growing talent and maturity.)
- Have you completed one song with a cowriter?
- Have you completed one song on your own?
- Could you pass a mini-quiz on who does what in Nashville? Are you getting to know who the decision makers are?

How do you really measure your progress? Everything you have read in this book, all of the interviews with songwriters and industry professionals, have told you that it is all about networking and developing relationships. If you are meeting people, getting out and performing, attending some industry functions and events, and getting in to see some top professionals occasionally, then you are doing great. If you are spending time fine-tuning songs in a home studio in your basement all by yourself, then you are not making any progress, *even if* those songs are awesome! In Nashville, the music business is a community effort.

Remember also that it's going to take a lot longer than you ever imagined. There are many wonderfully talented people who finally gave up after ten years of trying. There is no gold ring to try for—it's all about going for the ride. Just keep yourself out there and you'll do fine!

HOW TO SUCCEED WITHOUT MOVING TO NASHVILLE
If the decision to move to Nashville would cause hardship on you and/or your family, then it would not be a wise choice to move here. Your success will be measured by how content you are on a day-to-day level; it won't be about hearing yourself or your song on the radio for the first time, even

though, admittedly, that is a pretty awesome experience. Doing something that you really truly love on a daily basis will be your greatest reward, even if you never get a song recorded or sign a record contract. That is only one step in the process. One very gifted singer actually signed three different recording contracts at three different times; they all fell apart for different reasons. The first record company (Casablanca) completed an album, put it on the market, then went bankrupt for other reasons. The second record company completed the first single (they used to put singles out before they did an album), mailed it to radio, then the company was bought by a bigger company, and current developing artists were terminated. The third time the artist and record label couldn't come to terms on a producer; the artist was under contract to one producer, but the label wanted a different producer. You would think by this time the artist would have given up! But she made a great living as a backup singer both in the studio and on the road, and she wrote a few hit songs recorded by other artists. You've got to love what you're doing and keep on doing it, and don't get discouraged by the obstacles that stand in the way.

It doesn't make sense, either, to put your real life on hold and try your hand in the music industry for a few years. Songwriters have actually left their spouses at home for a few years while they came to Nashville to get established. One songwriter had a very unusual financial windfall—a lovely house on the beach *free of charge*. All he had to do was live there and take care of the house. He was considering giving that up in order to try to make it in Nashville. When life gives you a wonderful gift—a loving spouse, a beautiful house, a great job—it doesn't make much sense to give that up in order to go searching for another gift. Moving to Nashville to follow your dreams has to fit into your real world.

If you are struggling with "should I or shouldn't I," then you probably already have your answer. You shouldn't. Here is what you can do to pursue a career in country music and still live outside of Nashville.

Songwriters

Here's the real problem. Even if you read this book from cover to cover, especially the interviews, and clearly understand what it means, you still will be very, very surprised when you finally start interacting with people on a professional level. Things will be a lot different from what you thought they were going to be. That's why people have such a hard time breaking through the system when they are not residents. They don't have access to the right information. It's not really something you read about; it's something you experience. And it isn't really revealed to you on a one-week or two-week trip; it's unveiled slowly over time. So how do you get to the inside track in Nashville without living there?

Spend as much time in Nashville as you possibly can. Bring the family for vacations (as long as they understand that you'll be working and they'll be on their own). Actually, it will be easier to get appointments when you are from out of town. Publishers, producers, and A&R reps are always looking for fresh new material, so they are receptive to meeting with someone new. They also are very tuned into everything that is going on in Nashville and tend to meet with only the cream of the crop. When you live in town, everyone knows who's hot and who's not, and if you're not knocking them dead at the Bluebird then it's going to be hard to get into someone's office. If you don't live here, people won't expect there to be a buzz going on about you, but if you live here, then it is expected. That is the main reason it is so difficult for even very good writers to move to the next plateau of "hot" writer. Just good isn't good enough in Nashville. Spend your time in Nashville networking with as many people on as high a level as possible. Try to plan your trips around NSAI and SGA songwriter seminars; not just the workshops, but the three-day events. It's not about learning something, it's about meeting people, and the top executives participate in these seminars. Make it a goal to meet all those people listed in "In Charge." Open a Nashville "office." Best choice: open a P.O. Box and get an 800 number. Everyone here has a P.O. Box and uses the Acklen Station Post Office (37212). When people see the return address on your CD or cassette tape, they'll think you live in Nashville. Of course, the 800 number gives it away that you don't. A 615 area code would be preferable, which you may be able to get through a cell phone. Second choice: use a mailbox service. Some of Nashville's top songwriters and artists use Star Station, Nine Music Square South, Nashville, TN 37203, tel. (615) 321-3554. This is a great company and is very popular with out-of-town songwriters (in-town songwriters, too). The only problem is that publishers and producers will recognize the address and realize that you don't really have an office in Nashville, but Star Station has lots of other services that you might need when you are in town, including faxing, desktop publishing, and mailing services, and they will forward the mail that is sent to your private mailbox. Instead of a P.O. Box address, your address will be Nine Music Square South. Star Station also writes professional bios (Alan Jackson is one famous client) and lyric sheets, and will put together a great press kit.

Why do you need a Nashville address? For your CDs and cassette tapes. If your demo package is professionally done and your address is local, it will most probably get heard.

Find someone to drop off tapes for you. Even if you meet a publisher or producer in Nashville and they agree to accept your songs through the mail, the chances of your package ever getting to them are slim. Tapes sent through the mail get rejected before they ever get to the person for whom they were intended. Maybe that songwriter you met at the Bluebird would be willing to drop off tapes for you in exchange for something. Maybe you could subscribe to a tip sheet and share the information with him. Or maybe you could include some of his songs when you demo your songs. Another idea would be to hire a Belmont music industry student for next to nothing. Songs that are dropped off usually get heard, if they are packaged correctly and look like all the other tapes sitting on the listener's desk. Songs that are mailed rarely get out of the envelope.

Look for a mentor. Eventually you will connect with someone on the inside who will take you under their wing. Nurture that relationship.

Be aware that top Nashville executives travel to other cities looking for new talent. If there is a music conference or songwriters' seminar somewhere in your vicinity, be sure to go! It isn't recommended that you skip a trip to Nashville in exchange for a conference because time spent in Nashville has more value; but music conferences are fun, and interesting, and loaded with top music executives.

Subscribe to Star Station's biweekly publication, the *Nashville Newsletter.* Call (615) 321-0486 or e-mail *NashNews@aol.com.* ($24 for 24 issues, sample issue $2.) Published by California writer/artist Jeannie Johnson, the newsletter was founded to give those outside of Nashville information that will help make them feel in touch with Music Row. Many of the publication's readers are music industry insiders who say it gives them a digest of what's happening in Nashville.

Aspiring Artists

A talented artist has the best chance of making it outside of Nashville. In fact, if you don't write songs and just want to sing and play, there's no need at all to move to Nashville. Just concentrate on building up your fan base from where you live. Create a local and regional buzz about yourself and your music. Your live performance speaks for itself. However, here are some marketing ideas to get more exposure.

Hire a publicist. You will be amazed at all the different ideas they will come up with to help promote your act. They will also prepare professional packages for you, including bios and tear sheets (professional reproductions) of any print coverage you receive, like local newspaper reviews, etc.

If you don't have the money right now to hire a publicist, then be sure to prepare these materials yourself; a one-page bio, tear sheets on any print coverage, 8″ × 10″ glossy photograph, and a demo tape or CD. Call and invite local music reviewers to come and see your act.

Play in the best club(s) in your area. The Nashville music industry is aware of the hot country clubs across the United States and will make a trip to see acts they have heard about. Get to know the club owner or manager and find out if they interact with the music industry at all (probably not, but it's possible that they might, or might be interested in trying to in the future).

Be aware of the music scene around you. There may be other artists in your area who have attracted label attention. You might be able to open for them if the industry is coming to town to see them, or be sure to put on your own showcase on the same night. If you have several great live music venues located in one area, you might want to talk to your chamber of commerce about putting on a music conference. These are very popular and draw a decent crop of out-of-town visitors.

Start a fan club. Keep track of everyone who walks in the door to come and see your act. Get their name and address, and then start regular mailings of postcards with your tour schedule listed on the back. Mail these postcards to the database listings at the end of this book—they won't know who you are yet, but you just may stir their curiosity.

Get a booking agent. There might be one in your vicinity, or you might have to be your own booking agent when you are just starting out. Get booked in the regional areas surrounding your hometown.

Play at as many music conferences as you possibly can. Music industry professionals attend these conferences regularly.

Start a Web site. It doesn't have to be anything fancy; it's just a way to expand your fan base and help create a buzz about yourself, so when people hear about you they can look you up on the Internet.

Invite the music industry to your hometown. Once you have established a strong local following, have a great review written up in the local newspaper, and have enough of a fan base to be confident of a packed house, invite Nashville execs to come and see you.

Visit Nashville. Proceed with caution. Now you have to decide how you want to approach the Nashville record industry on their own turf. If your strong point is your demo tape or CD, talk to a Nashville entertainment attorney about shopping it for you. If you are really confident in your live performance, then put on a showcase in Nashville. If you can possibly afford it on top of the expense of everything else, hire a Nashville publicist to help you get an industry turnout.

Aspiring Musicians

It's going to be tough to get a gig as a musician in the country music industry without living in Nashville, because it's all about networking. Your personality and how you interact with other musicians is just as important as how talented you are, so you must be present to win! Nevertheless, here are a few things you might try if moving to Nashville is out of the question.

Visit Nashville in January, February, and/or March. That's when auditions take place for touring bands. By May, all of the artists have hired their musicians. When you are in town, get out and play every single night. Try to meet as many other musicians as you possibly can.

Subscribe to Dick McVey's Musician's Referral Service. Call (615) 322-9997 or look it up on the Internet at *www.members.aol.com/luv1hit.* ($30 application fee and $15 per month) The referral service operates in every possible way to secure employment for its musicians—a printed listing, a hotline, a Web site, e-mail, and fax. Once a month a printed list is mailed and faxed directly into the offices of over a thousand potential employers in Nashville, Branson, Myrtle Beach, and other areas. McVey has been helping musicians find gigs and artists find musicians since 1986.

19

Your
Personal
References

O ne of the most important things you can do to advance your career as a songwriter or artist/musician is to establish your own personal list of contacts you have made in Nashville (and other places) and keep it as up-to-date as possible. Right now, as you begin to pursue your dream career, you can use the information lists in this book as the basis for your own personal database.

CREATING A DATABASE

As you start to use the listings in this book, transfer them to your own computer, using a file management software program, one that will allow you to sort by different categories such as last name, company name, or business category. Include an entry for business categories, like "Artist Manager," "Publisher," etc. You will be using your own personal database to invite people to your showcase or writers' night, and at first you might not want to mail to the entire directory. Another entry you might want to include would be one for general comments, like "met at the Bluebird Cafe"; something to help you remember that person over time.

You can go ahead and start monthly mailings to Nashville even before you actually make a trip there or move there, especially if you are a performing artist. The most successful bands send a monthly or quarterly post-card of their tour schedule, even if they are not going to be anywhere near

Nashville. That way, Music Row professionals will know a lot about you before they even meet you.

ABOUT BASIC LISTINGS

The listings in this book can serve as the basis for your own personal database. These are the top companies on Music Row and the ones you will want to contact about your songs or artist package. You should also use these listings to mail an invitation to your artist/musician showcase or a special writers' night at the Bluebird Cafe or Douglas Corner. For the most part, these companies have been around for at least a quarter of a century, and will probably be around for another decade. But people and locations change almost daily, and some of the contacts printed here will change before the ink even dries. You can fill in specific names for each company as you learn more about them and the people who work there.

All of the contact information you will need to start has been included in earlier chapters. Here I am just going to remind you of the categories you will want to add to your list, and refer you to the chapter of this book in which the information appears.

Nashville's Top Artist Managers

Contact information in chapter 6, "Nashville's Top Managers and Entertainment Attorneys," pages 87–95.

If you are looking for the manager of a specific artist, you can find that information in *Music Row*'s "Artist Roster" edition. When pitching songs to artist managers, you need to specify whom the tape or CD is going to and for which artist.

Nashville's Top Music Publishers

Contact information in chapter 5, "Nashville's Major Music Publishers," "Nashville's Hot Independent Music Publishers," pages 50–53, and "Other Important Independent Music Publishers," pages 57–73.

If you do a little research in *Music Row*'s "Publisher Special," you will find individual names in both the listing section and in the text and advertisements.

Nashville's Top Record Companies

Contact information in chapter 6, "Nashville's Major Record Labels," "Nashville's Hot Independent Record Labels," and "Other Important Independent Record Labels," pages 81–85.

If you do a little research in *Music Row*'s "In Charge" edition, you will find a complete listing of everyone who works at the label, including the A&R department.

Nashville's Top Record Producers

Contact information listed in chapter 11, "Nashville's Top Producers," pages 156–163.

REFERENCE DIRECTORIES

The people and companies here do not need to be entered into your own personal database, as you will be contacting them only if and when needed. Please keep in mind that any directory undergoes major changes every six months, so by the time you start to use this directory, some people may have moved. We have tried to include only those companies that have been doing business in Nashville for a long time and are known to provide excellent services. These directories only include complete contact information for those services that have not been included earlier in the book. Complete contact information for many Nashville organizations and services is already included elsewhere in the book and is listed in the table of contents.

For a more comprehensive and up-to-date directory of Nashville services, please consult the *Nashville Red Book* (to order, call (615) 256-5456). It is very reasonably priced and has been published for over thirteen years.

SECTION I: RECORDING SERVICES

It is strongly recommended that you use Nashville recording facilities to produce your songwriter or artist demo. You will not only get a superior product which is comparable to the best demos being pitched on Music Row, but you will meet and interact with important music industry professionals. There is a wide range of pricing from one studio to the other, and it is not necessary to spend a lot of money on your demos. Be sure to shop around for the best deal.

Nashville's Best Demo Studios

See the listings in chapter 11, "Nashville's Top Demo Studios," pages 148–151.

Nashville's Top Recording Studios

Crème de la crème! These studios are the best—their prices will reflect it! It's not necessary to use these top studios for your demo project, but they are included here for your information. As with demo studios, there are many, many more great studios that are not included here. We listed just a few from the top of the list.

Battery Studio
916 19th Avenue South
Nashville, TN 37212
Tel. (615) 329-0600 Fax (615) 321-4616

Bennett House
134 Fourth Avenue North
Nashville, TN 37064
Tel. (615) 790-8696 Fax (615) 790-9034

Bradley's Barn
P.O. Box 120838
Nashville, TN 37212
Tel. (615) 244-1060 Fax (615) 726-2945

Castle Recording Studio
1393 Old Hillsboro Road
Franklin, TN 37069
Tel. (615) 791-0810 Fax (615) 791-1324

Emerald Sound Studio
1033 16th Avenue South
Nashville, TN 37212
Tel. (615) 321-0511 Fax (615) 329-9417

Javelina Recording Studios
Thirty Music Square West, #100
Nashville, TN 37212
Tel. (615) 242-3493 Fax (615) 777-3496

Masterfonics Studios
28 Music Square East
Nashville, TN 37203
Tel. (615) 259-4452 Fax (615) 242-0101

Ocean Way Nashville
1200 17th Avenue South
Nashville, TN 37201
Tel. (615) 320-3900 Fax (615) 320-3910

Omnisound
1806 Division Street
Nashville, TN 37203
Tel. (615) 321-5526 Fax (615) 321-5527

Recording Arts
307 29th Avenue North
Nashville, TN 37212
Tel. (615) 321-5479 Fax (615) 321-0756

Sound Emporium
3100 Belmont Boulevard
Nashville, TN 37212
Tel. (615) 383-1982 Fax (615) 383-1919

Sound Kitchen
112 Seaboard Lane
Franklin, TN 37067
Tel. (615) 370-5773 Fax (615) 370-1712

Sound Stage Studio
Ten Music Circle South
Nashville, TN 37203
Tel. (615) 256-2676 Fax (615) 259-2942

Soundshop, Inc.
1307 Division Street
Nashville, TN 37203
Tel. (615) 244-4149 Fax (615) 242-8759

Starstruck Studios
Forty Music Square West
Nashville, TN 37203
Tel. (615) 259-5200 Fax (615) 259-5202

Treasure Isle Recorders, Inc.
2808 Azalea Place
Nashville, TN 37204
Tel. (615) 297-0700 Fax (615) 297-1024

Westwood Sound Studios
2714 Westwood Drive
Nashville, TN 37204
Tel. (615) 298-5256 Fax (615) 298-5273

Woodland Studios
1011 Woodland Street
Nashville, TN 37206
Tel. (615) 262-2222 Fax (615) 262-5800

Tape Duplication Services

Some of the companies listed below can do everything for you; design an attractive CD or cassette package, print J-cards and cassette labels, etc. Also remember that special cassette tapes are sold in ten- and twenty-minute sizes as well as the usual thirty- and sixty-minute lengths (measures both sides even though you record on one side only). You can purchase these special tapes in bulk.

Cassette Express
116 17th Avenue South
Nashville, TN 37203
Tel. (615) 244-5667 Fax (615) 242-2472

Nashville Tape Supply
19-S Music Square West
Nashville, TN 37203
Tel. (615) 254-8178 Fax (615) 256-1155

Sound Impressions, Inc.
1855 Airlane Drive
Nashville, TN 37210
Tel. (615) 777-3535 Fax (615) 777-3636
Web site: *www.soundimpressions.com*

Writers Tape Copy Service
1905 Division Street
Nashville, TN 37203
Tel. (615) 327-3196

SECTION II: SERVICES YOU WILL NEED TO COMPLETE YOUR WRITER/ARTIST PACKAGE

As you no doubt know, quick copy companies do just about everything, including graphic design, word processing, color copies, printing, etc. They also sell fancy stationery, envelopes, folders, whatever you need. Creating your own writer/artist package is something you probably will have done at home before you even come to Nashville, but here are some services close to Music Row.

Copying/Printing Facilities

For your basic needs near Music Row:

Copies Unlimited, Inc.
120 20th Avenue South
Nashville, TN 37203
Tel. (615) 327-1758
Web site: *www.midtownprinting.com*

Kinko's
2308 West End Avenue
Nashville, TN 37203
Tel. (615) 327-2120

Mailboxes Etc.
Hillsboro Village
(address & phone not available at print time)

Label Systems

Blank forms for your own computer. Design your own cassette labels, J-cards, and business cards.

Ace Label Systems
7101 Madison Avenue West
Minneapolis, MN 55427
Tel. (800) 383-8631
Web site: *www.acelabel.com*

Avery Dennison Office Products
P.O. Box 5244
Diamond Bar, CA 91765-4000
Tel. (800) 252-8379
Web site: *www.avery.com*

Great Photos

Alan Mayor Photography
3807 Murphy Road
Nashville, TN 37209
Tel. (615) 385-4706

Great J-Card/Cassette Labels

Music Services Unlimited
1609 Horton Avenue
Nashville, TN 37212
Tel. (615) 256-0200 Fax (615) 256-0212

Great Bios/Artist's Packages

Star Station
Nine Music Square South
Nashville, TN 37203
Tel. (615) 321-3554 Fax (615) 321-0384
E-mail: *StarPlace@aol.com*

SECTION III: PUBLICATIONS

Tip Sheets

Chuck Chellman's Parade of Stars
1201 16th Avenue South
Nashville, TN 37212
Tel. (615) 320-7270

Music Row Publications' Row Fax
1231 17th Avenue South
Nashville, TN 37212
Tel. (615) 321-3617 Fax (615) 329-0852
E-mail: *news@musicrow.com*
Web site: *www.musicrow.com*

Trade Publications

American Songwriter Magazine
1009 17th Avenue South
Nashville, TN 37212
Tel. (615) 321-6096 Fax (615) 321-6097
Web site: *www.songnet.com/asongmag/*

Billboard Country Airplay Monitor
49 Music Square West
Nashville, TN 37203
Tel. (615) 321-4290

Music Row Publications Inc.
1231 17th Avenue South
Nashville, TN 37212
Tel. (615) 321-3617 Fax (615) 329-0852
E-mail: *news@musicrow.com*
Web site: *www.musicrow.com*

The Nashville Newsletter
Nine Music Square South
Nashville, TN 37203
Tel. (615) 321-0486
E-mail: *NashNews@aol.com*

Nashville Red Book
1207 Fesslers Lane
Nashville, TN 37210
Tel. (615) 256-5456 Fax (615) 244-8260

Other Helpful Publications

The Nashville Scene
2120 Eighth Avenue South
Nashville, TN 37204-2204
Tel. (615) 244-7989 Fax (615) 244-8578
Web site: *www.nashvillescene.com*

The Nashville Yellow Pages
Web site: *www.yp.bellsouth.com*

The Tennessean
1100 Broadway
Nashville, TN 37203
Tel. (615) 259-8000
Web site: *www.tennessean.com*

SECTION IV: RECOMMENDED READING

Allworth Press publishes some great books that cover everything you need to know about writing and publishing, performing arts, business, money and law, and just about everything else in the creative fields. They can be reached at *www.allworth.com* or (800) 491-2808. Here are just a very few offerings:

How to Pitch and Promote Your Songs by Fred Koller. New York: Allworth Press, 1996.
A step-by-step guide to being your own publisher, targeting the right markets, building your own catalog, creating a demo package. The author is a highly respected Nashville songwriter whose credits include Kathy Mattea's hits "Goin' Gone" and "She Came From Fort Worth." Writing from an insider's point of view, he discusses the way the music business works (particularly in the Nashville country music market) and the strategies that have worked for him in getting songs cut. Geoffrey Himes of the *Washington Post* says, "Any songwriter with hopes of selling a song to a recording artist should read this book."

Creative Careers in Music by Josquin des Pres and Mark Landsman. New York: Allworth Press, 2000.
Talented people of all levels can find profitable careers in today's thriving music industry with the help of this definitive guide. From songwriters to producers, solo artists to band members, a wide variety of careers in the music business are fully described, outlining the skills and training required for each and ways to target the right markets and income sources. The book thoroughly examines today's record business, detailing the pros and cons of starting your own label, major-label versus independent-label careers, and where and when to find professional help.

Making It in the Music Business by Lee Wilson. New York: Allworth Press, 1999.
Both a practical business manual and a prized legal companion, this authoritative guide contains solid information and advice that songwriters and performers need to make it in today's competitive music industry. This updated edition covers current copyright law and protection, copyright infringement and how to avoid it, trademark law, business law for bands, the roles of bookers, managers, music publishers, and music lawyers, and the provisions of music publishing, management, and booking agreements.

Making and Marketing Music by Jodi Summers. New York: Allworth Press, 1999.
This thorough guide explains everything musicians need to know to make and market a hit album, from raising money, securing a record deal, and distributing on major and independent labels, to the latest strategies for promoting and selling music on the Internet.

The following list of great books on the music industry was compiled and reviewed by NSAI staff member Phil Goldberg. They are available from the

NSAI bookshop, which can be found on their Web site, *www.nashvillesongwriters.com*.

All You Need to Know about the Music Business by Donald S. Passman. New York: Simon & Schuster, 1997.
This is a very good book about the business side of the music industry. Its layout makes this book particularly useful. It is designed so that if you need just a little information on a specific topic, you only need to read key sections; this is for the reader on the "Extremely Fast Track." If you want to know a little more, you can read the sections for the "Fast Track" reader. The next level (with a little more depth) is the "Advance Overview," and lastly there's the "Expert Track" if you want to know the most. Topics covered include songwriting deals, publishing, record deals, royalties, and much more.

Music, Money, and Success: The Insider's Guide to the Music Industry by Jeffrey and Todd Brabec. New York: Simon & Schuster, 1994.
Jeffrey Brabec is an entertainment law attorney and vice president of business affairs for Chrysalis Music Group. His twin brother, Todd, a former recording artist and entertainment law attorney, is director of membership at ASCAP in Los Angeles. Together, the two have written a detailed examination of the music business. In particular, the book extensively explores the business aspects of alternative sources of songwriting income, such as television, motion pictures, commercials, and theater.

How to Be Your Own Booking Agent and Save Thousands of Dollars by Jeri Goldstein. Charlottesville, VA: New Music Times, Inc., 1998.
If you are a performer or working with an artist, this is an excellent book on booking gigs. The author—who has been an agent, manager, and promoter—lays out information in an extremely organized and systematic manner. This book covers the ins and outs of finding gigs, developing press kits, negotiating contracts for live performances, and dealing with the media.

Making It in Country Music: An Insider's Guide to Launching or Advancing Your Career by Scott Faragher. Secaucus, NJ: Citadel Press, 1996.
This is an easy-to-read, extremely down-to-earth guide to the Nashville music business. It's almost depressingly realistic. The book describes how all the pieces fit together—artists, songwriters, managers, record companies, etc. If you're a songwriter but not a performer, this book should still prove valuable. As a songwriter, you will ultimately have to deal not only with publishers, but artists, producers, and record companies. It's important to understand everyone's perspective.

Music Publishing: A Songwriter's Guide by Randy Poe. Cincinnati: Writer's Digest Books, 1997.
Randy Poe is the president of Leiber & Stoller's publishing companies. An excellent overview of music publishing, this book is for the songwriter who knows little about publishing but wants to learn. This is a clearly written, easy-to-understand book. It contains basic explanations of copyrights, sources of income, etc. It is not a book about pitching and placing songs.

The Songwriters' Guide to Collaboration by Walter Carter. Emeryville, CA: Mix Books, 1997.
Cowriting is extremely important in Nashville. Over 90 percent of songs recorded are the result of a collaboration. *The Songwriter's and Musician's Guide to Nashville* talks a lot about cowriting, but says nothing about what to do when a collaboration has gone sour. Songwriters should read this book before they begin cowriting. This book deals with the legal, psychological, and emotional aspects of cowriting. It explores proper etiquette in a collaboration as well as ways of finding a cowriter.

Nashville Red Book edited and published by Larry Pacheco. Nashville: 1999.
A miniature Yellow Pages of the Nashville music industry, printed annually with each new edition usually available in late winter. A comprehensive listing of arrangers/scorers, booking agencies, recording equipment, management, media, music publishing, photographers, record companies, and recording studios, to name a few. To obtain a copy, contact Larry Pacheco at 1207 Fesslers Lane, Nashville, TN 37210, Tel. (615) 256-5456, Fax (615) 244-8260.

The Nashville Number System written and published by Chas Williams. Brentwood, TN: 1997.
The Nashville Number System is a way of notating song charts for musicians when they play on demos or at performances. In this notational system used principally in Nashville, numbers are used to correspond with chords. The first half of the book explains the notation, and the second half gives examples of actual charts from a few songs. The book is not a music theory book. It requires some knowledge of chords, but even with a moderate knowledge of music theory, this book will probably enable you to write out a simple chart.

The Craft and Business of Songwriting by John Braheny. Cincinnati: Writer's Digest Books, 1995.
A practical guide to creating and marketing artistically and commercially successful songs. John Braheny was the cofounder and director of the Los

Angeles Songwriters Showcase (LASS). The book is divided into two broad areas, the Craft and the Business. The subjects under Craft include creativity and inspiration, subject matter, the media and the listeners, writing lyrics, constructing a song, writing music, and collaboration. The topics under Business include protecting your songs, knowing where your money comes from, publishing, self-publishing, demos, marketing yourself and your songs, additional markets, and getting a record deal.

Songs that Changed Our Lives by Bruce Burch.
An inspirational journey of personal testimony from country music fans who were touched and moved by the power of eleven country songs, including "The Dance" and "Achy-Breaky Heart." Written by hit songwriter and EMI Music song plugger Bruce Burch, who penned "It's Your Call" and "Rumor Has It" recorded by Reba McEntire, Burch's story is a songwriter's dream come true. He moved to Nashville following his dream of writing songs, waiting tables, and clerking at the Quality Inn Hall of Fame. He then went on to achieve his own fame! You can order his book by mailing a check for $15 to *Songs that Changed Our Lives,* 119 Bowling Avenue, Nashville, TN 37205.

6 Steps to Songwriting Success by Jason Blume. New York: Billboard Books, 1999.
Jason Blume is a multitalented songwriter who has had songs hit the pop, country, and R&B charts. His songs have been recorded by Britney Spears and The Backstreet Boys, and he had a Top 5 country hit with John Berry's "Change My Mind." Jason is also sought after for his teaching talents, conducting regular songwriting classes for NASI and BMI in Nashville. *6 Steps to Songwriting Success* includes many of the techniques he has incorporated into crafting his own hit songs. This is a book that the beginning songwriter can easily use before going on to more in-depth works. At the same time, this is certainly a book that can be recommended to the advanced songwriter as well. It is a good distillation of what the commercial market is looking for these days.

Index

ALLWORTH BOOKS

Making It in the Music Business: The Business and Legal Guide for Songwriters and Performers by Lee Wilson (softcover, 6 × 9, 288 pages, $18.95)

Creative Careers in Music by Josquin des Pres and Mark Landsman (softcover, 6 × 9, 224 pages, $18.95)

Making and Marketing Music: The Musician's Guide to Financing, Distributing, and Promoting Albums by Jodi Summers (softcover, 6 × 9, 256 pages, $18.95)

How to Pitch and Promote Your Songs, Revised Edition by Fred Koller (softcover, 6 × 9, 192 pages, $18.95)

Moving Up in the Music Business by Jodi Summers (softcover, 6 × 9, 224 pages, $18.95)

The Interactive Music Handbook: The Definitive Guide to Internet Music Strategies, Enhanced CD Production, and Business Development by Jodi Summers (softcover, 6 × 9, 296 pages, $19.95)

Booking and Tour Management for the Performing Arts by Rena Shagan (softcover, 6 × 9, 272 pages, $19.95)

The Copyright Guide by Lee Wilson (softcover, 6 × 9, 192 pages, $18.95)

The Trademark Guide by Lee Wilson (softcover, 6 × 9, 192 pages, $18.95)

Artists Communities, Second Edition by the Alliance of Artists' Communities (softcover, 6¾ × 10, 240 pages, $18.95)

The Business of Multimedia by Nina Schuyler (softcover, 6 × 9, 240 pages, $19.95)

Money Secrets of the Rich and Famous by Michael Reynard (hardcover, 6 × 9, 256 pages, $24.95)

Please write to request our free catalog. To order by credit card, call 1–800–491–2808 or send a check or money order to Allworth Press, 10 East 23rd Street, New York, NY 10010. Include $5 for shipping and handling for the first book ordered and $1 for each additional book or $10 plus $1 for each additional book if ordering from Canada. New York State residents must add sales tax.

If you would like to see our complete catalog on the World Wide Web, you can find us at: *www.allworth.com*.